MW00489643

Chennai &
Tamil Nadu

David Stott

Credits

Footprint credits
Editor: Stephanie Rebello
Production and layout: Emma Bryers
Maps: Kevin Feeney

Publisher: Patrick Dawson
Managing Editor: Felicity Laughton
Advertising: Elizabeth Taylor
Sales and marketing: Kirsty Holmes

Photography credits
Front cover: Jorisvo/Shutterstock
Back cover: Sergemi/Dreamstime

Printed in Great Britain by Alphaset,
Surbiton, Surrey

Every effort has been made to ensure that
the facts in this guidebook are accurate.
However, travellers should still obtain advice
from consulates, airlines, etc, about travel
and visa requirements before travelling.
The authors and publishers cannot accept
responsibility for any loss, injury or
inconvenience however caused.

Publishing information
Footprint *Focus Chennai & Tamil Nadu*
2nd edition
© Footprint Handbooks Ltd
February 2014

ISBN: 978 1 909268 74 6
CIP DATA: A catalogue record for this book
is available from the British Library

® Footprint Handbooks and the Footprint
mark are a registered trademark of
Footprint Handbooks Ltd

Published by Footprint
6 Riverside Court
Lower Bristol Road
Bath BA2 3DZ, UK
T +44 (0)1225 469141
F +44 (0)1225 469461
footprinttravelguides.com

Distributed in the USA by Globe Pequot
Press, Guilford, Connecticut

Tamil Nadu smells of sacrificial burning camphor and the perfume from jasmine garlands piled up before its beautifully carved granite gods, well oiled with gingelly smeared from the palms of centuries of devotees, then reddened with sandal powder and washed with devotional milk baths.

About 90% of the 60-million-strong Tamil population is Hindu and religious ritual here is lived and breathed: men's entire foreheads are daubed with potash, huge horizontal sweeps or fingernail-thin red edges drawn from the hair's centre-parting sideways, while women sprinkle intricate geometric designs of ground rice powder on their hearths every dawn. It's rare to find a temple that has outlived its religious purpose – seldom the shrine that is mere monument. But nor is worship confined to the feats of architecture that dot Tamil Nadu. Banyan trees are festooned with dangling sacred talismen; tridents are slammed into the ground to create makeshift mounds of worship; village gods in life-size stucco renderings bare their teeth and brandish knives at every roadside, and files of pilgrims pick their way along baked dirt tracks.

Here, then, is the heady temple trail: Kanchipuram, Mahabalipuram, Chidambaram, Thanjavur, Madurai, the second Varanasi of Rameswaram, and the holy toe-tip of India in Kanniyakumari. Here too, for serious seekers and dilettante yogis, the contrasting ashram atmospheres of introspective Tiruvannamalai, futuristic utopian Auroville, and the industrious urban campus of Sri Aurobindo in Puducherry.

Welcome antidotes to temple fatigue come in the form of Puducherry's charming French domestic architecture and the crumbling palatial homes of Chettinad, or in big breaths of nature in the blue Nilgiri mountains around the celebrated hill stations of Ooty and Kodaikanal.

Planning your trip

Best time to visit Chennai and Tamil Nadu

By far the most comfortable time to visit Tamil Nadu is from December to March, when the weather is dry and relatively cool. April and May are intensely hot along the coast and plains – this is peak season for the hill stations – with humidity building up as the monsoon approaches. The southwest monsoon hits the southern tip of India in early June, sweeping northward up the west coast and soaking the Nilgiri and Palani hills. A second monsoon travels up the east coast between October and December, frequently leaving coastal towns in Tamil Nadu knee-deep in water for hours at a time. If you're travelling during the monsoon you need to be prepared for extended periods of torrential rain and disruption to travel. The post-monsoon period comes with cool air and clear skies – this is the best time for mountain views – while winter temperatures can drop close to zero in the high points of the Western Ghats. Autumn and winter are also the time of some of India's great festivals, including the delightful and distinctly Tamil festival of Pongal, as well as national celebrations such as Dussehra and Diwali.

Getting to Chennai and Tamil Nadu

Air
India is accessible by air from virtually every continent, and thanks to excellent connections through the Gulf and Southeast Asia, it's as easy to fly straight into Tamil Nadu as to come via the usual international gateways of Mumbai and New Delhi.

Chennai is the most obvious gateway to the State, with direct flights from several European airports. There are also international airports in Tiruchirappalli (Trichy), a popular entry point for Asian low-cost airlines, **Coimbatore**, and **Thiruvananthapuram**, just across the Kerala border. Any one of these makes for a relatively mellow and stress-free entry to India. Several carriers permit 'open-jaw' travel, making it possible to fly into one airport and out of another – a great option if you want to explore the full length of Tamil Nadu without having to backtrack to your initial arrival point.

In 2013 the cheapest return flights to Chennai from London started from around £500, but leapt to £800+ as you approached the high seasons of Christmas, New Year and Easter.

From Europe Despite the increases to Air Passenger Duty, Britain remains the cheapest place in Europe for flights to India. **British Airways**, **Virgin Atlantic**, **Jet Airways** and **Air India** all fly direct from London to Mumbai, while BA also flies direct to Chennai, Bengaluru and Hyderabad.

Air India and **Jet Airways** offer direct services from Mumbai to several airports in mainland Europe, while major European flag carriers including **KLM** and **Lufthansa** fly to Mumbai from their respective hub airports.

If you're heading straight for Tamil Nadu, the cheapest and most convenient flights are generally with Middle Eastern or Central Asian airlines, transiting via airports in the Gulf. Several airlines from the Middle East (including **Emirates**, **Etihad**, **Gulf Air**, **Kuwait Airways**, **Qatar Airways** and **Oman Air**) offer good fares from a wide choice of British and European airports to Chennai or Trichy via their hub cities. This may add a couple of hours to the

Don't miss...

journey time, but allows you to avoid the more fraught route via Mumbai which involves long immigration queues and shuttling from the international to domestic terminal. Consolidators in the UK can quote some competitive fares, such as: www.skyscanner.net, www.ebookers.com; **North South Travel** ① *T01245-608291, www.northsouthtravel.co.uk (profits to charity)*.

From North America From the east coast, several airlines including **Air India**, **Jet Airways**, **Continental** and **Delta** fly direct from New York to Mumbai, from where you can pick up an internal flight to any of Tamil Nadu's main airports. American flies from Chicago. Discounted tickets on **British Airways**, **KLM**, **Lufthansa**, **Gulf Air** and **Kuwait Airways** are sold through agents, although they will invariably fly via their country's capital cities. From the west coast, your best option is to fly to Chennai via Hong Kong, Singapore or Bangkok using one of those countries' national carriers. **Air Canada** operates between Vancouver and Delhi, which also has good internal connections to Tamil Nadu. **Air Brokers International** ① *www.airbrokers.com*, is competitive and reputable. **STA** ① *www.statravel.co.uk*, has offices in many US cities, Toronto and Ontario. Student fares are also available from **Travel Cuts** ① *www.travelcuts.com*, in Canada.

From Australasia Qantas, Singapore Airlines, Thai Airways, Malaysian Airlines, Cathay Pacific and Air India are the principal airlines connecting the continents, although none have direct flights to the south. **Singapore Airlines** offer the most flexibility, with subsidiary **Silk Air** flying to Chennai and several other convenient South Indian airports. Low-cost carriers including **Air Asia** (via Kuala Lumpur), **Scoot** and **Tiger Airways** (Singapore) offer flights to Chennai and Trichy at substantial savings, though long layovers and possible missed connections make this a potentially more risky venture than flying with the mainstream airlines. **STA** and **Flight Centre** offer discounted tickets from their branches in major cities in Australia and New Zealand.

Airport information The formalities on arrival in India have been increasingly streamlined during the last few years and the facilities at the major international airports greatly improved. However, arrival can still be a slow process. Disembarkation cards, with an attached customs declaration, are handed out to passengers during the inward flight. The immigration form should be handed in at the immigration counter on arrival. The customs slip will be returned, for handing over to the customs on leaving the baggage collection hall. You may well find that there are delays of over an hour at immigration in processing passengers passing through immigration who need help with filling in forms. When departing, note that you'll need to have a printout of your itinerary to get into the airport, and the security guards will only let you into the terminal within three hours of your flight. Many airports require your to scan your bags before checking in, and in rare cases you may also be asked to identify your checked luggage after going through immigration and security checks.

Departure charges Several Indian airports have begun charging a Passenger Service Fee or User Development Fee to each departing passenger. This is normally included in international tickets, but some domestic airlines have been reluctant to incorporate the charge. Keep some spare cash in rupees in case you need to pay the fee on arriving at the terminal.

Transport in Chennai and Tamil Nadu

Air
India has a comprehensive network linking the major cities of the different states. Deregulation of the airline industry has had a transformative effect on travel within India, with a host of low-budget private carriers jockeying to provide the lowest prices or highest frequency on popular routes. On any given day, booking a few days in advance, you can expect to fly between Mumbai and Chennai for around US$100 one way including taxes, while booking a month in advance can reduce the price to US$60-70.

Competition from the efficiently run private sector has, in general, improved the quality of services provided by the nationalized airlines. It also seems to herald the end of the two-tier pricing structure, meaning that ticket prices are now usually the same for foreign and Indian travellers. The airport authorities too have made efforts to improve handling on the ground.

Although flying is comparatively expensive, for covering vast distances or awkward links on a route it is an option worth considering, though delays and re-routing can be irritating. For short distances (eg Thiruvananthapurm–Kochi), and on some routes where you can sleep during an overnight journey it makes more sense to travel by train.

The best way to get an idea of the current routes, carriers and fares is to use a third-party booking website such as **www.cheapairticketsindia.com** (toll-free numbers: UK T0800-101 0928, USA T1-888 825 8680), **www.cleartrip.com**, **www.makemytrip.co.in**, or **www.yatra.com**. Booking with these is a different matter: some refuse foreign credit cards outright, while others have to be persuaded to give your card special clearance. Tickets booked on these sites are typically issued as an email ticket or an SMS text message – the simplest option if you have an Indian mobile phone, though it must be converted to a paper ticket at the relevant carrier's airport offices before you will be allowed into the terminal. **Makemytrip.com** and **Travelocity.com** both accept international credit cards.

Rail
Trains can still be the cheapest and most comfortable means of travelling long distances saving you hotel expenses on overnight journeys. Above all, you have an ideal opportunity to meet local travellers and catch a glimpse of life on the ground.

High-speed trains There are several air-conditioned 'high-speed' Shatabdi (or 'Century') **Express** for day travel, and **Rajdhani Express** ('Capital City') for overnight journeys. These

Train touts

Many railway stations – and some bus stations and major tourist sites – are heavily populated with touts. Self-styled 'agents' will board trains before they enter the station and seek out tourists, often picking up their luggage and setting off with words such as "Madam!/Sir! Come with me madam/sir! You need top-class hotel …". They will even select porters to take your luggage without giving you any say.

If you have succeeded in getting off the train or even in obtaining a trolley you will find hands eager to push it for you.

For a first-time visitor such touts can be more than a nuisance. You need to keep calm and firm. Decide in advance where you want to stay. If you need a porter on trains, select one yourself and agree a price **before** the porter sets off with your baggage. If travelling with a companion one can stay guarding the luggage while the other gets hold of a taxi and negotiates the price to the hotel. It sounds complicated and sometimes it feels it. The most important thing is to behave as if you know what you are doing!

---

cover large sections of the network but due to high demand you need to book them well in advance (up to 90 days). Meals and drinks are usually included.

Classes A/c First Class, available only on main routes, is the choice of the Indian upper crust, with two- or four-berth carpeted sleeper compartments with washbasin. As with all a/c sleeper accommodation, bedding is included, and the windows are tinted to the point of being almost impossible to see through. **A/c Sleeper**, two and three-tier configurations (known as 2AC and 3AC), are clean and comfortable and popular with middle class families; these are the safest carriages for women travelling alone. **A/c Executive Class**, with wide reclining seats, are available on many daytime Shatabdi trains. They come at double the price of the ordinary a/c Chair Car, which is perfectly comfortable. **First Class (non-a/c)** is gradually being phased out, and is now restricted to a handful of routes through Tamil Nadu, but the run-down old carriages still provide a very enjoyable combination of privacy and openable windows. **Second Class (non-a/c)** two and three-tier (commonly called Sleeper), provides exceptionally cheap and atmospheric travel, with basic padded vinyl seats and open windows that allow the sights and sounds of India (not to mention dust, insects and flecks of spittle expelled by passengers up front) to drift into the carriage. On long journeys Sleeper can be crowded and uncomfortable, and toilet facilities can be unpleasant; it is nearly always better to use the Indian-style squat loos rather than the Western-style ones as they are better maintained. At the bottom rung is **Unreserved Second Class**, with hard wooden benches. You can travel long distances for a trivial amount of money, but unreserved carriages are often ridiculously crowded, and getting off at your station may involve a battle of will and strength against the hordes trying to shove their way on.

Indrail passes These allow travel across the entire Indian railway network, but you have to spend a high proportion of your time on the train to make it worthwhile. However, the advantages of pre-arranged reservations and automatic access to Foreign Tourist Quota tickets can tip the balance in favour of the pass for some travellers.

Tourists (foreigners and Indians resident abroad) may buy these passes from the tourist sections of principal railway booking offices and pay in foreign currency, major credit cards, traveller's cheques or rupees with encashment certificates. Fares range from US$57 to US$1060 for adults or half that for children.

Indrail passes can also conveniently be bought abroad from special agents. For people contemplating a single long journey soon after arriving in India, the Half- or One-day Pass with a confirmed reservation is worth the peace of mind; two- or four-day passes are also sold.

The UK agent is **SDEL** ① *103 Wembley Park Dr, Wembley, Middlesex HA9 8HG, UK, T020-8903 3411, www.indiarail.co.uk.* They make all necessary reservations and offer excellent advice. They can also book Air India and Jet Airways internal flights.

Cost A/c first class costs about double the rate for two-tier shown below, and non a/c Sleeper class about half. Children (aged five to 12) travel at half the adult fare. The young (12-30 years) and senior citizens (65 years and over) are allowed a 30% discount on journeys over 500 km (just show your passport).

Period	US$ A/c 2-tier	Period	US$ A/c 2-tier
½ day	26	21 days	198
1 day	43	30 days	248
7 days	135	60 days	400
15 days	185	90 days	530

Fares for individual journeys are based on distance covered and reflect both the class and the type of train. Higher rates apply on the Mail and Express trains and the air-conditioned Shatabdi and Rajdhani Expresses.

Internet services Much information is available online via **www.railtourismindia.com, www.indianrail.gov.in, www.erail.in** and **www.trainenquiry.com,** where you can check timetables (which change frequently), numbers, seat availability and even the running status of your train. Internet e-tickets can be bought and printed on **www.irctc.in** though it's a fiendishly frustrating system to use, and paying with a foreign credit card is fraught with difficulty. If you plan to do a lot of train travel on popular routes (e.g. from Chennai to Bengaluru or across to Mumbai) it might be worth the effort to get your credit card recognized by the booking system. This process changes often, so your best option is to consult the very active India transport forums at **www.indiamike.com.**

An alternative is to seek out a local agent who sells e-tickets, which can cost as little as Rs 10 (plus Rs 20 reservation fee, some agents charge up to Rs 150 a ticket, however), and can save hours of hassle; simply present the printout to the ticket collector. However, it is tricky if you then want to cancel an e-ticket which an agent has bought for you on their account.

Tickets and reservations It is possible to reserve tickets for virtually any train on the network from one of the 1000 computerized reservation centres across India. It is always best to book as far in advance as possible (usually up to 60 days). To reserve a seat on a particular train, note down the train's name, number and departure time and fill in a reservation form while you line up at the ticket window; you can use one form for up to four passengers. At busy stations the wait can take an hour or more.

You can save a lot of time and effort by asking a travel agent to get your tickets for a fee of Rs 50-100. If the class you want is full, ask if tickets are available under any of Indian Rail's special quotas. **Foreign Tourist Quota** (FTQ) reserves a small number of tickets on popular routes for overseas travellers; you need your passport and either an exchange certificate or ATM receipt to book tickets under FTQ. The other useful special quota is **Tatkal**, which releases a last-minute pool of tickets at 1000 on the day before the train departs.

If the quota system can't help you, consider buying a 'wait list' ticket, as seats often become available close to the train's departure time; phone the station on the day of departure to check your ticket's status. If you don't have a reservation for a particular train but carry an Indrail Pass, you may get one by arriving three hours early. Be wary of touts at the station offering tickets, hotels or exchange.

Timetables It's best to consult the websites listed above for the most up-to-date timetable information. Once you're on the ground, regional timetables are available cheaply from station bookstalls; the monthly Indian Bradshaw is sold in principal stations, and the handy but daunting Trains at a Glance (Rs 40) lists popular trains likely to be used by most foreign travellers. You can pick it up in the UK from SDEL (see page opposite)

Road

Road travel is often the only choice for reaching many of the places of outstanding interest in which India is so rich. For the uninitiated, travel by road can also be a worrying experience because of the apparent absence of conventional traffic regulations and also in the mountains, especially during the rainy season when landslides are possible. Vehicles drive on the left – in theory. Routes around the major cities are usually crowded with lorry traffic, especially at night, and the main roads are often poor and slow. There are a few motorway-style expressways, but most main roads are single track. Some district roads are quiet, and although they are not fast they can be a good way of seeing the country and village life if you have the time.

Bus Buses now reach virtually every part of India, offering a cheap, if often uncomfortable, means of visiting places off the rail network. Very few villages are now more than 2-3 km from a bus stop. Most services in Kerala are operated by the government-run **Kerala State Road Transport Corporation (SETC)** ⓘ www.keralartc.com. These buses depart from the central Bus Stand in every town. The most popular routes are also served by private bus operators, whose offices cluster around the main Bus Stand. The latter allow advance reservations, including booking printable e-tickets online (check www.redbus.in and www.viaworld.in) and, although tickets prices are a little higher, they have fewer stops and are a bit more comfortable. In the absence of trains, buses are often the only budget option, into the Himalaya for example. There are many sleeper buses (a contradiction in terms) running Mumbai–Goa or into the Himalaya – if you must take a sleeper bus, choose a lower berth near the front of the bus. The upper berths are almost always really uncomfortable.

Bus categories Though comfortable for sightseeing trips, apart from the very best 'sleeper coaches' even **air-conditioned luxury coaches** can be very uncomfortable for really long journeys. Often the air conditioning is very cold so wrap up. Journeys over 10 hours can be extremely tiring so it is better to go by train if there is a choice. **Express buses** run over long distances (frequently overnight), these are often called 'video coaches' and can be an appalling experience unless you appreciate loud film music blasting through the night. Ear plugs and eye masks may ease the pain. They rarely average more than 45 kph. **Local buses** are often very crowded, quite bumpy, slow and usually poorly maintained. However, over short distances, they can be a very cheap, friendly and easy way of getting about. Even where signboards are not in English someone will usually give you directions. Many larger towns have **minibus** services which charge a little more than the buses and pick up and drop passengers on request. Again very crowded, and with restricted headroom, they are the fastest way of getting about many of the larger towns.

Bus travel tips Some towns have different bus stations for different destinations. Booking on major long-distance routes is now computerized. Book in advance where possible and avoid the back of the bus where it can be very bumpy. If your destination is only served by a local bus you may do better to take the Express bus and 'persuade' the driver, with a tip in advance, to stop where you want to get off. You will have to pay the full fare to the first stop beyond your destination but you will get there faster and more comfortably. When an unreserved bus pulls into a bus station, there is usually an unholy scramble for seats, whilst those arriving have to struggle to get off! In many areas there is an unwritten 'rule of reservation' using handkerchiefs or bags thrust through the windows to reserve seats. Some visitors may feel a more justified right to a seat having fought their way through the crowd, but it is generally best to do as local people do and be prepared with a handkerchief or 'sarong'. As soon as it touches the seat, it is yours! Leave it on your seat when getting off to use the toilet at bus stations.

Car A car provides a chance to travel off the beaten track, and gives unrivalled opportunities for seeing something of India's great variety of villages and small towns. Until recently, the most widely used hire car was the romantic but notoriously unreliable Hindustan Ambassador. You can still find them for hire in parts of Tamil Nadu, but they're gradually giving way to more efficient (and boring) Tata and Toyota models with mod-cons like optional air-conditioning – and seat belts. A handful of international agencies offer self-drive car hire (**Avis, Sixt**), but India's majestically anarchic traffic culture is not for the faint-hearted, and emphatically not a place for those who value such quaint concepts as lane discipline, or indeed driving on your assigned side of the road. It's much more common, and comfortable, to hire not just the car but someone to drive it for you.

Car hire If you fancy the idea of being Lady Penelope and gadding about with your own chauffeur, dream no more. Hiring a car and driver is the most comfortable and efficient way to cover short to medium distances, and although prices have increased sharply in recent years car travel in India is still a bargain by western standards. Even if you're travelling on a modest budget a day's car hire can help take the sting out of an arduous journey, allowing you to go sightseeing along the way without looking for somewhere to stash your bags.

Local drivers often know their way around an area much better than drivers from other states, so where possible it is a good idea to get a local driver who speaks the state language, in addition to being able to communicate with you. The best way to guarantee a driver who speaks good English is to book in advance with a professional travel agency, either in India or in your home country. Recommended operators with English speaking drivers include **Milesworth Travel** ① *www.milesworth.com*, and **Intersight** ① *www. intersighttours.com*. You can, if you choose, arrange car hire informally by asking around at taxi stands, but don't expect your driver to speak anything more than rudimentary English.

On pre-arranged overnight trips the fee you pay will normally include fuel and inter-state taxes – check before you pay – and a wage for the driver. Drivers are responsible for their expenses, including meals (and the pervasive servant-master culture in India means that most will choose to sit separately from you at meal times). Some tourist hotels provide rooms for drivers, but they often choose to sleep in the car overnight to save money. In some areas drivers also seek to increase their earnings by taking you to hotels and shops where they earn a handsome commission; these are generally hugely overpriced and poor alternatives to the hotels recommended in this book, so don't be afraid to say no and insist on your choice of accommodation. If you feel inclined, a tip at the end of the tour of Rs 100 per day is perfectly acceptable.

	Tata Indica non-a/c	Tata Indigo non-a/c	Hyundai Accent a/c	Toyota Innova
8 hrs/80 km	Rs 1200	Rs 1600	Rs 2200	Rs 2500
Extra km	Rs 8	Rs 10	Rs 15	Rs 15
Extra hour	Rs 80	Rs 100	Rs 200	Rs 180
Out of town				
Per km	Rs 8	Rs 10	Rs 15	Rs 15
Night halt	Rs 200	Rs 200	Rs 300	Rs 250

Taxi Taxi travel in India is a great bargain, and in most cities in Kerala you can take a taxi from the airport to the centre for under US$15.

Yellow-top taxis in cities and large towns are metered, although tariffs change frequently. The latest rates are typically shown on a fare conversion chart which should be read in conjunction with the meter reading. Increased night time rates apply in most cities, and there might be a small charge for luggage.

Insist on the taxi meter being flagged in your presence. If the driver refuses, the official advice is to contact the police. When a taxi doesn't have a meter, you will need to fix the fare before starting the journey – ask at your hotel desk for a rough price. As a foreigner, it is rare to get a taxi in the big cities to use the meter – if they are eager to, watch out as sometimes the meter is rigged and they have a fake rate card. Also, watch out for the David Blaine-style note shuffle: you pay with a Rs 500 note, but they have a Rs 100 note in their hand.

Most airports and many major stations have booths where you can book a prepaid taxi. For slightly more than the metered fare these allow you to sidestep overcharging and give you the security of knowing that your driver will take you to your destination by the most direct route. You might be able to join up with other travellers at the booth to share a taxi to your hotel or a central point. It's OK to give the driver a small tip at the end of the journey.

At night, always have a clear idea of where you want to go and insist on being taken there. Taxi drivers may try to convince you that the hotel you have chosen 'closed three years ago' or is 'completely full'. Say that you have a reservation.

Rickshaw Auto-rickshaws (autos) are almost universally available in towns across India and are the cheapest and most convenient way of getting about. Autorickshaws in Chennai, once a notorious rip-off, now run on meters. Elsewhere you'll need to negotiate a price before getting in. It is best to walk a short distance away from a hotel gate before picking up an auto to avoid paying an inflated rate. In addition to using them for short journeys it is often possible to hire them by the hour, or for a half or full day's sightseeing. In some areas younger drivers who speak some English and know their local area well may want to show you around. However, rickshaw drivers are often paid a commission by hotels, restaurants and gift shops so advice is not always impartial. Drivers generally refuse to use a meter, often quote a ridiculous price or may sometimes stop short of your destination. If you have real problems it can help to note down the vehicle licence number and threaten to go to the police.

Cycle-rickshaws and **horse-drawn tongas** are more common in the more rustic setting of a small town or the outskirts of a large one. You will need to fix a price by bargaining. The animal attached to a tonga usually looks too undernourished to have the strength to pull the driver, let alone passengers.

Where to stay in Chennai and Tamil Nadu

India has an enormous range of accommodation, and you can stay safely and very cheaply by Western standards right across the country.

A lifeline for budget travellers are backpacker hotels, found in all major cities and traveller destinations, and nearly always located within walking distance to train and bus stations. Facilities can be sparse – a bed, a few hooks to hang clothes, and a shared bathroom – but they are great places to meet other travellers, and standards are quite good if there's competition in the area. Try to insist on clean sheets (ask for a top sheet, as often only a pillow case and one sheet are provided). Another mainstay for economy travellers is the ubiquitous Indian 'business hotel': anonymous but generally decent value, with en suite rooms of variable cleanliness and a TV showing 110 channels of cricket and Bollywood MTV.

At the top end, alongside international chains like ITC Sheraton (ostentatious) and Radisson Blu (dependable), India boasts several home-grown hotel chains. The exceptional heritage and palace hotels operated by the Taj group are the pick of the bunch, while Neemrana Hotels run several excellent, more humble heritage properties in Tamil Nadu.

Puducherry and Chettinad are two spots that offer particularly abundant opportunities to stay in fine style in converted mansions – a great way to help preserve architectural heritage while keeping your money in the local economy.

In the high season (October to April, peaking at Christmas/New Year and again at Easter) bookings can be extremely heavy in popular destinations such as Kovalam and Varkala. It is generally possible to book in advance by phone, fax or email, sometimes on payment of a deposit, but double check your reservation a day or two beforehand and always try to arrive as early as possible in the day to iron out problems.

Hotels

Price categories The category codes used in this book are based on prices of double rooms excluding taxes. They are **not** star ratings and individual facilities vary considerably. The most expensive hotels charge in US dollars only. Expect to pay more in Bengaluru (Bangalore) and Chennai. Prices away from large cities tend to be lower for comparable hotels. Away from the metropolitan cities, in South India, room rates tend to be lower than the North, and the standard of cleanliness is higher.

Off-season rates Large reductions are made by hotels in all categories out-of-season in many resorts. Always ask if any is available. You may also request the 10-15% agent's commission to be deducted from your bill if you book direct. Clarify whether the agreed figure includes all taxes.

Taxes In Tamil Nadu you'll pay an extra 10% on the quoted tariff for rooms between Rs 500-1000, and 12.5% for rooms over Rs 1000. Some hotels choose to add a service charge on top of this. Taxes are not necessarily payable on meals, so it is worth settling your meals bill separately. Most hotels in the **$$** category and above accept payment by credit card. Check your final bill carefully. Visitors have complained of incorrect bills, even in the most

Price codes

Where to stay

$$$$ over US$150	**$$$** US$66-150
$$ US$30-65	**$** under US$30

For a double room in high season, excluding taxes.

Restaurants

$$$ over US$12	**$$** US$6-12	**$** under US$6

For a two-course meal for one person, excluding drinks and service charge.

expensive hotels. The problem particularly afflicts groups, when last-minute extras appear mysteriously on some guests' bills. Check the evening before departure, and keep all receipts.

Hotel facilities You have to be prepared for difficulties which are uncommon in the West. It is best to inspect the room and check that all equipment (air conditioning, TV, water heater, flush) works before checking in at a modest hotel. Many hotels try to wring too many years' service out of their linen, and it's quite common to find sheets that are stained, frayed or riddled with holes. Don't expect any but the most expensive or tourist-savvy hotels to fit a top sheet to the bed.

In some states **power cuts** are common, or hot water may be restricted to certain times of day. The largest hotels have their own generators but it is best to carry a good torch.

In some regions **water supply** is rationed periodically. Keep a bucket filled to use for flushing the toilet during water cuts. Occasionally, tap water may be discoloured due to rusty tanks. During the cold weather and in hill stations, hot water will be available at certain times of the day, sometimes in buckets, but is usually very restricted in quantity. Electric water heaters may provide enough for a shower but not enough to fill a bath tub. For details on drinking water, see page 17.

Modest hotels may not have their own restaurant but will often offer 'room service', bringing in food from outside. In South and West India, and in temple towns, restaurants may only serve vegetarian food.

Hotels close to temples can be very **noisy**, especially during festivals. Music blares from loudspeakers late at night and from very early in the morning, often making sleep impossible. Mosques call the faithful to prayers at dawn. Some find ear plugs helpful. Some hotels offer 24-hour checkout, meaning you can keep the room a full 24 hours from the time you arrive – a great option if you arrive in the afternoon and want to spend the morning sightseeing.

Homestays

At the upmarket end, increasing numbers of travellers are keen to stay in private homes and guesthouses, opting not to book large hotel chains that keep you at arm's length from a culture. Instead, travellers get home-cooked meals in heritage houses and learn about a country through conversation with often fascinating hosts. Kerala leads the way in this field, but Tamil Nadu is steadily catching up, with new and smart family-run B&Bs springing up. Tourist offices have lists of families with more modest homestays. Companies specializing in homestays include **MAHout** ① *www.mahoutuk.com*, **Pyramid Tours** ① *www.pyramidtravelindia.com* and **Sundale Vacations** ① *www.sundale.com*.

Food and drink in Chennai and Tamil Nadu

Food

You find just as much variety in dishes crossing South India as you would on an equivalent journey across Europe. Varying combinations of spices and unique local ingredients give each region its distinctive flavour.

Tamil food is predominantly vegetarian, based around a steady diet of rice, rice and more rice. Typical dishes include *pongal*, a mellow rice-and-lentil breakfast dish cooked in milk and laced with ghee and cashews; Puliyodarai, a delicious fried rice dish cooked with tamarind paste and spices; and *puttu*, hard cylindrical cakes of rice flour and grated coconut, typically served with vegetable stew and washed down with Tamil Nadu's brew of choice, milky filter coffee.

Also ubiquitous throughout the state are the humble snacks that appear on menus in South Indian cafes the length and breadth of India: *masala dosa*, a crispy rice pancake folded over and stuffed with a lightly spiced potato filling; *utthapam*, a cross between a pancake and a pizza, topped with tomato and onion or slices of banana; and *idli*, soft steamed rice cakes served with a spicy stew called *sambar* and coconut chutney. Every town has a slew of places serving these staples, and for less than US$1 you can fuel yourself up for a full morning's sightseeing.

Throughout India the best value food comes in the shape of the traditional thali (called 'meals' in Tamil Nadu and neighbouring Kerala), a complete feast often served on a banana leaf. Several curries surround the central serving of rice. A typical lunchtime thali will include sambar (thick lentil and vegetable soup), rasam (a hot peppery consommé) two or three curries which can be quite hot and maybe a crisp poppadum. A variety of pickles are offered – mango and lime are two of the most popular. These can be exceptionally hot, and are designed to be taken in minute quantities alongside the main dishes. Plain *dahi* (yoghurt), or raita, usually acts as a bland 'cooler', and there's usually a bowl of sweet *payasam* (rice pudding) to finish off.

If you're unused to spicy food, go slow. Food is often spicier when you eat with families or at local places, and certain cuisines (notably those of Andhra Pradesh and the Chettinad region of Tamil Nadu) are notorious for going heavy on the chilli. Most restaurants are used to toning things down for foreign palates, so if you're worried about being overpowered, feel free to ask for the food to be made less spicy.

Food hygiene has improved immensely in recent years. However, you still need to take extra care, as flies abound and refrigeration in the hot weather may be inadequate and intermittent because of power cuts. It is safest to eat only freshly prepared food by ordering from the menu (especially meat and fish dishes). Be suspicious of salads and cut fruit, which may have been lying around for hours or washed in unpurified tap water – though salads served in top-end hotel restaurants and places primarily catering to foreigners (eg in Mahabalipuram and Puducherry) can offer a blissful break from heavily spiced curries.

Choosing a good restaurant can be tricky if you're new to India. Many local eateries sport a grimy look that can be off-putting, yet serve brilliant and safe food, while swish four-star hotel restaurants that attract large numbers of tourists can dish up buffet food that leaves you crawling to the bathroom at 0200. A large crowd of locals is always a good sign that the food is freshly cooked and good. Even fly-blown *dhabas* on the roadside can be safe, as long as you stick to freshly cooked meals and avoid timebombs like deep-fried samosas left in the sun for hours.

Many city restaurants and backpacker eateries offer a choice of so-called European options such as toasted sandwiches, stuffed pancakes, apple pies, fruit crumbles and cheesecakes. Italian favourites (pizzas, pastas) can be very different from what you are used to. Ice creams, on the other hand, can be exceptionally good; there are excellent Indian ones as well as some international brands.

India has many delicious tropical fruits. Some are seasonal (eg mangoes, pineapples and jackfruit), while others (eg bananas, grapes and oranges) are available throughout the year. It is safe to eat the ones you can wash and peel. Don't leave India without trying its superb range of indigenous sweets. A piece or two of milk-based *peda* or Mysore *pak* make a perfect sweet postscript to a cheap dinner.

Food hygiene has improved immensely in recent years. However, you still need to take extra care, as flies abound and refrigeration in the hot weather may be inadequate and intermittent because of power cuts. It is safest to eat only freshly prepared food by ordering from the menu (especially meat and fish dishes). Be suspicious of salads and cut fruit, which may have been lying around for hours or washed in unpurified tap water – although salads served in top-end hotel restaurants and places primarily catering to foreigners (eg in Mahabalipuram and Puducherry) can offer a blissful break from heavily spiced curries.

Drink
Drinking water used to be regarded as one of India's biggest hazards. It is still true that water from the tap or a well should never be considered safe to drink since public water supplies are often polluted. Bottled water is now widely available although not all bottled water is mineral water; most are simply purified water from an urban supply. Buy from a shop or stall, check the seal carefully (some companies now add a second clear plastic seal around the bottle top) and avoid street hawkers; when disposing bottles puncture the neck which prevents misuse but allows recycling.

There is growing concern over the mountains of plastic bottles that are collecting and the waste of resources needed to produce them, so travellers are being encouraged to use alternative methods of getting safe drinking water. In some towns purified water is now sold for refilling your own container. You may wish to purify water yourself. A portable water filter is a good idea, carrying the drinking water in a plastic bottle in an insulated carrier. Always carry enough drinking water with you when travelling. It is important to use pure water for cleaning teeth.

Tea and **coffee** are safe and widely available. Both are normally served sweet, and with milk. If you wish, say 'no sugar' (*chini nahin*), 'no milk' (*dudh nahin*) when ordering. Alternatively, ask for a pot of tea and milk and sugar to be brought separately. Freshly brewed coffee is a common drink in South India, but in the North, ordinary city restaurants will usually serve the instant variety. Even in aspiring smart cafés, espresso or cappuccino may not turn out quite as you'd expect in the West.

Bottled **soft drinks** such as Coke, Pepsi, Teem, Limca, Thums Up and Gold Spot are universally available but always check the seal when you buy from a street stall. There are also several brands of fruit juice sold in cartons, including mango, pineapple and apple – Indian brands are very sweet. Don't add ice cubes as the water source may be contaminated. Take care with fresh fruit juices or *lassis* as ice is often added.

Indians rarely drink **alcohol** with a meal. In the past wines and spirits were generally either imported and extremely expensive, or local and of poor quality. Now, the best Indian whisky, rum and brandy (IMFL or 'Indian Made Foreign Liquor') are widely accepted, as are good Champagnoise and other wines from Maharashtra. If you hanker after a bottle of imported wine, you will only find it in the top restaurants for at least Rs 800-1000.

For the urban elite, refreshing Indian beers are popular when eating out and so are widely available. 'Pubs' have sprung up in the major cities. Elsewhere, seedy, all-male drinking dens in the larger cities are best avoided for women travellers, but can make quite an experience otherwise – you will sometimes be locked into cubicles for clandestine drinking. If that sounds unsavoury then head for the better hotel bars instead; prices aren't that steep. In rural India, local rice, palm, cashew or date juice *toddy* and *arak* is deceptively potent.

Most states have alcohol-free dry days or enforce degrees of Prohibition. Some upmarket restaurants may serve beer even if it's not listed, so it's worth asking. In some states there are government approved wine shops where you buy your alcohol through a metal grille.

Festivals in Chennai and Tamil Nadu

India has a wealth of festivals with many celebrated nationwide, while others are specific to a particular state or community or even a particular temple. Many fall on different dates each year depending on the Hindu lunar calendar; there's an amazingly thorough calendar of upcoming major and minor festivals at www.drikpanchang.com. ›› *Local festivals are listed in the Festivals section throughout the book.*

The Hindu calendar
Hindus follow two distinct eras: The *Vikrama Samvat* which began in 57 BC and the *Salivahan Saka* which dates from AD 78 and has been the official Indian calendar since 1957. The *Saka* new year starts on 22 March and has the same length as the Gregorian calendar. The 29½-day lunar month with its 'dark' and 'bright' halves based on the new and full moons, are named after 12 constellations, and total a 354-day year. The calendar cleverly has an extra month (*adhik maas*) every 2½ to three years, to bring it in line with the solar year of 365 days coinciding with the Gregorian calendar of the West.

Some major national and regional festivals are listed below. A few count as national holidays: **26 January**: Republic Day; **15 August**: Independence Day; **2 October**: Mahatma Gandhi's Birthday; **25 December**: Christmas Day.

Major festivals and fairs
Jan New Year's Day (**1 Jan**) is accepted officially when following the Gregorian calendar but there are regional variations which fall on different dates, often coinciding with spring/harvest time in Mar and Apr.
Jan 13-16 The 4-day harvest festival of Pongal is celebrated with great fervour throughout the state. Doorsteps are decorated with kolam (geometric designs in coloured powder), cattle are worshipped, and vast pots of the eponymous rice dish are cooked.
Feb Vasant Panchami, the spring festival when people wear bright yellow clothes to mark the advent of the season with singing, dancing and feasting.
Feb-Mar Maha Sivaratri marks the night when Siva danced his celestial dance of

destruction (*Tandava*), which is celebrated with feasting and fairs at Siva temples, but preceded by a night of devotional readings and hymn singing.
14 Apr Tamil New Year The Tamil month of Chithirai (14 Apr-14 May) kicks off the Tamil year with huge parades at temples throughout the state, most famously in Madurai.
Apr/May Buddha Jayanti, the 1st full moon night in Apr/May marks the birth of the Buddha.
Jul/Aug Raksha (or Rakhi) Bandhan symbolizes the bond between brother and sister, celebrated at full moon. A sister says special prayers for her brother and ties coloured threads around his wrist to remind

him of the special bond. He in turn gives a gift and promises to protect and care for her. Sometimes *rakshas* are exchanged as a mark of friendship. Narial Purnima on the same full moon. Hindus make offerings of *narial* (coconuts) to the Vedic god Varuna (Lord of the waters) by throwing them into the sea.

15 Aug is **Independence Day**, a national secular holiday is marked by special events.

Vinayaka Chaturthi Known elsewhere in India as Ganesh Chaturthi, this is the day when the elephant-headed God of good omen is shown special reverence. The elephant-headed God of good omen is shown special reverence. On the last of the 5-day festival after harvest, clay images of Ganesh are taken in procession with dancers and musicians, and are immersed in the sea, river or pond.

Aug/Sep Janmashtami, the birth of Krishna is celebrated at midnight at Krishna temples.

Sep/Oct Dasara has many local variations. Celebrations for the 9 nights (*navaratri*) are marked with **Ramlila**, various episodes of the Ramayana story are enacted with particular reference to the battle between the forces of good and evil. In some parts of India it celebrates *Rama's* victory over the Demon king *Ravana* of Lanka with the help of loyal *Hanuman* (Monkey). Huge effigies of *Ravana* made of bamboo and paper are burnt on the 10th day (*Vijaya dasami*) of **Dasara** in public open spaces. In some regions the focus is on Durga's victory over the demon *Mahishasura*.

Oct/Nov Gandhi Jayanti (**2 Oct**), Mahatma Gandhi's birthday, is remembered with prayer meetings and devotional singing.

Diwali/Deepavali (*Sanskrit ideepa* lamp), the festival of lights. Some Hindus celebrate Krishna's victory over the demon *Narakasura*, some Rama's return after his 14 years' exile in the forest when citizens lit his way with oil lamps. The festival falls on the dark *chaturdasi* (14th) night (the one preceding the new moon), when rows of lamps or candles are lit in remembrance, and *rangolis* are painted on the floor as a sign of welcome. Fireworks have become an integral part of the celebration which are often set off days before Diwali. Equally, Lakshmi, the Goddess of Wealth (as well as Ganesh) is worshipped by merchants and the business community who open the new financial year's account on the day. Most people wear new clothes; some play games of chance.

Dec Christmas Day (25 Dec) sees Indian Christians celebrate the birth of Christ in much the same way as in the West; many churches hold services/mass at midnight. There is an air of festivity in city markets which are specially decorated and illuminated. Over New Year's Eve (**31 Dec**) hotel prices peak and large supplements are added for meals and entertainment in the upper category hotels. Some churches mark the night with a Midnight Mass.

Muslim holy days

These are fixed according to the lunar calendar. According to the Gregorian calendar, they tend to fall 11 days earlier each year, dependent on the sighting of the new moon.

Ramadan is the start of the month of fasting when all Muslims (except young children, the very elderly, the sick, pregnant women and travellers) must abstain from food and drink, from sunrise to sunset.

Id ul Fitr is the 3-day festival that marks the end of Ramadan.

Id-ul-Zuha/Bakr-Id is when Muslims commemorate Ibrahim's sacrifice of his son according to God's commandment; the main time of pilgrimage to Mecca (the Hajj). It is marked by the sacrifice of a goat, feasting and alms giving.

Muharram is when the killing of the Prophet's grandson, Hussain, is commemorated by Shi'a Muslims. Decorated *tazias* (replicas of the martyr's tomb) are carried in procession by devout wailing followers who beat their chests to express their grief. Shi'as fast for the 10 days.

Responsible travel in Chennai and Tamil Nadu

As well as respecting local cultural sensitivities, travellers can take a number of simple steps to reduce, or even improve, their impact on the local environment. Environmental concern is relatively new in India. Don't be afraid to pressurize businesses by asking about their policies.

Litter   Many travellers think that there is little point in disposing of rubbish properly when the tossing of water bottles, plastic cups and other non-biodegradable items out of train windows is already so widespread. Don't follow an example you feel to be wrong. You can immediately reduce your impact by refusing plastic bags and other excess packaging when shopping – use a small backpack or cloth bag instead – and if you do collect a few, keep them with you to store other rubbish until you get to a litter bin.

Plastic mineral water bottles, an inevitable corollary to poor water hygiene standards, are a major contributor to India's litter mountain. However, many hotels, including nearly all of the upmarket ones, most restaurants and bus and train stations, provide drinking water purified using a combination of ceramic and carbon filters, chlorine and UV irradiation. Ask for '*filter paani*'; if the water tastes like a swimming pool it is probably quite safe to drink, though it's best to introduce your body gradually to the new water. If purifying water yourself, bringing it to a boil at sea level will make it safe, but at altitude you have to boil it for longer to ensure that all the microbes are killed. Various sterilizing methods can be used that contain chlorine (eg Puritabs) or iodine (eg Pota Aqua) and there are a number of mechanical or chemical water filters available on the market.

Bucket baths or showers   The biggest issue relating to responsible and sustainable tourism is water. The traditional Indian 'bucket bath', in which you wet, soap then rinse off using a small hand-held plastic jug dipped into a large bucket, uses on average around 15 litres of water, as compared to 30-45 for a shower. These are commonly offered except in four- and five-star hotels.

Support responsible tourism   Spending your money carefully can have a positive impact. Sleeping, eating and shopping at small, locally owned businesses directly supports communities, while specific community tourism concerns provide an economic motivation for people to stay in remote communities, protect natural areas and revive traditional cultures, rather than exploit the environment or move to the cities for work.

Transport   Choose walking, cycling or public transport over fuel-guzzling cars and motorbikes.

Essentials A-Z

Accident and emergency

Contact the relevant emergency service (police T100, fire T101, ambulance T102) and your embassy (see under Directory in major cities). Make sure you obtain police/medical reports required for insurance claims.

Customs and duty free

Duty free

Tourists are allowed to bring in all personal effects 'which may reasonably be required', without charge. The official customs allowance includes 200 cigarettes or 50 cigars, 0.95 litres of alcohol, a camera and a pair of binoculars. Valuable personal effects and professional equipment including jewellery, special camera equipment and lenses, laptop computers and sound and video recorders must in theory be declared on a Tourist Baggage Re-Export Form (TBRE) in order for them to be taken out of the country, though in practice it's relatively unlikely that your bags will be inspected beyond a cursory x-ray. Nevertheless, it saves considerable frustration if you know the equipment serial numbers in advance and are ready to show them on the equipment. In addition to the forms, details of imported equipment may be entered into your passport. Save time by completing the formalities while waiting for your baggage. It is essential to keep these forms for showing to the customs when leaving India, otherwise considerable delays are very likely at the time of departure.

Prohibited items

The import of dangerous drugs, live plants, gold coins, gold and silver bullion and silver coins not in current use are either banned or subject to strict regulation. It is illegal to import firearms into India without special permission. Enquire at consular offices abroad for details.

Drugs

Certain areas, such as Mahabalipuram, have become associated with foreigners who take drugs. These are likely to attract local and foreign drug dealers but be aware that the government takes the misuse of drugs very seriously. Anyone charged with the illegal possession of drugs risks facing a fine of Rs 100,000 and a minimum 10 years' imprisonment. Several foreigners have been imprisoned for drugs-related offences in the last decade.

Electricity

Inida supply is 220-240 volts AC. Some top hotels have transformers. There may be pronounced variations in the voltage, and power cuts are common. Power back-up by generator or inverter is becoming more widespread, even in humble hotels, though it may not cover a/c. Socket sizes vary so take a universal adaptor; low-quality versions are available locally. Many hotels, even in the higher categories, don't have electric razor sockets. Invest in a stabilizer for a laptop.

Embassies and consulates

For information on visas and immigration, see page 27. For a comprehensive list of embassies (but not all consulates), see http://india.gov.in/overseas/indian_missions.php. Many embassies around the world are now outsourcing the visa process which might affect how long the process takes.

Health

Local populations in India are exposed to a range of health risks not encountered in the Western world. Many of the diseases are major problems for the local poor and destitute and, although the risk to travellers is more remote, they cannot be ignored. Obviously 5-star travel is going to carry less risk than backpacking on a budget.

Health care in the region is varied. There are many excellent private and government clinics/hospitals. As with all medical care, first impressions count. It's worth contacting your embassy or consulate on arrival and asking where the recommended (ie those used by diplomats) clinics are. You can also ask about locally recommended medical do's and don'ts. If you do get ill, and you have the opportunity, you should also ask your medical insurer whether they are satisfied that the medical centre/hospital you have been referred to is of a suitable standard.

Before you go

Ideally, you should see your GP or travel clinic at least 6 weeks before your departure for general advice on travel risks, malaria and vaccinations. Make sure you have travel insurance, get a dental check (especially if you are going to be away for more than a month), know your own blood group and if you suffer a long-term condition such as diabetes or epilepsy make sure someone knows or that you have a Medic Alert bracelet/necklace with this information on it. Remember that it is risky to buy medicinal tablets abroad because the doses may differ and India has a huge trade in false drugs.

Vaccinations

If you need vaccinations, see your doctor well in advance of your travel. Most courses must be completed by a minimum of 4 weeks. Travel clinics may provide rapid courses of vaccination, but are likely to be more expensive. The following vaccinations are recommended: typhoid, polio, tetanus, infectious hepatitis and diptheria. For details of malaria prevention, contact your GP or local travel clinic.

The following vaccinations may also be considered: rabies, possibly BCG (since TB is still common in the region) and in some cases meningitis and diphtheria (if you're staying in the country for a long time). Yellow fever is not required in India but you may be asked to show a certificate if you

have travelled from Africa or South America. Japanese encephalitis may be required for rural travel at certain times of the year (mainly rainy seasons). An effective oral cholera vaccine (Dukoral) is now available as 2 doses providing 3 months' protection.

Websites

British Travel Health Association (UK), www.btha.org This is the official website of an organization of travel health professionals.

Fit for Travel, www.fitfortravel.scot. nhs. uk This site from Scotland provides a quick A-Z of vaccine and travel health advice requirements for each country.

Foreign and Commonwealth Office (FCO) (UK), www.fco.gov.uk This is a key travel advice site, with useful information on the country, people, climate and lists the UK embassies/consulates. The site also promotes the concept of 'know before you go' and encourages travel insurance and appropriate travel health advice. It has links to Department of Health travel advice site.

The Health Protection Agency, www.hpa.org.uk Up-to-date malaria advice guidelines for travel around the world. It gives specific advice about the right drugs for each location. It also has useful information for those who are pregnant, suffering from epilepsy or planning to travel with children.

Medic Alert (UK), www.medicalalert.com This is the website of the foundation that produces bracelets and necklaces for those with existing medical problems. Once you have ordered your bracelet/necklace you write your key medical details on paper inside it, so that if you collapse, a medic can identify you as having epilepsy or a nut allergy, etc.

Travel Screening Services (UK), www.travelscreening.co.uk A private clinic dedicated to integrated travel health. The clinic gives vaccine, travel health advice, email and SMS text vaccine reminders and screens returned travellers for tropical diseases.

World Health Organisation, www.who.int

The WHO site has links to the *WHO Blue Book* on travel advice. This lists the diseases in different regions of the world. It describes vaccination schedules and makes clear which countries have yellow fever vaccination certificate requirements and malarial risk.

Language

Tamil, spoken as a mother tongue by million people, is the most widely spoken. See Language section, page 152, for useful words and phrases.

English now plays an important role across India. It is widely spoken in towns and cities and even in quite remote villages it is usually not difficult to find someone who speaks at least a little English. Outside of major tourist sites, other European languages are almost completely unknown. The accent in which English is spoken is often affected strongly by the mother tongue of the speaker and there have been changes in common grammar which sometimes make it sound unusual. Many of these changes have become standard Indian English usage, as valid as any other varieties of English used around the world. It is possible to study a number of Indian languages at language centres.

Money

Indian currency is the Indian Rupee (Re/Rs). It is **not** possible to purchase these before you arrive. If you want cash on arrival it is best to get it at the airport bank, although see if an ATM is available as airport rates are not very generous. Rupee notes are printed in denominations of Rs 1000, 500, 100, 50, 20, 10. The rupee is divided into 100 paise. Coins are minted in denominations of Rs 5, Rs 2, Rs 1 and 50 paise. **Note** Carry money, mostly as traveller's cheques, in a money belt worn under clothing. Have a small amount in an easily accessible place.

Exchange rates ➜ *£1 = Rs 101, €1 = Rs 83, US$1 = Rs 61 (Jan 2014)*

ATMs

By far the most convenient method of accessing money, ATMs are all over India, usually attended by security guards, with most banks offering some services to holders of overseas cards. Banks whose ATMs will issue cash against Cirrus and Maestro cards, as well as Visa and MasterCard, include **Bank of Baroda, Citibank, HDFC, HSBC, ICICI, IDBI, Punjab National Bank, State Bank of India (SBI), Standard Chartered** and UTI. A withdrawal fee is usually charged by the issuing bank on top of the conversion charges applied by your own bank. Fraud prevention measures quite often result in travellers having their cards blocked by the bank when unexpected overseas transactions occur; advise your bank of your travel plans before leaving.

Credit cards

Major credit cards are increasingly acceptable in the main centres, though in smaller cities and towns it is still rare to be able to pay by credit card. Payment by credit card can sometimes be more expensive than payment by cash, whilst some credit card companies charge a premium on cash withdrawals. **Visa** and **MasterCard** have a growing number of ATMs in major cities and several banks offer withdrawal facilities for Cirrus and Maestro cardholders. It is however easy to obtain a cash advance against a credit card. Railway reservation centres in major cities take payment for train tickets by Visa card which can be very quick as the queue is short, although they cannot be used for Tourist Quota tickets.

Currency cards

If you don't want to carry lots of cash, prepaid currency cards allow you to preload money from your bank account, fixed at the day's exchange rate. They look like a credit or debit card and are issued by specialist money changing companies, such as Travelex and Caxton FX. You can top up and check your balance by phone, online and sometimes by text.

Traveller's cheques (TCs)

TCs issued by reputable companies (eg Thomas Cook, American Express) are widely accepted. They can be easily exchanged at small local travel agents and tourist internet cafés but are rarely used directly for payment. Try to avoid changing at banks, where the process can be time consuming; opt for hotels and agents instead, take large denomination cheques and change enough to last for some days.

Changing money

The State Bank of India and several others in major towns are authorized to deal in foreign exchange. Some give cash against Visa/MasterCard (eg ANZ, Bank of Baroda who print a list of their participating branches, Andhra Bank). American Express cardholders can use their cards to get either cash or TCs in Chennai. They also have offices in Coimbatore and Thiruvananthapuram. The larger cities have licensed money changers with offices usually in the commercial sector. Changing money through unauthorized dealers is illegal. Premiums on the currency black market are very small and highly risky. Large hotels change money 24 hrs a day for guests, but banks often give a substantially better rate of exchange. It is best to exchange money on arrival at the airport bank or the Thomas Cook counter. Many international flights arrive during the night and it is generally far easier and less time consuming to change money at the airport than in the city. You should be given a foreign currency encashment certificate when you change money through a bank or authorized dealer; ask for one if it is not automatically given. It allows you to change Indian rupees back to your own currency on departure. It also enables you to use rupees to pay hotel bills or buy air tickets for which payment in foreign exchange may be

required. The certificates are only valid for 3 months.

Cost of travelling

Most food, accommodation and public transport, especially rail and bus, is exceptionally cheap, although inflation in 2010 was 16.3% and basic food items such as rice, lentils, tomatoes and onions have skyrocketed. There is a widening range of moderately priced but clean hotels and restaurants outside the big cities, making it possible to get a great deal for your money. Budget travellers sharing a room, taking public transport, avoiding souvenir stalls, and eating nothing but rice and dhal can get away with a budget of Rs 400-600 (about US$8-12 or £5-8) a day. This sum leaps up if you drink alcohol (still cheap by European standards at about US$2, £1 or Rs 80 for a pint), smoke foreign-brand cigarettes or want to have your own wheels (you can expect to spend between Rs 150 and 200 to hire a Honda per day). Those planning to stay in fairly comfortable hotels and use taxis sightseeing should budget at US$50-80 (£30-50) a day. India can be a great place to pick and choose, save a little on basic accommodation and then treat yourself to the type of meal you could only dream of affording back home. Also, be prepared to spend a fair amount more in Chennai, where not only is the cost of living significantly higher but where it's worth coughing up extra for a half-decent room: penny-pinch by the beach when you'll be spending precious little time indoors anyway. A newspaper costs Rs 5 and breakfast for 2 with coffee can come to as little as Rs 50 in a South Indian 'hotel', but if you intend to eat banana pancakes by the sea, you can expect to pay more like Rs 50-150 a plate.

Opening hours
Banks Mon-Fri 1030-1430, Sat 1030-1230. Top hotels sometimes have a 24-hr money changing service. **Post offices** Mon-Fri 1000-1700, often shutting for lunch, and

Sat mornings. **Government offices** Mon-Fri 0930-1700, Sat 0930-1300 (some open on alternate Sat only). **Shops** Mon-Sat 0930-1800. Bazars keep longer hours.

Safety
Personal security

In general the threats to personal security for travellers in India are remarkably small. However, incidents of petty theft and violence directed specifically at tourists have been on the increase so care is necessary in some places, and basic common sense needs to be used with respect to looking after valuables. Follow the same precautions you would when at home. There have been incidents of sexual assault in and around the main tourist beach centres, particularly after full moon parties in South India. Avoid wandering alone outdoors late at night in these places. During daylight hours be careful in remote places, especially when alone. If you are under threat, scream loudly. Be very cautious before accepting food or drink from casual acquaintances, as it may be drugged – though note that Indians on a long train journey will invariably try to share their snacks with you, and balance caution with the opportunity to interact.

Travel advice

It is better to seek advice from your consulate than from travel agencies. Before you travel you can contact: **British Foreign & Commonwealth Office Travel Advice Unit**, T0845-850 2829 (Pakistan desk T020-7270 2385), www.fco.gov.uk. **US State Department's Bureau of Consular Affairs**, Overseas Citizens Services, Room 4800, Department of State, Washington, DC 20520-4818, USA, T202-647 1488, http://travel.state.gov. **Australian Department of Foreign Affairs Canberra**, Australia, T02-6261 3305, www.smartraveller.gov.au. Canadian official advice is on www.voyage.gc.ca.

Theft

Theft is not uncommon. It is best to keep TCs, passports and valuables with you at all times. Don't regard hotel rooms as being automatically safe; even hotel safes don't guarantee secure storage. Avoid leaving valuables near open windows even when you are in the room. Use your own padlock in a budget hotel when you go out. Pickpockets and other thieves operate in the big cities. Crowded areas are particularly high risk. Take special care of your belongings when getting on or off public transport.

If you have items stolen, they should be reported to the police as soon as possible. Keep a separate record of vital documents, including passport details and numbers of TCs. Larger hotels will be able to assist in contacting and dealing with the police. Dealings with the police can be very difficult and in the worst regions, such as Bihar, even dangerous. The paperwork involved in reporting losses can be time consuming and irritating and your own documentation (eg passport and visas) may be demanded.

In some states the police occasionally demand bribes, though you should not assume that if procedures move slowly you are automatically being expected to offer a bribe. The traffic police are tightening up on traffic offences in some places. They have the right to make on-the-spot fines for speeding and illegal parking. If you face a fine, insist on a receipt. If you have to go to a police station, try to take someone with you.

If you face really serious problems (eg in connection with a driving accident), contact your consular office as quickly as possible. You should ensure you always have your international driving licence and motorbike or car documentation with you.

Confidence tricksters are particularly common where people are on the move, notably around railway stations or places where budget tourists gather. A common plea is some sudden and desperate calamity; sometimes a letter will be produced in English to back up the claim.

The demands are likely to increase sharply if sympathy is shown.

Telephone

The international code for India is +91. International Direct Dialling is widely available in privately run call booths, usually labelled on yellow boards with the letters 'PCO-STD-ISD'. You dial the call yourself, and the time and cost are displayed on a computer screen. Cheap rate (2100-0600) means long queues may form outside booths. Telephone calls from hotels are usually more expensive (check price before calling), though some will allow local calls free of charge. Internet phone booths, usually associated with cybercafés, are the cheapest way of calling overseas.

A double ring repeated regularly means it is ringing; equal tones with equal pauses means engaged (similar to the UK). If calling a mobile, rather than ringing, you might hear music while you wait for an answer.

One disadvantage of the tremendous pace of the telecommunications revolution is the fact that millions of telephone numbers go out of date every year. Current telephone directories themselves are often out of date and some of the numbers given in this book will have been changed even as we go to press. Our best advice is if the number in the text does not work, add a '2'. Directory enquiries, T197, can be helpful but works only for the local area code.

Mobile phones are for sale everywhere, as are local SIM cards that allow you to make calls within India and overseas at much lower rates than using a 'roaming' service from your normal provider at home – sometimes for as little as Rs 0.5 per min. Arguably the best service is provided by the government carrier BSNL/MTNL but security provisions make connecting to the service virtually impossible for foreigners. Private companies such as Airtel, Vodafone, Reliance and Tata Indicom are easier to sign up with, but the deals they offer can be befuddling and are frequently changed. To connect you'll need to complete a form, have a local address or receipt showing the address of your hotel, and present photocopies of your passport and visa plus 2 passport photos to an authorized reseller – most phone dealers will be able to help, and can also sell top-up. Univercell, www.univercell.in, and The Mobile Store, www.themobilestore.in, are 2 widespread and efficient chains selling phones and sim cards.

India is divided into a number of 'calling circles' or regions, and if you travel outside the region where your connection is based you will pay higher charges for making and receiving calls, and any problems that may occur – with 'unverified' documents, for example – can be much harder to resolve.

Time

India doesn't change its clocks, so from the last Sun in Oct to the last Sun in Mar the time is GMT +5½ hrs, and the rest of the year it's +4½ hrs (USA, EST +10½ and +9½ hrs; Australia, EST -5½ and -4½ hrs).

Tipping

A tip of Rs 10 to a bellboy carrying luggage in a modest hotel (Rs 20 in a higher category) would be appropriate. In upmarket restaurants, a 10% tip is acceptable when service is not already included, while in places serving very cheap meals, round off the bill with small change. Indians don't normally tip taxi drivers but a small extra is welcomed. Porters at airports and railway stations often have a fixed rate displayed but will usually press for more. Ask fellow passengers what a fair rate is.

Tourist information

There are Government of India tourist offices in the state capitals, as well as state tourist offices (sometimes Tourism Development Corporations) in the major cities and a few important sites. They produce their own tourist literature, either free or sold at a nominal price, and some also have lists of city hotels and paying guest options. The quality of material is improving though maps are often poor. Many offer tours of the city, neighbouring sights and overnight and regional packages. Some run modest hotels and midway motels with restaurants and may also arrange car hire and guides. The staff in the regional and local offices are usually helpful.

Visas and immigration

Virtually all foreign nationals, including children, require a visa to enter India. Nationals of Bhutan and Nepal only require a suitable means of identification. The rules regarding visas change frequently and arrangements for application and collection also vary from town to town so it is essential to check details and costs with the relevant embassy or consulate. These remain closed on Indian national holidays. Many consulates and embassies are currently outsourcing the visa process; it's best to find out in advance how long it will take. Note that visas are valid from the date granted, not from the date of entry. Recently the Indian government has decided to issue 'visas on arrival' for some 40 countries (including the UK, the USA, France and Germany), as well as for citizens of all countries who are over the age of 60. The exact time frame for the change is not yet clear, so check the latest situation online before travelling. No foreigner needs to register within the 180-day period of their tourist visa. All foreign visitors who stay in India for more than 180 days need to get an income tax clearance exemption certificate from the Foreign Section of the Income Tax Department in Delhi, Mumbai, Kolkata or Chennai. Applications for visa extensions should be made to the Foreigners' Regional Registration Offices at New Delhi or Kolkata, or an office of the Superintendent of Police in the District Headquarters. After 6 months, you must leave India and apply for a new visa – the Nepal office is known

to be difficult. Anyone staying in India for a period of more than 180 days (6 months) must register at a convenient Foreigners' Registration Office.

Weights and measures

Metric is in universal use in the cities. In remote areas local measures are sometimes used. One lakh is 100,000 and 1 crore is 10 million.

Contents

Footprint features

Chennai & Tamil Nadu

Chennai (Madras)

Chennai, South India's sprawling metropolis and India's fourth largest city, is dubbed 'India's Detroit' thanks to its chiefly automotive industrial revolution. The analogy is apt in more ways than one. Chennai's beautiful Indo-Saracenic buildings now stand like islands of elegance in a sea of concrete sprawl, and seen from the back of a taxi crawling along Anna Salai in the rush hour, the city can seem to be little more than a huge, sweltering traffic jam.

Nevertheless, modern Chennai remains the de facto capital of Indian high culture – complex dances such as Bharatnatyam are still widely taught and practised here – and the city retains an air of gentility that's missing from the other Indian metros. Despite attempts to carpet-bomb the southern suburbs with IT parks and malls, you'll find little here of the boom of Mumbai or the overheated dynamism of Bengaluru. Chennai's urban elite of textile magnates, artists and web entrepreneurs still maintain their networks around the bars and walking tracks of the city's Raj-era clubs, where chinos and loafers rule and *churidars* and *lungis* are checked at the door.

Outside the gates of these green refuges, Chennai can be a hard city to love. It's polluted, congested, tricky to negotiate and lacks anything resembling a centre. Nevertheless, there are reasons to stick around for more than the customary pre- or post-flight overnight stay, particularly if you base yourself near the old Brahmin suburb of Mylapore, which with its beautiful temple towers, old-time silk emporia and dingy cafés, makes a worthy introduction or postscript to the Tamil temple circuit.

Arriving in Chennai → *Phone code: 044. Population: 5.36 million.*

Getting there Chennai's international and domestic air terminals are next to each other about 15 km from the city: allow 50 minutes, although it may take as little as half an hour. Airport buses run the circuit of the main hotels, and include Egmore station; otherwise it's best to get a pre-paid taxi: either yellow-topped government taxis or the more comfortable and expensive private cabs (note the number written on your charge slip). Trains from the north and west come into the Central Station behind the port, while lines from the south terminate at Egmore; both stations have abundant hotels nearby. State-owned buses terminate at the Koyembedu Moffusil terminus, 10 km west of the centre, and private buses at the nearby Omni terminus; it's worth asking whether the driver can drop you closer to your destination.

Getting around Chennai is very spread out and walking is usually uncomfortably hot so it's best to find an auto-rickshaw. Chennai's autos, once a notorious rip-off, are now required by law to run by the meter, though the rule is flexibly followed. With patience you should be able to find a driver who will use the meter.

Taxis are comparatively rare and a bit more expensive. The best option are call / radio taxis, which you call and book in advance rather than hail on the street. You can use these simply to get from one point to another, or for a set number of hours – a cheap (as little as Rs 100 per hour) and convenient way to cover a lot of sights in a morning or a day. There are a number of companies, all charging similar rates; **Fast Track** ① *T044-24732020*, is a reliable one. The bus network is extensive with frequent services, but it's often very crowded. ▸ *See Transport, page 52.*

Orientation Chennai is far from an 'organized' city. The main harbour near the old British military zone of **George Town** is marked by cranes for the cargo business. Nearby is the **fort**, the former headquarters of the British and now the Secretariat of the Tamil Nadu Government, and the High Court. The **Burma bazar**, a long line of pokey shops, runs between the two near Parry's Corner, while the two main rail stations lie to the west of George Town. From the fort, **Anna Salai** (Mount Road of old) cuts a southwest-ward swathe through the city, passing through or near to most areas of interest to visitors: **Triplicane**, where most of Chennai's cheap accommodation can be found; **Thousand Lights** and **Teynampet**, where ritzier hotels and malls dominate; and the commercial free-for-all of **T Nagar**. Just south of the central area between Anna Salai and the long sweep of Marina Beach lies **Mylapore**, older than Chennai itself and the cultural heart of the city. Further south still, industrial and high-tech sprawl stretches down the coast almost as far as Mahabalipuram.

Tourist information Most tourist offices are located in the the new **Tourism Complex** ① *2 Wallajah Rd, near Kalaivanar Arangam*. **Tamil Nadu Tourism (TN)** ① *T044-2536 8358, www.tamilnadutourism.org*, also has offices opposite Central station (T044-2535 3351), in Egmore (T044-2819 2165), and at the Domestic and International airports. **Tamil Tourist Development Corporation (TTDC)** ① *T044-2538 9857, www.ttdconline.com*.

Possibly the best organized office is **Government of India Tourism** ① *154 Anna Salai, T044-2846 0285, Mon-Fri 0915-1745, Sat until 1300*. **India Tourism Development Corporation (ITDC)** ① *29 Ethiraj Salai, T044-2821 1782, Mon-Sat 1000-1800, Sun closed*. For city information see also **www.chennaionline.com**.

Background

Armenian and Portuguese traders had settled the San Thome area before the arrival of the British. In 1639, **Francis Day**, a trader with the East India Company, negotiated the grant of a tiny plot of sandy land to the north of the Cooum River as the base for a warehouse or factory. The building was completed on 23 April 1640, St George's Day. The site was chosen partly because of local politics – Francis Day's friendship with Ayyappa Nayak, brother of the local ruler of the coast country from Pulicat to the Portuguese settlement of San Thome – but more importantly by the favourable local price of cotton goods.

By 1654 the patch of sand had grown into Fort St George, complete with a church and English residences – the 'White Town'. To its north was 'Black Town', referred to locally as Chennaipatnam, after Chennappa Nayak, Dharmala Ayyappa Nayak's father. The two towns merged and Madraspatnam grew with the acquisition of neighbouring villages of Tiru-alli-keni (meaning Lily Tank, and Anglicized as Triplicane), in 1676. In 1693, Governor Yale (founder of Yale University in the USA) acquired Egmore, Purasawalkam and Tondiarpet from Emperor Aurangzeb, who had by then extended Mughal power to the far south. In 1746 Madras was captured by the French, to be returned to British control as a result of the Treaty of Aix-la-Chapelle in 1748. Villages like Nungambakkam, Ennore, Perambur, San Thome and Mylapore (the 'city of the peacock') were absorbed by the mid-18th century with the help of friendly Nawabs. In 1793, the British colonial administration moved to Calcutta, but Madras remained the centre of the East India Company's expanding power in South India.

It was more than 150 years after they had founded Fort St George at Madras (in 1639) before the East India Company could claim political supremacy in South India. Haidar Ali, who mounted the throne of Mysore in 1761, and his son Tipu Sultan, allied with the French, won many battles against the English. The 1783 Treaty of Versailles forced peace. The English took Malabar in 1792, and in 1801 Lord Wellesley brought together most of the south under the Madras Presidency.

The city continues to grow, although many services, including water and housing, are stretched to breaking point. Since Independence an increasing range of heavy and light goods industries, particularly automotive, has joined the long-established cotton textiles and leather industries.

Places in Chennai → For listings, see pages 42-55.

Apart from anomalous little pockets of expats, such as Chetpet's Jamaican and South African communities, life in Chennai continues much as it always has done: brahminical neighbourhoods still demand strict vegetarianism of all tenants; and flat sharing, a commonly accepted practice among the young in Bengaluru (Bangalore), is taboo. Superstition is important here too: rents are decided according to vasthu, India's equivalent of feng shui, and a wrong-facing front door can slash your payments.

You have to squint hard today to picture the half-empty grandeur that was the Madras of the East India Presidency. Triplicane has some of the finest architectural remains but the derelict district is better known today as 'Bachelors' Neighbourhood' due to its popularity with young men who come to make their fortune in the city.

The long expanse of Marina Beach, just seaward of Triplicane, made Chennai's residents tragically vulnerable to the 2004 tsunami, which devastated this public land – the city's cricket pitch, picnic ground and fishing shore. There's no trace of the ferocity of the waves today, but here alone it took about 200 lives.

The fort and port: St George and George Town

Madras began as nothing more than a huddle of fishing villages on the Bay of Bengal, re-christened Madras by British 17th-century traders after they built the Factory House fortifications on the beach. The present fort dates from 1666. The 24 black

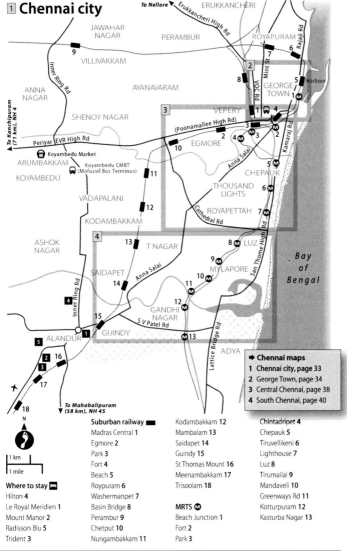

1 Chennai city

To Nellore ► Erukkancheri High Rd   ERUKKANCHERI

JAWAHAR
NAGAR

PERAMBUR   ROYAPURAM

9   6   Rajaji Rd   7

VILLIVAKKAM

ANNA
NAGAR   AYANAVARAM   8   GEORGE   5   Harbour

Inner Ring Rd   2   TOWN   1

SHENOY NAGAR   VEPERY   1   4

To Kanchipuram
(71 km), NH 4   3   (Poonamallee High Rd)   3   2

Periyar EVR High Rd   10   EGMORE   4   3

Koyambedu Market   Anna Salai   5

ARUMBAKKAM   Koyambedu CMBT   CHEPAUK   Kamaraj Rd

(Mofussil Bus Terminus)   11

KOYAMBEDU   THOUSAND   6

LIGHTS

VADAPALANI   12

ROYAPETTAH   7

KODAMBAKKAM   Cathedral Rd

ASHOK   4   13   T NAGAR   8   LUZ   Bay
NAGAR   of
9   MYLAPORE   San Thome High Rd   Bengal

SAIDAPET   Anna Salai   10

14   11

Inner Ring Rd   12

4   GANDHI
NAGAR

15   S V Patel Rd   13

ALANDUR   1   GUINDY   ADYA   Lattice Bridge Rd

5   2   16   ➡ Chennai maps
3   1 Chennai city, page 33
✈   17   2 George Town, page 34
3 Central Chennai, page 38
To Mahabalipuram   4 South Chennai, page 40
18   ▼ (58 km), NH 45

N

1 km

1 mile

Where to stay
Hilton 4
Le Royal Meridien 1
Mount Manor 2
Radisson Blu 5
Trident 3

Suburban railway ▬
Madras Central 1
Egmore 2
Park 3
Fort 4
Beach 5
Roypuram 6
Washermanpet 7
Basin Bridge 8
Perambur 9
Chetput 10
Nungambakkam 11

Kodambakkam 12
Mambalam 13
Saidapet 14
Guindy 15
St Thomas Mount 16
Meenambakkam 17
Trisoolam 18

MRTS Ⓜ
Beach Junction 1
Fort 2
Park 3

Chintadripet 4
Chepauk 5
Tiruvellikeni 6
Lighthouse 7
Luz 8
Tirumailai 9
Mandaveli 10
Greenways Rd 11
Kotturpuram 12
Kasturba Nagar 13

Charnockite pillars, were reclaimed by the British in 1762 after the French had carried them off to Puducherry in 1746. Now the site of state government, the **State Legislative Hall** has fine woodwork and black and white stone paving. You can also see the old barracks and officers' quarters including Lord Clive's house, which he rented from an Armenian merchant. One room, Clive's Corner, has small exhibits. The house once occupied by Arthur Wellesley, the future Duke of Wellington, is 100 m further along.

The fort's governor Streynsham Master was responsible for the most interesting building in the compound, **St Mary's Church** ① *T044-2538 2023*. Built between 1678 and 1680, it ranks as the first English church in India and the oldest British building to survive. It's unusually well fortified for a house of God – all solid masonry with semi-circular cannon-proof roofs and 1.3-m-thick walls – so that in times of siege it could function as a military dormitory and storehouse, and had to be almost entirely rebuilt in 1759 after military action in a siege. **Governor Elihu Yale** and **Robert Clive** were both married in the church. Yale, an American (born to English parents), who worked as a writer for the East India Company from the ages of 24 to 39, rose to become governor; his son David is buried under the Hynmers Obelisk in the old burial ground. The famous missionary **Schwartz**, at one time the intermediary between the British and Haidar Ali, is also celebrated here for his role just 'going about doing

2 George Town

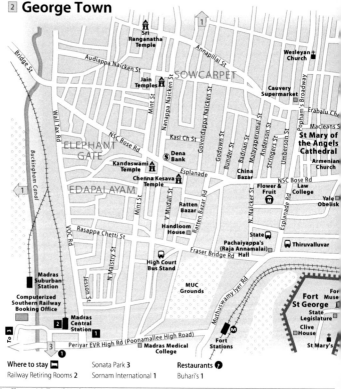

Where to stay 🛏
Railway Retiring Rooms 2

Sonata Park 3
Sornam International 1

Restaurants 🍴
Buhari's 1

good'. Job Charnock is commemorated for carrying a Hindu widow from the funeral pyre she was about to burn herself on and whereupon he took her as his wife. You can also learn the unhappy end of poor Malcolm McNeill, a colonel of the Madras Light Cavalry, who died at Rangoon in 1852 from neither battle nor disease but from a case of sunstroke. Nor is he alone: many Britishers appear to have fallen "a martyr to an ungenial climate".

The original black font, made from 3000-million-year-old Charnockite from Pallavaram, has been in continuous use since the church was consecrated. Outside the west entrance lies one of the oldest British inscriptions in India: the tombstone of Elizabeth Baker.

Also in the compound is an 18th-century building housing the **Fort Museum** ① *Sat-Thu 1000-1700, US$2, photography prohibited*, with exhibits from 300 years of British Indian history including brilliant portraits of Madras governors. It includes prints, documents, paintings, sculpture, arms (medieval weapons with instructions on their use) and uniforms. The Indo-French gallery has some Louis XIV furniture and clocks. Clive Corner, which includes letters and photographs, is particularly interesting. The building itself was once an exchange for East India Company merchants, becoming an officers' mess later.

Within walking distance of the compound, to the north, is the city's long-standing commercial centre, **George Town**. The area was renamed after the future King George V when he visited India in 1905. You first reach the grand Indo-Saracenic complex of the **High Court** ① *Mon-Sat 1045-1345, 1430-1630, contact registrar for visit and guide, Rs 10*, developed in the style of the late 19th-century architects like **Henry Irwin**, who was also responsible for the National Art Gallery. You are allowed to visit the courtrooms by using the entrance on the left. A fine example is Court No 13 which has stained glass, fretted woodwork, carved furniture, silvered panels and a painted ceiling. The huge red central tower, nearly 50 m tall (you can climb to the top), built like a domed minaret to serve as a lighthouse, can be seen 30 km out at sea. It was in use from 1894 until 1977. The original **Esplanade Lighthouse** ① *open to visitors Tue-Sun 1000-1300 and 1500-1700, Rs 10*, southeast of the High Court, is in the form of a large Doric pillar and took over from the fort lighthouse in 1841.

Cross NSC Bose Road from the High Court's north gate to walk up Armenian Street for the beautiful Armenian **Church** of the Holy Virgin Mary (1772) ① *0930-1430, bells rung on Sun at 0930*. Solid walls and massive 3-m-high wooden doors conceal the pleasant open courtyard inside, which contains a pretty belltower and many Armenian tombstones, the oldest dating

Map labels:
Kalikambar Kameshwarar Temple
Office St
Shipping Corp of India (Tickets for Andaman Islands)
M Nalla Muthu St
Beach Station
Lingi Chetty St
Rajaji Rd (North Beach Rd)
Burma Bazaar
Beach Junction
Thomas Cook
Parry's Corner
City
High Court
Esplanade Lighthouse
PORT AREA

➜ **Chennai maps**
1 Chennai city, page 33
2 George Town, page 34
3 Central Chennai, page 38
4 South Chennai, page 40

N

200 metres
200 yards

from 1663. The East India Company praised the Armenian community for their 'sober, frugal and wise' lifestyle and they were given the same rights as English settlers in 1688. Immediately north again is the Roman Catholic cathedral, **St Mary of the Angels** (1675). The inscription above the entrance (1642) celebrates the date when the Capuchin monks built their first church in Madras.

Popham's Broadway, west from the St Mary cathedral, takes its name from a lawyer called Stephen (in Madras 1778-1795) who was keen to improve the city's sanitation, laying out what was to become Madras's main commercial street. Just off Popham's Broadway in Prakasham Road is the **Wesleyan Church** (1820).

In the 18th century there was major expansion between what is now First Line Beach (North Beach Road) and **Mint Street** to the west of George Town. The Mint was first opened in 1640, and from the late 17th century minted gold coins under licence for the Mughals, but did not move to Mint Street until 1841-1842.

The 19th-century growth of Madras can be traced north from **Parry's Corner. First Line Beach**, built on reclaimed land in 1814 fronted the beach itself. The **GPO** (1844-1884) was designed by Chisholm. The completion of the harbour (1896), transformed the economy of the city.

Central Chennai and the marina

Triplicane and **Chepauk** contain some of the finest examples of late 19th-century Indo-Saracenic architecture in India, concentrated in the area around the University of Madras. The Governor of Madras, Mountstuart Elphinstone Grant-Duff (1881-1886), decided to develop the marina as a promenade, since when it has been a favourite place for thousands of city inhabitants to walk on a Sunday evening.

Until the harbour was built at the end of the 19th century the sea washed up close to the present line of Kamaraj Salai (South Beach Road). However, the north-drifting current has progressively widened **Marina Beach**, which now stands as one of the longest urban beaches in the world – a fact that fills Chennai with great pride, if little sense of urgency about keeping the beach itself clean. The area just south of the malodorous mouth of the River Cooum is dedicated to a series of memorials to former state governors: **Anna Park** is named after the founder of the DMK party, CN Annadurai, while pilgrims converge on the **MGR Samadhi** to celebrate **MG Ramachandran** – the charismatic 1980s film star-turned-chief minister (see box, page 148). **Chepauk Palace**, 400 m away on South Beach Road, was the former residence of the Nawab of the Carnatic. The original four-domed Khalsa Mahal and the Humayun Mahal with a grand *durbar* hall had a tower added between them in 1855. The original building is now hidden from the road by the modern Public Works Department (PWD) building, Ezhilagam. Immediately behind is the Chepauk **cricket ground** where test matches are played. Further south, opposite the clunky sculpture entitled 'the Triumph of Labour', the elegant circular **Vivekenanda Illam** was Madras's first ice house, and now hosts a **museum** ① *Thu-Tue 1000-1200, 1500-1900, yoga and meditation classes are currently stopped, may resume from Jan 2014, Rs 2*, devoted to the wandering 20th-century saint, Swami Vivekananda. There are weekend yoga classes at the ice house (weekends, 0630-0830) and regular meditation classes (T044-2844 6188, Wednesday at 1900) run by the Sri Ramakrishna Math.

Inland from here lies the **Parthasarathi Temple** ① *0630-1300, 1500-2000*, the oldest temple structure in Chennai. It was built by eighth-century Pallava kings, then renovated in the 16th by Vijayanagara rulers. Dedicated to Krishna as the royal charioteer, it shows five of Vishnu's 10 incarnations, and is the only temple dedicated to Parthasarathi. Further north in the heart of Triplicane, the **Wallajah Mosque** ⓘ *0600-1200, 1600-2200*, or 'Big Mosque', was built in 1795 by the Nawab of the Carnatic. There are two slender minarets with golden domes on either side. North again, near the Round Thana which marks the beginning of Anna Salai, is the Greek temple-style banqueting hall of the old Government House, now known as **Rajaji Hall** (1802), built to mark the British victory over Tipu Sultan.

Egmore

A bridge across the Cooum at Egmore was opened in 1700, and by the late 18th century, the area around Pantheon Road became the fulcrum of Madras's social and cultural life, a 'place of public entertainment and balls'. Egmore's development, which continued for a century, started with the building of Horden's garden house in 1715. The original pantheon (public assembly rooms) was completely replaced by one of India's National Libraries. The **Connemara Library** (built 1896) traces its roots back to 1662, when residents exchanged a bale of Madras calico for books from London. At the southwest corner of the site stands Irwin's Victoria Memorial Hall, now the **Government Museum and Art Gallery** ⓘ *486 Pantheon Rd, T044-2819 3238, Sat-Thu 0930-1630, closed Fri, foreigners Rs 250, Indians Rs 15, camera Rs 500*. The red-brick rotunda surrounded by an Italianate arcade was described by Tillotson as one of "the proudest expressions of the Indo-Saracenic movement". There are locally excavated Stone and Iron Age implements and striking bronzes including a 11th-century Nataraja from Tiruvengadu, seated images of Siva and Parvati from Kilaiyur, and large figures of Rama, Lakshmana and Sita from Vadak-kuppanaiyur. Buddhist bronzes from Nagapattinam have been assigned to Chola and later periods. The beautiful Ardhanariswara statue here is one of the most prized of all Chola bronzes: Siva in his rare incarnation as a hermaphrodite. There are also good old paintings including Tanjore glass paintings, Rajput and Mughal miniatures and 17th-century Deccan paintings. Contemporary art is displayed at the **Gallery of Modern Art** ⓘ *Government Museum, T044-2819 3035*.

Egmore has other reminders of the Indo-Saracenic period of the 19th and early 20th centuries, the station itself being one of the last to be built, in the 1930s. Northeast of the station is the splendid **St Andrew's Church** ⓘ *Poonamalle High Rd, T044-2561 2608*. With a façade like that of London's St Martin-in-the-Fields, it has a magnificent shallow-domed ceiling. Consecrated in 1821, it has an active congregation.

Mylapore and South Chennai

Mylapore, which is technically older than Chennai and is the seat of city's urban elite, is more charming than the city centre. The present **Basilica of San Thomas** (1898) ⓘ *24 San Thome High Rd, T044-2498 5455*, surrounded now by the tenement rehousing scheme of a fishermen's colony, is claimed as one of the very few churches to be built over an apostle's tomb. St Thomas Didymus (Doubting Thomas) is believed to have come to India in AD 52. According to one legend, he crossed the peninsula from his landing on the west coast to reach Mylapore (the 'town of peacocks') where he proceeded to live and preach, taking shelter from persecution in Little Mount (see page 41). An alternative story argues King Gondophernes invited him to Taxila, where he converted the king and his court before moving to South India. Some claim that his body was ultimately buried in the Italian town of Ortona. Marco Polo in his travels in 1293 recorded the chapel on the seashore and a Nestorian monastery on a hill to the west where the apostle was put to death. In 1523, when the Portuguese started to rebuild the church they discovered the tomb containing the relics consisting of a few bones, a lance head and an earthenware

3 Central Chennai

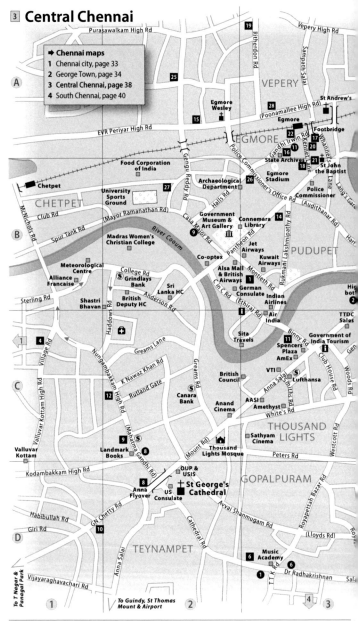

→ Chennai maps
1 Chennai city, page 33
2 George Town, page 34
3 Central Chennai, page 38
4 South Chennai, page 40

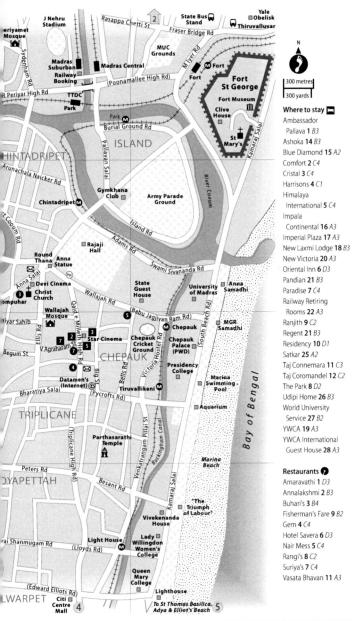

Where to stay

Ambassador
  Pallava **1** *B3*
Ashoka **14** *B3*
Blue Diamond **15** *A2*
Comfort **2** *C4*
Cristal **3** *C4*
Harrisons **4** *C1*
Himalaya
  International **5** *C4*
Impala
  Continental **16** *A3*
Imperial Plaza **17** *A3*
New Laxmi Lodge **18** *B3*
New Victoria **20** *A3*
Oriental Inn **6** *D3*
Pandian **21** *B3*
Paradise **7** *C4*
Railway Retiring
  Rooms **22** *A3*
Ranjith **9** *C2*
Regent **21** *B3*
Residency **10** *D1*
Satkar **25** *A2*
Taj Connemara **11** *C3*
Taj Coromandel **12** *C2*
The Park **8** *D2*
Udipi Home **26** *B3*
World University
  Service **27** *B2*
YWCA **19** *A3*
YWCA International
  Guest House **28** *A3*

Restaurants

Amaravathi **1** *D3*
Annalakshmi **2** *B3*
Buhari's **3** *B4*
Fisherman's Fare **9** *B2*
Gem **4** *C4*
Hotel Savera **6** *D3*
Nair Mess **5** *C4*
Rangi's **8** *C2*
Suriya's **7** *C4*
Vasata Bhavan **11** *A3*

pot containing bloodstained earth. The church was replaced by the neo-Gothic structure which has two spires and was granted the status of a basilica in 1956. The relics are kept in the sacristy and can be seen on request. There are 13th-century wall plaques, a modern stained glass window, a 450-year-old Madonna brought from Portugal and a 16th-century stone sundial. The basilica is now subject to an ambitious US$164,400 restoration project. To stop the Mangalore tile roof leaking, concrete reparations are being peeled back and replaced with original lime mortar.

Kapaleeswarar Temple ⓘ *0600-1300, 1600-2200*, to the west, is a 16th-century Siva temple with a 40-m *gopuram* (gateway), built after the original was destroyed by the Portuguese in 1566. Sacred to Tamil Shaivites, non-Hindus are only allowed in the outer courtyard. It's absolutely worth a visit, especially at sunset when worshippers gather for the evening *puja*, conducted amidst ropes of incense smoke and swirling pipe music.

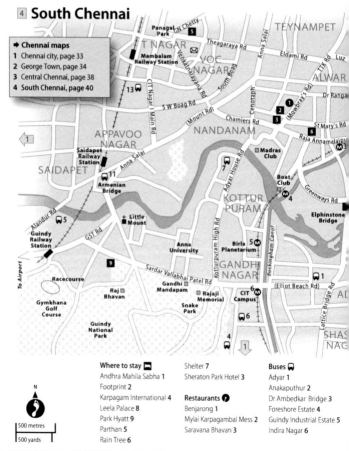

4 South Chennai

➡ **Chennai maps**
1 Chennai city, page 33
2 George Town, page 34
3 Central Chennai, page 38
4 South Chennai, page 40

Where to stay 🛏
Andhra Mahila Sabha 1
Footprint 2
Karpagam International 4
Leela Palace 8
Park Hyatt 9
Parthan 5
Rain Tree 6
Shelter 7
Sheraton Park Hotel 3

Restaurants 🍴
Benjarong 1
Mylai Karpagambal Mess 2
Saravana Bhavan 3

Buses 🚌
Adyar 1
Anakaputhur 2
Dr Ambedkar Bridge 3
Foreshore Estate 4
Guindy Industrial Estate 5
Indira Nagar 6

N

500 metres
500 yards

The nearby **Sri Ramakrishna Math** ① *31 Ramakrishna Mutt Rd, www.sriramakrishna math.org, 0500-1145, 1500-2100*, is one of the city's more appealing quiet corners, with a spectacular multi-faith temple, a quieter memorial to Ramakrishna in a prettily tiled Chettinad-style house, and a bookshop packed with writings by Ramamkrishna and notable devotees, including Swami Vivekananda.

The diminutive Portuguese **Luz Church**, 1547-1582 (the 1516 date in the inscription is probably wrong), is possibly the oldest church in Chennai. Its Tamil name, *Kattu Kovil*, means 'jungle temple'. Legend has it that Portuguese sailors lost at sea in a storm followed a light to the shore, where it disappeared. In gratitude they built the church. There are a number of 19th-century marble plaques to wives of the Madras civil service in the church and an ornate crypt.

To the south of Elphinstone Bridge, the **Theosophical Society** ① *Mon-Fri 0830-1000, 1400-1600, Sat 0830-1000, bus 5 from Central Chennai, ask taxi for Ayappa Temple on San Thome High Rd,* is set in large and beautifully quiet gardens. There are several shrines of different faiths and a Serene Garden of Remembrance for Madame Blavatsky and Colonel Olcott who founded the society in New York in 1875 and moved its headquarters to Madras in 1882. There's a huge 400-year-old banyan past the kitchen garden, a library and a meditation hall. The brackish river attracts waders and seabirds.

Tucked away near Saidapet is the **Little Mount** area. The older of the two churches (1551), with its small vaulted chapel, was built by the Portuguese. The modern circular church was built in 1971. St Thomas is believed to have been martyred and bled to death in AD 52 on the **Great Mount**, though others believe he was accidentally killed by a hunter's arrow. On top of the 90-m-high 'mount' is the **Church of Our Lady of Expectation**. The altar marks the spot where, according to legend, Thomas fell. Some legends suggest that after St Thomas had been martyred on the Little Mount, near Saidapet Bridge, his body was brought back to the beach which had been his home and was buried there.

Chennai listings

For hotel and restaurant price codes and other relevant information, see pages 14-18.

⊖ Where to stay

Chennai has seen a major increase of luxury accommodation options in the last few years, all pitched at the city's ever-growing business sector. These include the ITC Grand Chola, Leela Palace, Hyatt Regency, Park Hyatt, Hilton and the Westin. There continue to be excellent mid-range options, including a slew of service apartments and 1 solitary but wonderful B&B. Cheap hotels congregate around Central and Egmore stations and on hectic Triplicane High Rd, but even here you'll tramp a long way to find an acceptably clean room for under Rs 400. For more atmosphere, up your budget a little and stay near the temple in Mylapore.

Chennai airport

These hotels offer free airport transfers. Other hotels are 12-15 km from the airport.
$$$$ Hilton, JN Salai, near the Kathipara Grade Separator, T044-2225 5555, www. chennaiguindy.hilton.com. Flashy design, great restaurants, popular rooftop bar, and just 15 minutes from the airport.
$$$$ Trident, 1/24 GST Rd, T044-2234 4747. 166 rooms in characterless but functional hotel. Pleasant swimming pool in the garden.
$$$ Le Royal Meridien, 1 GST Rd, St Thomas Mount, T044-2231 4343, www.leroyal meridien-chennai.com. Plush hotel with all facilities including good restaurants and bars.
$$$ Radisson Blu, 531 GST Rd, Saint Thomas Mount, T044-2231 0101, www. radissonblu.com. Excellent value if rather anonymous rooms just 2 km from the airport. With amenable staff and a good variety of restaurants and bars, plus free airport pick-up, this is a good choice if you just want to flop for a night off the plane.

$$ Mount Manor, 14, GST Rd, St Thomas Mount, T044-2231 0975. New business-style hotel with modern facilities and free airport transfers, but guests warn drivers may try to take you to inferior nearby hotels (eg Mount Heera) for commission.

George Town *p33, map p34*

Good location for Central Station and State bus stands. Many cheap hotels are along VOC (Walltax) Rd, while slightly more salubrious places jostle for space with cheap restaurants and travel agencies along EVR Periyar (Poonamallee) High Rd.
$ Railway Retiring Rooms, Central Station, T044-2535 3337. Some a/c rooms, dorms.
$ Sonata Park, 41 Sydenhams Rd, T044-4215 2272. Simple but well-looked-after rooms and excellent-value suites, within walking distance of the station, but away from the usual budget hotel belt.
$ Sornam International, 7 Stringer St, T044-2535 3060. Pleasant, 50 rooms with TV and balcony, hot water, rooftop vegetarian restaurant.
$ Youth Hostel (TTDC), EVR Park (near Central Railway Station), T044-2538 9132. Reasonably quiet.

Central Chennai *p32, map p38*

Many accommodation options are within 1 km of Anna Salai (Mount Rd). **$$$-$** hotels charge an extra 19.42% tax.
$$$$ The Park, 601 Anna Salai, T044-4267 6000, www.theparkhotels.com. Converted from the site of the Gemini Film Studios, this is a quintessentially film hotel. Conran interiors, original film posters on the walls, world-class business facilities and restaurants and lovely rooftop pool with magnificent views over Chennai.
$$$$ Taj Connemara, 2 Binny Rd (off Anna Salai), T044-6600 0000, www.tajhotels.com. Supremely comfortable hotel with 148 renovated rooms that retain splendid art deco features. Excellent restaurants, bar

FOOTPRINT B&B

Calm & private 9-room bed & breakfast.
Urban retreat in the heart of Chennai.

- Behind Park Sheraton in Chennai
- Close to best sights, dining & shopping
- Ideal for women travelers

Email: bookings@footprint.in
Web: www.footprint.in
Call: +91 98400 37483

Disclaimer: Footprint B&B is not affiliated with Footprint Handbooks Limited whatsoever.

and good **Giggles** bookshop – so heavily stocked you can't get in the door. Heavily booked Dec-Mar.

$$$$ Taj Coromandel, 37 Mahatma Gandhi Rd, Nungambakkam, T044-6600 2827, www.tajhotels.com. 201 rooms, fine restaurants, good pool. Recommended but Western tours dominate.

$$$ Ambassador Pallava, 53 Montieth Rd, T044-2855 4476, www.ambassadorindia. com. Enormous, frumpy wedding cake of a hotel, with 120 rooms split between 'Heritage' (red carpet, quirky old furniture, antique bathroom fittings) and slightly cheaper, tile-floored 'Executive'. Neither are brilliant value, but good restaurants (especially Chinese), a pool and health club make it a viable choice if you want a taste of retro Indian high-end hospitality.

$$$ Harrisons, 315 Valluvar Kottam High Rd, T044-4222 2777, www.harrisonshotels. com. A new 4-star tower bock stands on the site of one of the city's classic hotels. Though it's all a bit slick and soulless, the rooms are large and new enough to qualify as spotless, with great views from the upper floors, and there are 2 good restaurants (South Indian and Chinese) plus a bar.

$$$-$$ Oriental Inn, 71 Cathedral Rd, T044-2811 4941, www.orientalgroup.in. The older rooms here come with crisp sheets and unusually fragrant bathrooms, but the studio apartments in the new wing are the real steal, with huge amounts of space and designer fittings. Wi-Fi available in both wings, and a slew of good restaurants right downstairs. Price includes breakfast.

$$ Ranjith, 15 Nungambakkam High Rd, T044-2827 0521, hotelranjith@yahoo.com. 51 threadbare but spacious and cool rooms, some a/c, restaurant (good non-vegetarian continental), reasonable bar, travel desk.

$$ Residency, 49 GN Chetty Rd (convenient for airport), T044-2825 3434, www.the residency.com. 112 very comfortable spacious rooms, 4th floor upwards have good views (9th floor, plush **$$$** suites). Excellent **Ahaar** restaurant (good

buffet lunches), exchange, car hire with knowledgeable drivers. Better rooms and service than some more expensive hotels. Highly recommended, book ahead.

$ Comfort, 22 Vallabha Agraharam St, Triplicane, T044-2858 7661. 40 rooms, some a/c, friendly and a good deal more salubrious than most other options in the area.

$ Cristal, 34 CNK Rd, Triplicane, T044-2851 3011. Clean basic rooms with tiled bath, very helpful service, better and cheaper than some others in the area.

$ Himalaya International, 91 Triplicane High Rd, T044-2854 7522. Modern, bright, welcoming, 45 rooms with nice bath, some a/c, clean. No food but available from **Hotel Gandhi** next door.

$ Paradise, 17/1 Vallabha Agraharam St, Triplicane, T044-2859 4252, paradisegh@ hotmail.com. Spacious clean rooms with fans (some with 2), shower, good value, very friendly and helpful owners. A firm budget-traveller favourite.

Egmore *p37, map p38*
Many hotels (including several good budget options) are around the station and along EVR Periyar (Poonamallee) High Rd, an auto-rickshaw ride away to the north of the railway line. Try to book ahead as budget hotels opposite the station and down Kennet Lane often fill up by midday.

$$$-$$ New Victoria, 3 Kennet Lane (200 m from station), T044-2819 3638. 51 a/c rooms, restaurant (excellent breakfast), bar, spacious, quiet, ideal business hotel. Recommended.

$$ Ashoka, 47 Pantheon Rd, T044-2855 3377, www.ballalgrouphotels.com. The funky 1950s flavour and encouraging whiff of disinfectant run out of steam before they make it to the rooms, but this is one of Egmore's more appealing mid-range options, set back from the street and right opposite the museum, with an in-house restaurant and 'Ice Cream Park'. Popular wedding venue, so ring ahead.

$$ Pandian, 15 Kennet Lane, T044-2819 1010, www.hotelpandian.com. A decent budget choice that's cornered the foreign-traveller market, with a host of handy facilities including travel desk, multiple internet cafés and an a/c restaurant and bar. But the 90 rooms are small and poky for what you're paying, and the whole place could do with a lick of paint.

$$-$ Udipi Home, Udipi Junction (corner of Hall's Rd and Police Commissioner's Rd), T044-6454 6555, uhome@redifmail.com. Some excellent business-class 'Deluxe' rooms with colourful glass dividers separating sleeping and meeting areas, plus more basic doubles, some windowless, at the cheaper end. There's an internet café and a superb restaurant downstairs. Book ahead – walk-ins rarely get a room.

$ Blue Diamond, 934 EVR Periyar High Rd, T044-2641 2244. 33 rooms, some a/c, quieter at rear, good a/c restaurant (busy at peak times), exchange.

$ Impala Continental, opposite station, T044-2819 1778. Near Vasanta Bhavan restaurant, 50 excellent clean rooms with TV, good service.

$ Imperial Plaza, 6 Gandhi Irwin Rd, T044-4214 7362. A friendly mid-priced option, set back from the street in a complex of 5 'Imperial' hotels, each owned by a different member of the same family. Rooms are average for the area – clean enough, but don't expect sparkling value, and there's a huge markup if you want the a/c switched on.

$ New Laxmi Lodge, 16 Kennet Lane, T044-2819 4576. Old building, set back in garden, with 50 rooms around courtyard.

$ Railway Retiring Rooms, Egmore Station, T044-2819 2527.

$ Regent, 11 Kennet Lane, T044-2819 1801. 45 renovated clean rooms set motel-style around a leafy courtyard/car park. The friendly owner makes this the pick of the Egmore cheapies.

$ Satkar, 65 Ormes Rd (junction of Flowers Rd and Miillers Rd), T044-2642 5179. Spotless rooms with bath, some a/c, good

vegetarian Suryaprakash restaurant, helpful staff, good value but very noisy.

$ Silver Star, 5 Purasawalkam High Rd, T044-2642 6818. Set back from the road, 38 simple clean rooms, open-air restaurant in courtyard, helpful and friendly staff.

$ World University Service, East Spur Tank Rd, T044-2836 4422. Some rooms with bath, dorm, International student cards needed, couples not allowed to share a room, cheap canteen for Indian snacks, good value, well situated for Egmore and south central Chennai.

$ YMCA, 74 Ritherdon Rd, T044-2532 2628. Good rooms and an extensive range of sports facilities including badminton, snooker, table tennis.

$ YWCA International Guest House, 1086 EVR Periyar High Rd, T044-2532 4234. Restaurant (rate includes breakfast), 60 rooms with bath and a/c, available to both men and women, popular so book early, excellent value, also campsite and plenty of parking – good for bikers.

South Chennai *p37, map p40*

$$$$ The Leela Palace, Adyar Seaface, M.R.C Nagar, T044-3366 1234, www.theleela.com. Chennai's only luxury hotel with an ocean view offers the gorgeous, over-the-top glamour for which Leela hotels are renowned. Rooms have lovely views of the Adyar River Estuary and Bay of Bengal. Recommended.

$$$$ Park Hyatt, Velachery Rd near the Governors residence, T044-7177 1234. Chennai's uber-cool design hotel is understated, elegant and packed with the young and beautiful. Their multi-level restaurant and lounge bar, Flying Elephant, is all the rage, and the rooftop pool has spectacular views over Guindy National Park. Highly recommended.

$$$$-$$$ Sheraton Park Hotel & Towers (Adyar Gate Hotel), 132 TTK Rd, T044-2499 4101. Good pool, 160 rooms, Dakshin Chettinad restaurant.

$$$$-$$$ Rain Tree, 120 St Mary's Rd, T044-4225 2525, www.raintreehotels.com. Beautiful luxury hotel, and Chennai's 1st to be run on an environmentally sustainable basis.

$$$ Footprint Bed and Breakfast, behind Park Sheraton, off TTK Rd, T(0)98400-37483, www.chennaibedandbreakfast.com. Beautifully cool, peaceful and intimate retreat from the city, with 9 stylish but unfussy rooms, decorated with handmade paper from Auroville, spread over 2 floors of a residential apartment block. Indian and continental breakfasts come with fresh newspapers, and there's a small library, free internet and Wi-Fi. Owner, Rucha, pops in every day to check on things, and will negotiate weekly and monthly rates if you want to stay longer. Highly recommended.

$$ Parthan, 75 GN Chetty Rd (near Panagal Park), T044-2815 8792. Restaurant (Chinese), 29 clean, large, comfortable and quiet rooms, exchange. Recommended.

$$ Shelter, 19-21 Venkatesa Agraharam St, T0411-2495 1919, T(0)9840-037483, www.hotelshelter.com. Business hotel located in Mylapore. Clean rooms with hot water, central a/c, very helpful staff, internet café, exchange, restaurant.

$ Andhra Mahila Sabha, 12 D Deshmukh Rd, T044-2493 8311. Some a/c rooms, vegetarian restaurant.

$ Karpagam International, 41 South Mada St, Mylapore, T044-2495 9984. Basic but clean rooms amid the Mylapore temple madness; the best ones face straight across the lake. Book 2 weeks in advance.

🍴 Restaurants

Central Chennai *p32, map p38*
Most restaurants are in Central Chennai and are open 1200-1500, 1900-2400. Those serving non-vegetarian dishes are often more expensive.

$$$ 601, The Park (see Where to stay). Possibly the best choice in town for a night out, with fantastic fusion food in a super

elegant setting. Also at The Park, **Aqua**, serves excellent Mediterranean dishes and cocktails in poolside cabanas, and lays on a barbeques with live music on Wed nights.

$$$ Copper Chimney, Oriental Inn (see Where to stay). Rich Mughlai and tandoori offerings in very clean setting. In the same building you can eat Chinese at **Chinatown** and good Spanish tapas at **Zara** (see Bars and clubs).

$$$ Hotel Savera, 146 Dr Radhakrishnan Rd, T044-2811 4700. Atmospheric rooftop restaurant with superb views, excellent Indian food, friendly service and live Indian music in the evenings. The hotel pool is open to non-residents, Rs 150.

$$$ Raintree, Taj Connemara (see Where to stay). Romantic outdoor restaurant with good food, atmosphere and ethnic entertainment but cavalier service. Very good buffet dinner on Sat night.

$$$ Southern Spice, Taj Coromandel (see Where to stay). Very good South Indian, along with evening dance recitals and freezing a/c.

$$ Annalakshmi, Anna Salai (near Higginbotham's bookshop). Wholesome, health-restoring offerings, Southeast Asian specialities (profits to charity, run by volunteers). Closed Mon. Recommended.

$$ Buhari's, 83 Anna Salai, and EVR Periyar Rd opposite Central Station. Good Indian. Dimly lit a/c restaurant, with terrace and unusual decor. Try crab curry, egg *rotis* and Muslim dishes; also in Park Town near Central Station.

$$ Dynasty, Harrisons (see Where to stay). Highly regarded Chinese, a popular venue for business lunchers.

$$ Rangi's, Continental Chambers, 142 Nungambakkam High Rd. Tiny but excellent hole-in-the-wall Chinese bistro.

$ Amaravathi, corner of TTK Rd and Cathedral (Dr Radhakrishan) Rd. Great value for spicy Andhra food, but relatively little joy for vegetarians.

$ Gem, Triplicane High Rd. Tiny non-veg Muslim place.

$ Nair Mess, 22 Mohammed Abdullah 2nd St, Chepauk. Fast and furious Kerala 'meals' joint, dishing out rice and *sambhar* in mountain-sized portions until 2100 sharp.

$ Saravana Bhavan, branches all over the city including Cathedral Rd opposite Savera Hotel, both railway stations, Spencer Plaza Mall and Pondy Bazar. Spotlessly clean Chennai-based chain restaurant, serving excellent snacks and 'mini tiffin', fruit juices (try pomegranate), sweetmeats, all freshly made.

$ Suriyas, 307 Triplicane High Rd. Shiny and clean vegetarian restaurant, with North and South Indian options.

Egmore *p37, map p38*

$$ Jewel Box, Blue Diamond (see Where to stay). Cool a/c, good for breakfasts, snacks and main courses.

$ Fisherman's Fare, 21 Spur Tank Rd. Outstanding value fish and seafood cooked in Indian, Chinese and Western styles.

$ Mathsya, Udipi Home, 1 Hall's Rd (corner of Police Commissioner's Rd). Chennai's night-owl haunt par excellence has been burning the oil (the kitchen stays open until 0200) by government order since the Indo-Chinese war. It also happens to serve some of the city's best pure veg food; their Mathsya *thali* comes with tamarind and sweetened coconut *dosas* and will keep you going all day. Recommended.

$ Vasanta Bhavan, 1st floor, 10 Gandhi Irwin Rd, opposite Egmore station. Very clean and super cheap, excellent food, friendly staff, downstairs bakery does delicious sweets.

South Chennai *p37, map p40*

$$$ Dakshin, Sheraton Park Hotel (Adyar Gate Hotel) (see Where to stay). High on the list of the best South Indian restaurants in the city, with Kanchipuram silk draped everywhere and a huge range of veg and non-veg choices. Book ahead.

$$ Benjarong & Teppan, 537 TTK Rd, Alwarpet, T044-2432 2640. 2 great

restaurants in the same building: one an upscale Thai affair, doing very passable renditions of *tom kha* and *pad thai* (and plenty of vegetarian options) amid a collection of Buddhas in glass cases; the other a smart new teppanyaki restaurant with live cooking.

$ Mylai Karpagambal Mess, 80 East Mada St, Mylapore. If you can handle the all-round dinginess, this place serves superb, simple food – *vada*, *dosas* and a sweet *pongal* to die for – to an avid Tamil Brahmin crowd.

$ Saravana Bhavan, north of the temple tank, Mylapore. Similarly excellent food in a more salubrious if less interesting environment.

🎧 Bars and clubs

Central Chennai *p32, map p38*

Alcohol can be purchased only through government-run TASMAC shops. Generally unsavoury locations with a street-bar on the side. Not recommended for women travellers. Instead go to TASMAC air-con shops located at Alsa Mall in Egmore or at Parsns Complex near Park Hotel Chennai

10 Downing, Kences Inn, BN Rd, T Nagar, T044-2815 2152. Noisy and popular bolthole, with live jazz and classic rock bands, but not a place for a quiet conversation.

365 A.S., Hyatt Regency, 365 Anna Salai, Teynampet, T044-6100 1234. Want to meet the city's expats? Head out to this popular centrally located lounge bar on the weekend. Lots of intimate seating options and excellent, well-priced drinks and snacks.

Bike and Barrel, Residency Towers, Sri Thyagaraya Rd, T044-2815 6363. Split-level restaurant and bar, playing rock, trance and house.

Dublin, Sheraton Park Hotel & Towers (see Where to stay). A notionally Irish pub by day, at night Dublin turns into a pulsating nightclub, pumping out the tunes until the early hours.

Flying Elephant, Park Hyatt, Velachery, T044-7177 1234. Chennai's hottest restaurant, built on three floors with central sunken bar. Converts into a nightclub from Thu-Sat after 2300. Move over Leather Bar (Park Hotel). Chennai's young and hip congregate at this watering hole now. Reservations needed.

Havana, Rain Tree (see Where to stay). Lounge bar with dance floor, hosts various theme nights.

Leather Bar, The Park (see Where to stay). Not as kinky as the name suggests, but this dark womb of a bar, with black leather floors and olive suede walls, is still one of the city's sexiest.

Oakshott Bar, Taj Connemara (see Where to stay). A large, bright bar, offering huge tankards of beer, great snacks and a huge TV.

Pasha, The Park (see Where to stay). The city's sleekest dance club.

The Tapas Bar, Oriental Inn (see Where to stay). Cocktails and Indian-style Spanish classics are the order of the day at this buzzing tapas bar, where you can lounge on leather banquettes with the trendies of Chennai.

❸ Entertainment

Chennai *p30, maps p34, p38 and p40*
Although Chennai is revered for its strong cultural roots, much of it is difficult for tourists to access. Events are often publicized only after they have passed. Check the free *Cityinfo* guide, published fortnightly, and www. explocity.com, for upcoming events.

Cinemas

Cinemas showing foreign (usually English-language) films are mostly in the centre of town on Anna Salai.

Escape, Express Avenue Mall, Whites Rd. Sathyam's swanky new multiplex located on the top-floor of Chennai's new city-centre mall. 30 mins from both Central and Egmore stations, the food-court and restaurants make this a great place to while away an afternoon with food and a movie before your train.

Sathyam, 8 Thiru-vi-ka Rd, Royapettah, T044-4392 0200. Chennai's first multiplex is also India's highest grossing cinema, with 6 screens and a mix of new-release Hollywood, Bollywood and Tamil films. Worth visiting if only to overload on chocolate and caffeine at Michael Besse's Ecstasy bakery.

Music, dance and art galleries

Sabhas are membership societies that offer cultural programmes 4 times a month to their members, but occasionally tickets are available at the door.

Chennai Music Academy, TTK Rd, T044-2811 2231, www.musicacademymadras.in. The scene of many performances of Indian music, dance and theatre, not only during the prestigious 3-week music festival from mid-Dec but right through the year.

FOCUS Art Gallery, 59 TTK Rd (close to Amaravathi Restaurant/Hotel Savera), T044-2498 6611. Good place to pick up affordable contemporary art by South Indian artists and prints of famous Indian painters.

Kalakshetra, Tiruvanmiyur, T044-2446 1943. Daily 0900-1700, entry Rs 50. A temple of arts founded by Rukmani Devi Arundale in 1936 to train young artists to revive the dance form *Bharatnatyam*. The foremost exponents of the art are now trained here, and you can have a peek at lessons in progress between 0930 and 1130.

Shree Bharatalaya, Mylapore. One of the key dance fine arts institutes run by respected guru Sudharani Raghupathy, Sura Siddha, 119 Luz Church Rd, T044-2499 4460.

❀ Festivals

Chennai *p30, maps p34, p38 and p40*
Jan 14 Pongal Makara Sankranti, the harvest thanksgiving, is celebrated all over Tamil Nadu for 3 days (public holiday). After ritually discarding old clothes and clay pots, festivities begin with cooking the first harvest rice in a special way symbolizing good fortune, and offering

it to the Sun god. The 2nd day is devoted to honouring the valuable cattle; cows and bulls are offered special 'new rice' dishes prepared with jaggery or nuts and green lentils. You will see them decorated with garlands, bells and balloons, their long horns painted in bright colours, before being taken out in procession around villages. Often they will pull carts decorated with foliage and flowers and carrying children, accompanied by noisy bands of musicians. On the final day of feasting, it is the turn of the 'workers' to receive thanks (and bonuses) from their employers.

O Shopping

Chennai *p30, maps p34, p38 and p40*
The main shopping areas are **Parry's Corner** in George Town and **Anna Salai. Khader Nawaz Khan Rd** is a very pleasant and (for a change) walkable street, with several elegant boutiques.

Note that many drivers – even those from reputable agents and companies – see little wrong in collecting a sweetening kickback from Kashmiris staffing huge shopping emporia, in exchange for dumping you on their doorstep. These are expert salesmen and although they do have some beautiful items, will ask at least double. The commission comes out of whatever you buy, so exercise restraint.

Most shops open Mon-Sat 0900-2000, some close for lunch 1300-1500. Weekly holidays may differ for shops in the same locality. There are often discount sales during the festival seasons of Pongal, Diwali and Christmas. The weekly *Free Ads* (Rs 5, Thu) has listings for second-hand cameras, binoculars, etc, which travellers might want to buy or sell.

Books
Most bookshops open 0900-1900; many upmarket hotels also have a selection of books for sale.

Higginbotham's, 814 Anna Salai and F39 Anna Nagar East, near Chintamani Market. **Landmark**, Apex Plaza, 3 Nungambakkam High Rd, T044-2822 1000.

Clothes and crafts
Amethyst, next to Corporation Bank, Whites Rd, Royapettah, T044-6499 3634. Open 1100-2000. Elegant Indian couture and jewellery, plus a lovely café set in a converted factory warehouse, surrounded by fabulous gardens and foliage. Don't miss the delicious ginger-lime sugarcane juice!
Atmosphere, K Nawaz Khan Rd. Beautiful modern furniture, fabrics and curtains – mostly silks – which can be shipped anywhere within India within 72 hrs.
Central Cottage Industries, 118 Nungambakkam High Rd, opposite **Taj Coromandel**. Wide variety of handicrafts, fixed prices.
Chamiers, 85 Chamiers Rd. Home to the beloved Anokhi store, for tribal-style block print fabrics and jewellery, plus a nice-looking but terrible-value outdoor café.
Evoluzione, 30 Khader Nawaz Khan Rd. High-end brands and cutting-edge Indian designers.
Fabindia, Besant Nagar/Woods Ro/ Express Ave Mall. India's best loved ethnic apparel brand. Their biggest choice is on the 2-storied outlet located opposite the Velankani Church off Elliots Beach in Besant Nagar in South Chennai.
Habitat, K Nawaz Khan Rd nearby. Good for special, unusual gifts.
Kalakshetra at Thiruvanmiyur (see Entertainment). Excels in *kalamkari* and traditional weaving, good household linen.
Kalpa Druma, 61 Cathedral Rd (opposite Chola Sheraton). Attractive selection of wooden toys and panels.
Khazana, Taj Coromandel (see Where to stay). Good for special, unusual gifts.
Naturally Auroville, Khader Nawaz Khan Rd. Products from the new-age colony of Auroville, including incense,

handmade papers, clothing and delicious breads and cheeses.

New Kashmir Arts, 111 Anna Salai. Good carpets.

Poompuhar, 818 Anna Salai. Tamil Nadu crafts store, specializes in first-class bronzes.

Tiffany's, 2nd floor, Spencer's Plaza. Antiques and bric-a-brac.

Vatika, 5 Spur Tank Rd. Good for special, unusual gifts.

Victoria Technical Institute, Anna Salai near **Taj Connemara** hotel and opposite the Life Insurance Corporation of India. This fixed-rate, government-backed operation is the best for South Indian handicrafts (wood carving, inlaid work, sandalwood). Other government emporia are along Anna Salai.

Department stores and malls

Most open 1000-2000.

Burma Bazar, Rajaji Salai, George Town. For imports, especially electronic. Bargain hard.

Citi Centre, 10-11 Dr Radhakrishnan Salai, Mylapore. Huge new mall packed with international names, plus **Lifestyle** department store, bookshop, food court.

Express Avenue Mall, Whites Rd, Royapettah. Centrally located, fabulous new mall with a luxury good section, but also excellent Indian brands. Well-maintained, a/c, and has the city's best multiplex cinema on the top floor. Great for whiling away time between hotel check-out and your overnight train!

Ispahani Centre, 123/4 Nungambakkam High Rd. Where the hip Madrasis hang out. Very snazzy designer 'ethnic' clothes shops.

Phoenix Market City Mall, Velachery. Located about 25 mins from the airport, this is Chennai's newest and largest mall, with several luxury brands and excellent international chain restaurants. Again, a good place to spend time between flights.

Spencer's Plaza, Anna Salai near Taj Connemara, is a dizzyingly huge mall with loads of choice, but suffering from power cuts and poor maintenance. Patronage from locals has declined, but there are plenty of small independent stores that offer good bargains.

Supermarket, 112 Davidson St and TNHB Building, Annanagar (closed Fri).

Fabrics

Chennai was founded because of the excellence of the local cotton.

Co-optex (government run) shops, 350 Pantheon Rd. These stock handloom silks and cottons. The alleyway directly to the north is Cotton St, where piles of export surplus fabrics are sold at less than half the normal shop prices.

Khadi, 44 Anna Salai. Stores specialize in handspun and handwoven cotton.

Shilpi or **Urvashi**, TTK Rd. Good for cottons.

Jewellery

Radha Gold Jewellers, 43 North Mada St, Mylapore, T044-249 1923. Open 0930-1300 and 1600-2100. 'Antique'-finished items and dance jewels.

Sri Sukra Jewels, 42 North Mada St, Mylapore, T044-2464 0699, www.sukra.com. Brilliant temple and costume jewellery. Fixed price.

Silk and saris

Look out for excellent Kanchipuram silk and saris. Recommended for quality and value:

Handloom House, 7 Rattan Bazar.

Nalli, opposite Panagal Park, with excellent selection, both in T Nagar.

Radha, 1 Sannadhi St, Mylapore (near east gate of temple). 4 floors of silk and cotton saris, *salwar kameez* sets, men's *kurtas* and children's clothes. Great old-fashioned department store atmosphere.

Rupkala, 191 Anna Salai. Good prices, helpful.

⊙ What to do

Chennai *p30, maps p34, p38 and p40*
Body and soul
Krishnamacharya Yoga Mandiram,
New No 31 (Old No13), Fourth Cross St,
R K Nagar (near Tirumailai MRT station),
T044-2493 7998, www.kym.org. Runs 2-
and 4-week intensive courses in yoga, plus
an extended Diploma course, and a very
well-regarded yoga therapy program.

Cultural centres
These have libraries, daily newspapers
from home and cultural programs including
film shows and photo exhibitions.
Alliance Française, 24 College Rd,
Nungambakkam, T044-2827 9803.
American Center, 561 Anna Salai, T044-
2827 7825. Library 0930-1800, closed Sun.
British Council, 737 Anna Salai, T044-
4205 0600. Tue-Sun 1000-1900.
InKo, 51 6th Main Rd, Raja Annamalaipuram,
T044-2436 1224. Run workshops in
traditional Korean arts, eg calligraphy.
Max Müeller Bhawan, 4 5th St, Rutland
Gate, T044-2833 1314. Mon-Sat 0900-1900.

Golf
Cosmopolitan Club, 334 Anna Salai, T044-
2432 2759. The best course in town, though
you may need an invitation to play. Also
offers tennis, billiards, library and bar.
   There's another, less exclusive golf course
at Guindy Race Course.

Sports clubs and associations
Most clubs are members-only domains,
though temporary membership may be
available for sports facilities. The Chennai
Cricket Club in Chepauk and the Gymkhana
Club at the racecourse on Anna Salai both
offer tennis, swimming, cricket, billiards,
library and a bar – definitely worth
experiencing if you can make friends with
a member.

Chennai Riders' Club, Race View, Race
Course, Velachery Rd. Riding (including
lessons) throughout the year except Jun.
Tamil Nadu Sailing Association, 83 East
Mada Church Rd, Royapuram, T044-2538
2253. Open to the public.
Wildertrails Adventure Club, T044-2644
2729. Camping and hiking trips.

Swimming
The pool at the **Savera** hotel is open to
non-residents. Others open to the public
are at Marina Beach and the YMCA pool
at Saidapet. Sea bathing is safe at Elliot's
Beach, though no longer attractive.

Tennis
Clubs allowing members' guests and
temporary members to use courts are:
**Chennai Club, Gymkhana Club, Cricket
Club, Cosmopolitan Club, Presidency
Club** and **Lady Willingdon Club**. YMCA
at Saidapet also has courts.

Tours and tour operators
Cox & Kings, 10 Karuna Corner, Spur Tank
Rd, T044-2820 9500.
Mercury, 191 Anna Salai, T044-2852 2993.
Milesworth Holidays, RM Towers,
108 Chamiers Rd, T044-2432 0522,
www.milesworth.com. Tamil Nadu
specialists, but cover all of India.
Favourite among Chennai's expats.
STIC, 672 Anna Salai, T044-2433 0211
Surya, 1st floor, Spencer's Plaza, Anna Salai,
T044-2849 3934. Very efficient, friendly,
personal service.
Tamil Nadu Tourism, sales counters at:
Tourism Complex, 2 Wallajah Rd, T044-
2536 8358; 4 EVR Periyar High Rd (opposite
Central Station), T044-2536 0294; and
Express Bus Stand near High Ct compound,
T044-2534 1982 (0600-2100). You can book
the some tours online, www.ttdconline.com.
The following tours are on deluxe coaches
and accompanied by a guide.

City sightseeing half-day, daily 0800-1300, 1330-1830. Fort St George, Government Museum (closed Fri), Valluvar Kottam, Snake Park, Kapaleeswarar Temple, Elliot's Beach, Marina Beach. Rs 120, a/c Rs 170.
Mahabalipuram and Kanchipuram, 0730-1900, Rs 200 (a/c Rs 350) and Tirupati, 0630-2200, Rs 375 (a/c Rs 600).
Hop-On Mahabalipuram tours leave hourly 0900-1600, returning 1040-1740; the ticket (Rs 250) lets you stop at several points along the way, eg at Dakshinachitra and the Crocodile Bank, and catch a later bus.
Thomas Cook, 45 Monteith Rd, opposite Ambassador Pallava hotel, T044-2855 4600.
Welcome, 150 Anna Salai, near India Tourist Office, T044-2846 0614. Open 24 hrs.

Walking tours
Detours, T(0)9000-850505, www.detours india.com. Off-beat walking and car-based thematic city experiences covering British history, religions and spirituality, food and bazaars. Exclusive and guided by local experts.
Story Trails, T(0)9940-040215, www.story trails.in. Themed walking tours that allow the city to unfold through its stories, including Spice Trail, Mystic Trail and Bazar Trail.

⊖ Transport

Chennai *p30, maps p34, p38 and p40*
Air
The **Arignar Anna International Airport** (named after CN Annadurai), T044-2234 6013 with 2 terminals and the **Kamaraj Domestic Airport**, T044-2256 0501, are on one site at Trisulam in Meenambakkam, 12 km from the centre. Enquiries, T140, arrivals and departures, T142. **Pre-paid taxis** from both; to Chennai Central or Egmore, Rs 600-800 (yellow taxis are cheaper than private), 45-60 mins; Rs 1500-1800 to Mahabalipuram. Buses to centre Rs 75 (day), Rs 100 (night). **Auto-rickshaws** to Chennai Central, Rs 200, but you have to walk to the main road to catch one. **Suburban railway** the cheapest way into town, from Trisulam

suburban line station to Egmore and Fort, but trains are often packed. Free phone in the main concourse, after collecting baggage in the international airport, to ring hotels. Railway bookings 1000-1700.
Domestic Flights to **Bengaluru (Bangalore), Bhubaneswar, Coimbatore, Delhi, Goa, Hyderabad, Kochi, Kolkata, Madurai,** via **Tiruchirappalli; Mumbai, Port Blair** and **Pune, Puttaparthy, Thiruvananthapuram, Visakhapatnam.**
Indian Airlines (Marshalls Rd, Egmore, T044-2345 3301 (daily 0800-2000). Reservations, all 24 hrs: T044-2855 5209, airport T044-2256 6065.
International Connections with: **Abu Dhabi, Bangkok, Colombo, Doha, Dubai, Frankfurt, Hong Kong, Kuala Lumpur, Kuwait, London, Male, Mauritius, Muscat, Paris, Reunion** and **Singapore.**
Air France, 42 Kubers, Pantheon Rd, T1800-180 0044. Air India, 19 Rukmani Lakshmipathy Rd (Marshalls Rd), T044-2345 3301 (0930-1730, avoid 1300-1400), airport T044-2256 6065. British Airways, 10/11 Dr Radha Krishnan Salai, T98-4037 7470. Cathay Pacific, 47 Spur Tank Rd, T044-4298 8400; airport, T044-2256 1229. Emirates, 12 Nungambakkam High Rd, T044-6683 4444. Gulf Air, 52 Montieth Rd, T044-2815 6244. Jet Airways, 43 Montieth Rd, Egmore, T044-3989 3333, airport T044-2256 1818. Kuwait Airways, 476, Anna Salai, Nandanam, T044-2431 5162. Malaysian Airlines, 90 Dr Radha Krishnan Salai, T044-4219 1919. Singapore Airlines, 108 Dr Radhakrishna Rd, T044-4592 1921; airport, T044-2256 0409. Sri Lankan, 4 Vijaya Towers, Kodambakkam High Rd, T044-4392 1100. Thai, at ITC Park Sheraton, TTK Rd, T044-4206 3311.
General Sales Agents (GSA): **Air Kenya, Garuda Airways, Japan Airlines, Global** Travels, 703 Anna Salai, T044-4295 9633. **Air Canada, Bangladesh Biman** and **Royal Jordanian**, Thapar House, 43 Montieth Rd, T044-2856 9232. **Delta**, at Interglobe, 1, 4th St, Dr Radhakrishnan Salai, T044-2824 0073. **Continental, Iberian**

and **Royal Nepal Airlines**, at STIC Travels, 672 Anna Salai, T044-2433 0211.

Bus

Local The cheap and convenient local bus service is not overcrowded and offers a realistic alternative to auto-rickshaws and taxis outside the rush hour (0800-1000, 1700-1900). Make sure you know route numbers as most bus signs are in Tamil (timetables from major bookshops).

Metropolitan Transport Corp (MTC), Anna Salai, runs an excellent network of buses from 0500-2300 and a skeleton service through the night. 'M' service on mini-buses are good for the route between Central and Egmore stations and journeys to the suburban railway stations. The 'V' service operates fast buses with fewer stops and have a yellow board with the route number and LSS (Limited Stop Service). PTC has a half-hourly 'luxury' mini-bus service between Egmore Station, Indian Airlines' Marshall's Rd office and the airports at Meenambakkam picking up passengers from certain hotels (inform time keeper at Egmore in advance, T044-2536 1284). The fare is about Rs 20.

Long-distance For long-distance journeys, the state highways are reasonably well maintained but the condition of other roads varies. The fast new highways leading north and south of Chennai and the East Coast Rd (ECR) have helped to cut some journey times. Fast long-distance a/c buses now run on some routes, giving a comfortable ride on air-cushioned suspension.

Chennai is amazingly proud of its bus station – Asia's biggest, with 30 arrival and 150 departure terminals. Officially titled the **Chennai Mofussil Bus Terminus (CMBT)** it is known to rickshaw drivers as Koyambedu CMBT, Jawaharlal Nehru Rd near Koyambedu Market, T044-2479 4705.

Tamil Nadu Govt Express, T044-2534 1835, offers good connections within the whole region and the service is efficient and inexpensive. Best to take a/c coaches or super deluxe a/c. Bookings 0700-2100. Other state and private companies cover the region but you may wish to avoid their video coaches which make listening, if not viewing, compulsory as there are no headphones.

Beware of children who 'help' you to find your bus in the expectation of a tip; they may not have a clue. There have also been reports of men in company uniforms selling tickets, which turn out to be invalid; it is best to buy on the bus. The listings given are for route number, distance. **Coimbatore** *No 460*, 500 km; **Chidambaram** and **Nagapattinam** *326*; **Kanchipuram** *76B*; **Kanniyakumari** *282 and 284*, 700 km; **Kumbakonam** *303F*, 289 km, 6½ hrs; **Madurai** *137*, 447 km, 10 hrs; **Mahabalipuram** *109*, Rs 19, 1½ hrs (*108B* goes via Meenambakkam airport, 2½ hrs) can be very crowded; **Nagercoil** *198*, 682 km, 14 hrs; **Ooty** *468*, 565 km, 13 hrs; **Puducherry** *803*, 106 km, 3 hrs; **Thanjavur** *323*, 320 km, 8 hrs; Tiruchirappalli *123*, 320 km and Route *124*, 7 hrs; **Tiruvannamalai** 180 km, 5 hrs; **Yercaud** *434*, 360 km, 8 hrs; **Bengaluru** **(Bangalore)** via **Vellore** and **Krishnagiri** *831*, 360 km, 8 hrs; **Bengaluru (via Kolar)** 350 km, 7½ hrs; **Tirupati** via **Kalahasti** *802*, 150 km, 3½ hrs.

Car

A/c or ordinary cars with drivers are good value and convenient for sightseeing, especially for short journeys out of the city when shared between 3 and 5 people. Large hotels can arrange, eg **Ganesh Travels**, 35/1 Police Commisioner Office Rd, T044-2819 0202; **Milesworth**, 108 Chamiers Rd, Alwarpet, T044-2436 2557, vacations@ milesworth.com. Efficient and friendly company, good touring cars and English speaking drivers); **Regency** (Rs 600 per 8 hrs; Rs 750 for Mahabalipuram). TTDC, 2 Wallajah Rd, T044-2536 8358.

Ferry

Passenger ships leave every 7-10 days to the **Andaman** and **Nicobar Islands**, taking 3 days, and as visas are now issued on arrival at Port Blair the process of getting a ticket is less complicated than it used to be. Ships are operated by the **Shipping Corporation of India**, Jawahar Building, Rajaji Salai, T044-2523 1401, and the **Deputy Directorate of Shipping Services**, 6 Rajaji Salai, T044-2522 6873. Check sailing schedules, then take 4-5 passport photos, originals plus 3 copies of your passport and visa, and queue up for a ticket, 1000-1300. Women have an advantage when queuing.

Motorbike hire or purchase
Southern Motors, 995A Koleth Court, 11th Main Rd, 2nd Ave, Anna Nagar, T044-2616 4666, T044-2499 0784, is a good modern garage with efficient service. The YWCA, EVR Periyar Rd, is a good hotel for bikers and has a big shaded garden to park bikes securely.

MRTS
The **Mass Rapid Transit System** (raised, above-ground railway) runs from Chennai Beach south to Velacheri in the IT belt, passing through Chepauk, Triplicane (Thiruvallikeni) and Mylapore on the way. Station facilities are minimal, and there's little information about when the next train might depart.

Rickshaws
Three-wheeler scooter taxis are the most common form of transport around the city. A recent court ruling has forced rickshaw drivers, in defiance of the age-old Chennai tradition of radical price gouging, to charge by the meter. Look out for the Namma Auto rickshaw fleet (reliable and safe). Minimum charge Rs 25 for up to 1.8 km, additional km Rs 12. As always, drivers get kickbacks from emporium owners to encourage detours via shops.

Taxi
Taxis are better than rickshaws for extended trips and sightseeing. Many companies offer 'packages' of fixed times and distances –

Rs 700 for 40 km and 4 hrs, Rs 1200 for 80 km and 8 hrs, plus Rs 100 for each extra hour. Expect to pay more for a/c. **Bharati Call Taxi**, T044-2814 2233. **Chennai Call Taxi**, T044-2598 4455. **Fast Track**, T044-2473 2020. **Thiruvalluvar Travels**, T044-2474 5807.

Train
Suburban railway Inexpensive and handy, but very crowded at peak times. Stops between Beach Railway Station and Tambaram (every 5 mins in rush hour) include Fort, Park, Egmore, Chetpet, Nungambakkam, Kodambakkam, Mambalam, Saidapet, Guindy, St Thomas Mt. Also serves suburbs of Perambur and Villivakkam. Convenient stop at Trisulam for the airports, 500-m walk from the terminals.
Long distance Chennai has 2 main stations **Chennai Central (MC)** for broad gauge trains to all parts of India and **Egmore (ME)** for trains to the south; a few significant trains also start from Tambaram, in the southern suburbs. Egmore and Central are linked by minibus; taxis take 5 mins. There is a reservations counter at the domestic airport, as well as at the stations. **Chennai Central** enquiry, T131, reservations, T132, arrivals and departures, T133, then dial main no. Advance Reservations Centre, Mon-Sat 0800-1400, 1415-2000, Sun 0800-1400, is in a separate building in front of the suburban station, to the left of the main station. Indrail Passes and booking facilities for foreigners and NRIs on the 1st floor. From Chennai Central to **Coimbatore** *Kovai Exp 12675*, 0615, 7¾ hrs; *West Coast Exp 16627*, 1100, 8¼ hrs; *Cheran Exp 12673*, 2145, 8½ hrs. **Kochi (Cochin)** *Chennai-Alleppey Exp 16041*, 1945, 13¾ hrs; *Guwahati Cochin Exp 15624*, 1210, Fri, 14¾ hrs. **Mettupalayam** *Nilgiri Exp 16605*, 2015, 10 hrs.

Egmore enquiry, T135, arrivals and departures, T134. No counter for foreign tourist quota bookings. To **Kanniyakumari** *Chennai-Kanniyakumari Exp 16121*, 1900, 15 hrs. **Madurai** *Chennai-Kanniyakumari Exp 16121*, 1815, 10 hrs; *Vaigai Exp 12635*,

1225, 8 hrs; *Pandyan Exp 16717*, 2100, 9½ hrs via Kodai Rd (this connects with the bus service at **Kodaikanal** arriving at midday). **Tiruchirappalli** *Vaigai Exp 12635*, 1225, 5½ hrs; *Pallavan Exp 12606*, 1530, 5½ hrs.

❶ Directory

Chennai *p30, maps p34, p38 and p40*
Embassies and consulates For Indian visa extensions go to **Foreigners' Registration Office**, Shastri Bhavan Annexe, 26 Haddows Rd, T044-2345 4970, Mon-Fri 0930-1800. For details of foreign embassies in Chennai, go to embassy.goabroad.com.

Medical services Ambulance (Government), T102; **St John's Ambulance**, T044-2819 4630, 24-hr. **Dental hospital** (Government), T044-2534 0441; **All-in-One**, 34 Nowroji Rd, T044-2641 1911, 0400-2000, 0900-1200 Sun. **Chemists:** Apollo Pharmacy, many branches including 320 Anna Salai, Teynampet; 52 Usman Rd South, T Nagar. SS Day & Night Chemists, 106D, 1st Main Rd, Anna Nagar. **Hospitals:** Apollo Hospital, 21 Greams Rd, T044-2829 3333. **CSI Rainey**, GA Rd, RA Puram, T044-2595 3322, with 24-hr pharmacy. **Deviki Hospital**, 148 Luz Church Rd, Mylapore, T044-2499 2607. **National Hospital**, 2nd Line Beach Rd, T044-2524 0131.

Around Chennai

South of the capital, easily reached in a day but worthy of at least a weekend, lies Mahabalipuram, an intriguing little beachside town given over entirely to sculpture, both ancient and modern. Part open-air museum and part contemporary workshop, its seventh-century bas-reliefs are some of the world's largest and most intricate, telling the Indian flood myth, the *Descent of the Ganga*. Within earshot of the old shore temples you can find modern-day masons industriously piling their shacks and yards high with freshly and beautifully chiselled deities. Inland from Chennai, the former Pallava capital of Kanchipuram is one of India's seven sacred cities, chock-full of temples and overflowing with silks spun straight from the loom.

Chennai to Mahabalipuram → *For listings, see pages 64-67.*

If travelling from Chennai, there are three good stop-off points before Mahabalipuram.

Cholamandal Artists' Village

ⓘ *East Coast Rd, Enjampakkam, T044-2449 0092, 0900-1900, free.*

The first of three good stop offs, travelling from Chennai to Mahabalipuram, is 19 km from Chennai. The artists' community, started in 1969, gives living, working and exhibition space for artists creating sculptures, pottery and batik. They sometimes hold dance performances in a small open-air theatre, and there are some simple cottages for hire if you want to stick around for a workshop or residency.

Dakshinchitra

ⓘ *East Coast Rd, T044-2747 2603, www.dakshinachitra.net, Wed-Mon 1000-1830, Rs 200, Indians Rs 75.*

The second stop is the **Madras Craft Foundation**'s model village, which showcases the rich cultural heritage of the four southern states against a backdrop of 17 authentic buildings, each relocated piece by piece from their original homes around South India. There's a regular programme of folk performances, including puppet shows, plus a newly opened art gallery with an excellent collection of tribal art from across India, a small textile museum, a restaurant and a fortune-telling parrot.

Madras Crocodile Bank

ⓘ *Tue-Sun 0830-1730, RRs 35, camera Rs 20, video Rs 100.*

Finally, 14 km before Mahabalipuram, is Romulus Whitaker's captive breeding centre for Indian crocodiles. Established by the American-born herpetologist (known as the Snake Man of India), you can now see several rare species from India and beyond, including

Siamese and African dwarf crocodiles, basking around the open pools. There's a small extra charge to visit the snake venom bank, where snakes donate small quantities of poison for use in antivenins before being released back to the wild.

Mahabalipuram (Mamallapuram) → *For listings, see pages 64-67.*

Mahabalipuram's mix of magnificent historic rock temples, exquisite alfresco bas reliefs and inviting sandy beach bestows a formidable magnetism, and it has matured into a buzzing backpacker hamlet, complete with all the high-power Kashmiri salesmanship and insistent begging that such a role implies. Though the beach and ocean are dirty enough to make you think twice about swimming, the craftsmanship that built the

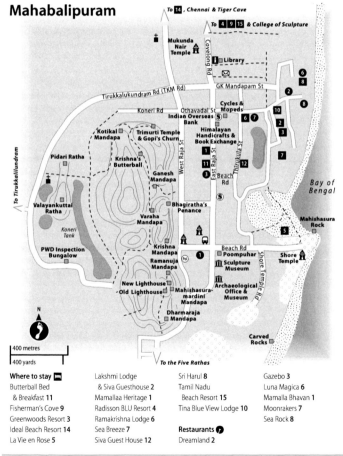

Mahabalipuram

temples continues today and the whole place echoes with the sound of chisels tapping industriously on stone.

Arriving in Mahabalipuram → *Phone code: 044. Population: 12,345.*

Getting there Buses from Chennai take around 1½ hours to the bus stand in the centre of the small village. They may stop at hotels north of Mahabalipuram, on the way, otherwise autos from anywhere in the village will ferry you there for Rs 50. Arriving by car, you may have to pay a Rs 20 toll at the booth near the post office on Kovalam Road.

Getting around The town is small enough to explore on foot, but hiring a bike can get you further afield. ►► *See Transport, page 66.*

Tourist information Tamil Nadu Tourist Office ① *Kovalam Rd, 300 m north of Othavadai St, T044-2744 2232, Mon-Fri 1000-1745,* can arrange guides, car and cycle hire. The best time to visit is early morning, for the best light on Bhagiratha's Penance. Allow two hours for a circuit. It's hard to get lost but the paths on the top of the rock are not always clear.

Background

The coastal temple town Mahabalipuram is officially known as Mamallapuram after 'Mamalla' ('great wrestler'), the name given to Narasimhavarman I Pallavamalla (ruled AD 630-668). The Pallava ruler made the port famous in the seventh century and was largely responsible for the temples. There are 14 cave temples and nine monolithic *rathas* (shrines in the shape of temple chariots), three stone temples and four relief sculptured rock panels.

The **Dravida** or Dravidian style underwent several changes over the course of the different dynasties that ruled for about 1000 years from the time of the Pallavas who laid its foundations. In Mahabalipuram, rock-cut cave temples, *mandapas* (small excavated columned halls), and *rathas* were carved out by the early Pallavas. These were followed by structural temples and bas relief sculptures on giant rocks. The Ekambaresvara Temple in Kanchipuram (see page 62) shows the evolution of the Dravidian style – the shrine with its pyramidal tower and the separate *mandapa* (pillared portico) all within the courtyard with its high enclosure wall made up of cells. Six centuries later the two separate structures were joined by the *antarala* (covered hall). A large subsidiary shrine, which took the place of an entrance gateway, also hinted at the later *gopuram*.

A characteristic feature of the temples here was the system of water channels and tanks, drawn from the **Palar River**, which made it particularly suitable as a site of religious worship. The *naga*, or serpent cult associated with water worship, can be seen to be given prominence at Bhagiratha's Penance.

Carving in stone is still a living art; stone masons can be heard chipping away from dawn to dusk along the dusty roadsides, while students at the **Government School of Sculpture** ① *near the bus stand, Wed-Mon 0900-1300, 1400-1830,* continue to practise the skills which flourished centuries ago.

Places in Mahabalipuram

Bhagiratha's Penance *Descent of the Ganga*, also called **Arjuna's Penance**, is a bas relief sculpted on the face of two enormous adjacent rocks, 29 m long and 7 m high. It shows realistic life-size figures of animals, gods and saints watching the descent of the river from the Himalaya. Bhagiratha, Rama's ancestor, is seen praying to Ganga. A man-made waterfall,

Stone temple pilot

When the British Council sponsored Bristol-born artist Stephen Cox to scout India for a place to make his huge-scale stone works for the national art prize, the Indian Triennale, he chose not the country's best art schools, but a little fishing village on the Coromandel coast of Tamil Nadu. It may sound bloody minded, until you arrive in Mahabalipuram, where the whole air clatters with the sound of chisel on rock. It must be the most industrious seat of Hindu idol-making the world over; everywhere you look masons sit on their haunches hammering away at the local dolerite rock.

As Cox explains: "I didn't go to India to work with like-minded contemporary artists, I wanted people who could work with great big blocks of stone without fear. Mahabalipuram is totally unique in having this unbroken, living tradition of making idols for people to pray to, and that means that they are also used to working with huge monolithic stone so no-one's daunted by making my 14-tonne sculptures." Although he has kept a studio there from that first year, 1986, you won't find any of his sculpture in the town itself – these are mainly kept for cities: the British High Commission at Delhi, the British Council's office in Chennai and dotted about London's Square Mile. Indeed his work – too minimalist for Hindu temple carving purists – has been received with something less than gusto by some of the local craftsman, and

journalist Mark Tully, branded Cox's use of Indian labour a form of 'neo-colonialism'. One sculpture alone can take up to a year to make and will have passed through, on average, 20 pairs of Indian hands before being shipped for exhibition. "At the end of the day of course, I wouldn't be working in India over Carrara in Italy if it wasn't economically viable," Cox concedes, but he also says "my raison d'être for working in India is because, in working amongst and with the temple carvers, I can immerse myself in a living antique tradition. It is not just the cost factor. The hand skills of the silpies have been lost to the rest of the world."

The town has changed dramatically since he arrived in 1986, but Cox spares the burgeoning tourist industry infrastructure to reserve his criticism for the Architectural Survey of India's maintenance of the monuments themselves. "Since it was declared a World Heritage Site, they've buggered the Shore Temple up; it's not a shore temple anymore, instead it sits in a bijou plot of grassland, while the five *rathas* are fenced off, destroying the whole beauty of these wonderful monuments in a natural environment."

And his favourite piece of sculpture in a town teeming with them? It's the Pallava's flair for observation that still gets him: "the naturalism that Giotto was supposed to have invented you find in a ninth-century relief carving here. It is amazing. I only hope fewer and fewer people come."

fed from a collecting chamber above, issues from the natural crack between the two rocks. Some see the figure of an ascetic (to the top left-hand side of the rock, near the cleft) as representing Arjuna's penance when praying for powers from Siva, though this is disputed. There are scenes from the fables in the *Panchatantra* and a small shrine to Vishnu.

A path north goes to the double-decker rectangular **Ganesh** *ratha* with a highly decorative roof and two pillars with lions at their base – an architectural feature which was to become significant. The Ganesh image inside is mid-20th century. To the west are the **Valayankuttai** and twin **Pidari** *rathas*. The path continues past the precariously balanced

Krishna's Butterball through some huge boulders at the north end of the hillock to the **Trimurti Temple** caves that hold three shrines to Brahma, Vishnu and Siva, the last with a lingam.

Mandapas The 10 *mandapas* are shallow, pillared halls or porticos in the rocky hillside which hold superb sculptures from mythological tales, and illustrate the development of the Dravidian (South Indian) temple style.

On the south is a **Durga niche** (AD 630-660), while next door is the **Gopi's Churn**, a Pallava cistern. Walk back along the ridge, passing Krishna's Butterball on your left and boulders with evidence of incomplete work. The **Varaha Mandapa** (AD 640-674) on the left of the ridge shows two incarnations of Vishnu – Varaha (boar) and Vamana (dwarf) – among scenes with kings and queens. The base forms a narrow water pool for pilgrims to use before entering the temple. From here you can walk to the top of Bhagiratha's Penance.

Krishna Mandapa (mid-seventh century) has a bas relief scene of Krishna lifting Mount Govardhana to protect a crowd of his kinsmen from the anger of the Rain God, Indra. The cow licking its calf during milking is remarkably realistic.

Kotikal Mandapa (early seventh century) may be the earliest of the *mandapas*, roughly carved with a small shrine with no image inside. **Ramanuja Mandapa** was originally a triple-cell Siva temple, converted later into a Vaishnava temple.

South of the new lighthouse the simple **Dharmaraja cave** (early seventh century) contains three empty shrines. To its west is **Isvara Temple** (or Old Lighthouse), a truncated Siva temple still standing like a beacon on the highest summit, with a view for miles around. (To the south, across the Five Rathas, is the nuclear power station of Kalpakkam; to the west is the flat lagoon and the original port of Mahabalipuram.)

Mahishasuramardini Mandapa (mid-seventh century) is immediately below. It has fine bas relief and carved columns with lion bases. The main sculpture shows the goddess Durga slaying the buffalo demon Mahishasura while another relief shows Vishnu lying under Adishesha, the seven-hooded serpent.

Pancha Rathas ⓘ *Rs 250, Indians Rs 10*. These mid-seventh-century monolithic temples, 1.5 km south of the Old Lighthouse, were influenced by Buddhist architecture as they resemble the *vihara* (monastery) and *chaitya* (temple hall). They imitate in granite temple structures that were originally built of wood and are among the oldest examples of their type.

The five *rathas* to the south of the hill are named after the Pancha Pandava (five Pandava brothers) in the epic *Mahabharata* and their wife Draupadi. The largest is the domed **Dharmaraja** with many images including an interesting Ardhanarishvara (Siva-Parvati) at the rear. The barrel-vaulted **Bhima** nearby has a roof suggestive of a thatched hut, while next to it the dome-shaped ratha **Arjuna** imitates the Dharmaraja. **Draupadi ratha** is the smallest and simplest and is again in the form of a thatched hut. The base, now covered by sand, conceals a lion in front which appears to carry it, which suggests that it may be a replica of a portable shrine. Immediately east is a large unfinished *Nandi*. To its west is the apsidal **Nakula-Sahadeva ratha** with a freestanding elephant nearby. The Bhima and Nakula–Sahadeva follow the oblong plan of the Buddhist *chaitya* hall and are built to two or more storeys, a precursor to the *gopuram*, the elaborate entrance gateway of the Dravidian temple.

Shore Temple ⓘ *0900-1730, foreigners Rs 250, Indians Rs 10, video Rs 25, includes Panch Rathas if visited on same day*. This beautiful sandstone World Heritage Site, built in the seventh century by King Rajasimha, is unusual for holding shrines to both Siva and Vishnu. Its gardens have been laid out to ape their ancient antecedents. Its base is granite and it has a basalt *kalasha* at its top. Its position on the water's edge, with an east-facing altar designed to catch the rising sun and a stone pillar to hold the beacon for sailors at night, meant that there was no space for a forecourt or entrance gateway, but two additional shrines were built to the west. The second smaller spire adds to the temple's unusual structure. The outer parapet wall has lines of *Nandi* (Siva's sacred bull) and lion pilasters.

Saluvankuppam Some 5 km north of Mahabalipuram, on the coast, is the temple at Saluvankuppam. It holds the **Tiger Cave** *mandapa* with carvings of tiger heads. The cave, not signposted from the beach, is secluded and peaceful – perfect for a picnic. On the way you will see the **Mukunda Nayar Temple**.

Beaches Mahabalipuram's beach is far from pristine, particularly north of the temples towards the **Ashok** and in the rocky area behind the *Descent of the Ganga* where it serves as an open latrine. To sunbathe undisturbed by hawkers pay Rs 200 to use the small pools at **Crystal Shore Palace** or **Sea Breeze**, or the bigger pool, 1 km north at **Tamil Nadu Beach Resort**.

Around Mahabalipuram

Tirukkalukundram is a small Siva temple dedicated to Vedagirishvara on top of the 3000-million-year-old rock, 14 km west of Mahabalipuram. About 400 steps take you to the top of the 160-m hill which has good views, plus money-conscious priests and 'guides'. Be prepared for a hot barefoot climb, 'donations' at several shrines and Rs 10 for your shoes. The Bhaktavatsleesvara in town with its *gopuram* (gateway) stands out like a beacon. The tank is considered holy and believed to produce a conch every 12 years. Small shops in the village sell cold drinks. Buses from Mahabalipuram take 30 minutes or you can hire a bike.

Sriperumbudur, 44 km from Chennai on National Highway 4, is the birthplace of the 11th-century Hindu philosopher Ramanuja, and is where Rajiv Gandhi was assassinated on 21 May 1991. There is a memorial at the site in a well-kept garden.

Kanchipuram → *For listings, see pages 64-67.*

What Darjeeling is to tea, and Cheddar is to cheese, so Kanchipuram is to silk. One of Hinduism's seven most sacred cities, 'the Golden City of a Thousand Temples', dates from the early Cholas in the second century. The main temple complexes are very spacious and only a few of the scattered 70 or so can be seen in a day's visit. The town itself is relatively quiet except for crowds of pilgrims. **Tourist information** ① *Hotel Tamil Nadu, T044-2722 2553, 1000-1700.*

Background

The **Pallavas** of Kanchi came to power in the fourth century AD and were dominant from AD 550 to 869. Possibly of northern origin, under their control Mahabalipuram became an important port in the seventh century. Buddhism is believed to have reached the Kanchipuram area in the third century BC. Successive dynasties made it their capital and built over 100 temples, the first as early as the fourth century. As well as being a pilgrimage site, it was a centre of learning, culture and philosophy. Sankaracharya and the Buddhist monk Bodhidharma lived and worked here.

Places in Kanchipuram → *Phone code: 044. Population: 153,000.*

ⓘ *Temples are usually open from 0600 and closed 1200-1600, but very few allow non-Hindus into the inner sanctum. Have change ready for 'donations' to each temple you visit.*

Ekambaresvara Temple ⓘ *small entry fee, cameras Rs 3, only Hindus are allowed into the inner sanctuary.* The temple has five enclosures and a 'Thousand-pillared Hall' (if you're pedantically inclined, the number is actually 540). Dedicated to Siva in his ascetic form it was begun by the Pallavas and developed by the Cholas. In the early 16th century the Vijayanagara king Krishna Deva Raya built the high stone wall which surrounds the temple and the 59-m-tall *rajagopuram* (main tower) on which are sculpted several figures of him and his consort.

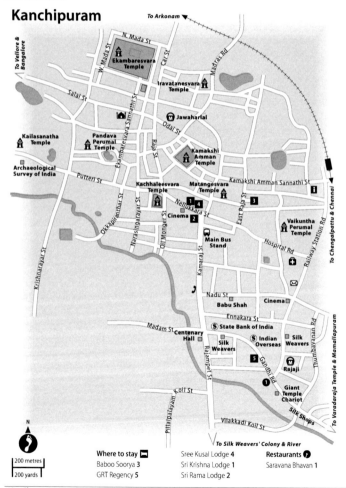

Kanchipuram

Where to stay
Baboo Soorya 3
GRT Regency 5
Sree Kusal Lodge 4
Sri Krishna Lodge 1
Sri Rama Lodge 2

Restaurants
Saravana Bhavan 1

The main sanctuary has a *lingam* made of earth (Siva as one of the elements) and the story of its origin is told on a carved panel. The teasing Parvati is believed to have unthinkingly covered her husband Siva's eyes for a moment with her hands which resulted in the earth being enveloped in darkness for years. The enraged Siva ordered Parvati to do severe penance during which time she worshipped her husband in the form of an earth *lingam* which she created. When Siva sent a flood to test her, she clung to the *lingam* with her hands until the waters subsided. Some believe they can see her fingerprints on the *lingam* here. On 18 April each year the sun's rays enter the sanctum through a small square hole.

Kailasanatha Built in the early seventh century, this is considered to be the most beautiful of the town's temples. It was built of sandstone by the Pallava king Narasimha Varman II with the front completed by his son Mahendra III. The outer structure has a dividing wall with a shrine and doorways, separating a large courtyard from a smaller one. The unusual enclosure wall has 58 small raised shrines with a *Nandi* in most pavilions and some frescoes have survived. The seven shrines in the temple complex have images of different Siva forms. The intricately carved panels on the walls depict legends about Siva with accompanying text in ancient Grantha script. It has been extensively restored. The festival **Mahashivaratri** is held here in February.

Vaikuntha Perumal Eighth century and dedicated to Vishnu, this temple was built by the Pallava king Nandivarman just after the Kailasanatha and illustrates the progress of Dravidian temple architecture. The sanctuary is separated from the *mandapa* by an open space. The cloisters are built from rows of lion pillars. Panels of bas relief accompanied by lines in old Tamil trace the history of the wars between the Pallavas and Chalukyas. There is an unusual *vimana* (tower) with shrines in three tiers with figures of Vishnu in each.

Varadaraja (Devarajasvami) ① *0630-1200, 1530-2000, Rs 5, camera Rs 5, video Rs 100.* Built by the Vijayanagara kings (circa 16th century), 3 km southeast of town, it has superb sculpture in its marriage hall (with 96 pillars). Figures on horseback wear half North Indian/ half South Indian costumes. Note the rings at each corner and the massive flexible chain supposedly carved out of one piece of granite, although it is no longer in one piece. The main shrine is on an elephant-shaped rock, Hastagiri. The **Float Festival** is in February and November, **Brahmotsavam** in May and **Garuda Sevai** in June.

Chengalpattu (Chingleput) The fort here was built by the Vijayanagar king Thimmu Raya after his defeat at the Battle of Talikotta in 1565. After 1687 it was absorbed into the Mughal Empire. Then in 1750 it was taken by the French, who held it until it was captured by Clive in 1752; British control was only finally established after the defeat of Haidar Ali in 1781. Although the fort is now almost totally destroyed (the railway runs through the middle of it), the Raja Mahal ('King's Palace') remains.

Around Kanchipuram

On the Trichy Road, 87 km from Chennai and 60 km from Mahabalipuram, the **Vedanthangal Bird Sanctuary** ① *0530-1800, Rs 5, camera Rs 50, see Transport, page 67,* and **Karikili Tank** are thought to have existed as a protected area for about 250 years. The marshy site attracts numerous water fowl and provides their main nesting place. Visitors and residents include crested cormorants, night herons, grey pelicans, sand pipers, white wagtails, open-billed storks, white ibis, egrets, little grebe and purple moorhens. The best time to visit is November to February, at dawn and from 1500 to 1800; avoid weekends and holidays. Afternoons are best because the sun is behind you for clear views, and you get to see large flocks of birds returning home to roost.

Marakkanam, mentioned in Roman records as an important port in the first century AD, has an ancient Siva temple with many inscriptions. Immediately inland is the Kaliveli Tank, an extremely important staging post and wintering area for about 40,000 migratory water fowl, including over 200 pelicans.

Around Chennai listings

For hotel and restaurant price codes and other relevant information, see pages 14-18.

🛏 Where to stay

Mahabalipuram *p57, map p57*
Even modest hotels charge 20% luxury tax. Several new places in the Othavadai St area. It's busy during the Jan dance festival.
$$$$ Fisherman's Cove (Taj), Kovalam Rd, 8 km north, T044-6741 3333, www.taj hotels.com. A beautiful resort, recently expanded and given a sleek and thoroughly modern fit-out. Pick of the rooms are the beachfront cottages with private sit-outs and open-air showers.
$$$$ Radisson BLU Resort, off the northern entry point into town, T044-27443636, www.radissonblu.com. 100 rooms on 44 acres, beachfront. Best luxury resort in town. Top-notch service and food. Excellent seafood restaurant on the beach. Best rooms are the Pool View Chalets.
$$$$-$$$ Ideal Beach Resort, Kovalam Rd (3.5 km north), T044-2744 2240, www.ideal resort.com. 30 rooms in cottages, some a/c (limited hours), good restaurant, exchange, spa with Ayurvedic massage, pool and gardens, clean, comfortable.
$$$-$$ Sea Breeze, Othavadai Cross, T044-2744 3035, www.hotelseabreeze.in. Clean, spacious, well-furnished rooms (some a/c with fridge, Rs 700), direct beach access, pool (non-residents Rs 200), good food. Iffy 'hot water', mediocre upkeep. Next door annexe is cheaper, see below.

$$ Butterball B&B, East Raja St, T(0)9094-792525, bbbb@gatsby.in. 9-room B&B located in town centre next to Nilgiris Supermarket. Rooms are small but clean. Holds music and art events, a weekly sandhai (flea market). Good food at their restaurant called Burger Shack. Avoid rooms at the rear which face Krishna's butterball – big noisy coaches park there. Recommended.
$$-$ Lakshmi Lodge, Othavadai St, T044-2744 2463. Friendly, popular with backpackers, 26 clean rooms in main building, upstairs small but light, downstairs dark and poor, plus an annexe out the back with larger, brighter a/c rooms and a pool (which you pay extra to use if you stay in the cheap rooms). Restaurant with beach view.
$ Greenwoods Beach Resort, 7 Othavadai Cross St, T044-2744 2212, greenwoods_ resort@yahoo.com. Basic but good and clean rooms with mosquito nets in a rambling building lushly shaded by banana and mango trees. The family owners are genuinely welcoming, and there's a well-regarded Ayurvedic clinic on site.
$ La Vie en Rose, 9 Old College Rd, near bus stand, T(0)9444-877544. Small, quiet hotel slowly going to rack and ruin, but it's a genuine cheapie and the manager is friendly.
$ Mamalla Heritage, 104 East Raja St, T044-2744 2060. Spotless, friendly and reasonable value, 43 clean spacious rooms, 17 a/c, nice balconies, pool, excellent vegetarian restaurant, exchange, travel, 24-hr hot water, and complimentary toiletries. Recommended.

$ Ramakrishna Lodge, 8A Othavadai St, T044-2744 2431. Friendly, good value, 31 well-kept, clean rooms with fan, shower, Western toilets, no nets, courtyard, good rooftop restaurant with travellers' menu and music; contact Vijay for informal yoga classes. Possibly the best cheap deal in town.
$ Sea Breeze Annexe, see above. Clean doubles with fan and deck, but rates don't include access to the **Sea Breeze** hotel pool.
$ Siva Guest House, 2 Othavadai Cross St, T044-2744 3534, www.sivaguesthouse.com. 11 very clean rooms, taxi hire, internet, friendly. Highly recommended.
$ Sri Harul Guest House, 181 Bajanai Koil St, T(0)9384-620173, lings6@rediffmail.com. Friendly little guesthouse right on the beach, with interesting views over the fishermen's colony. Rooms on the ground floor have private balconies.
$ Tamil Nadu Beach Resort, north of town on Covelong Rd, T044-2744 2361. Beautiful setting, 48 cottages, some a/c but neglected, damp, restaurants, bar (limited hours), exchange, good pool (non-residents Rs 75).
$ Tina Blue View Lodge, 1 Othavadai St, T044-2744 2319. Very friendly, 25 rooms with bath and balcony (Room 9 best), cottages for long-term stays, garden and rooftop restaurant, massage. Recommended.

Kanchipuram *p61, map p62*
$$-$ Baboo Soorya, 85 East Raja St, T044-2722 2555. Set back off main road down palm-fringed lane. 38 clean, spacious rooms, some a/c, restaurant, snack bar, glass 'bubble' lift, friendly staff, quiet.
$$-$ GRT Regency, Gandhi Rd, T044-2722 5250, www.grthotels.com. The best in town by a long chalk, with smart, spotless rooms and all the facilities of a luxury business hotel.
$ Sree Kusal Lodge, 68C Nellukkara St, T044-2722 3356. 25 clean and good-value rooms, TV, vegetarian restaurant.
$ Sri Krishna Lodge, 68A Nellukkara St, T044-2722 2831. Helpful, friendly manager, 28 good, clean rooms, some with bath.

$ Sri Rama Lodge, 20 Nellukkara St, near Bus Stand, T044-2722 2435. Fairly basic rooms, some a/c and TV, a/c restaurant, relatively quiet, helpful staff.

Around Kanchipuram *p63*
$$ Karadi Malai Camp, 5 km east of Chengalpattu, T(0)8012-033087, www.draco-india.com. Wildlife film-maker and croc man Romulus Whittaker and his wife Janaki have opened up their home and farm in the Vallam Reserve Forest. There are just 3 bamboo cottages here, plus a campsite and a delightful pool. Rich in small mammals (and the occasional leopard), birds, amphibians and reptiles. Set camera traps, search for snakes and other critters with Irula tribal guides. The best base for visiting Vedanthangal Sanctuary too.
$ Forest Rest House, 1 km from Vedanthangal Sanctuary gates, contact Wildlife Warden, T044-2432 1471 in Chennai, or ask a local agency to help with bookings. Rest house with 4 well-kept rooms (2 with a/c), meals available on request.

ⓟ Restaurants

Mahabalipuram *p57, map p57*
Beachside cafés are pleasant for a drink: **Sea Rock** and **Luna Magica** in particular. In top hotels waterfront cafés are especially attractive in the evening.
$$ Curiosity, Othavadai St. Wide range, excellent food, very willing to please.
$$ Gazebo, East Raja St. Charcoal-grilled fish, pleasant seating.
$$ Moonrakers, Othavadai St, www.moonrakersrestaurant.com. Long-established backpacker favourite. Pleasant and friendly vibe during the week, but very rushed at weekends – you may be ordered out of your seat to make way for incoming diners.
$$ Temple View, GRT Temple Bay Kovalam Rd, T044-2744 3636. Multi-cuisine restaurant overlooking shore temple, breakfast lunch and dinner, plus less formal, open-air **Beach Comber** and **High Tide** bars (1000-2200).

$ Dreamland, Othavadai St. Western favourites, very friendly, relaxed.
$ Mamalla Bhavan, opposite bus stand. Classic high-ceilinged South Indian restaurant, excellent for cheap breakfasts.

Kanchipuram *p61, map p62*
Baboo Soorya (see Where to stay). A/c, cheap Indian vegetarian restaurant, good *thalis*.
Bakery Park Place, Odai St. Cakes and sweets.
Saravana Bhavan, next to Jaybala International 504 Gandhi Rd (50 m off the road). "Best in town".
Sri Rama Lodge, a/c, and **Sri Vela**, Station Rd. Good breakfasts.

❋ Festivals

Mahabalipuram *p57, map p57*
Dec-early Feb 6-week Dance Festival starting on 25 Dec; at Bhagiratha's (Arjuna's) Penance, classical 1800-2030, folk 2030-2100, every Sat, Sun and holidays. Long speeches in Tamil on opening (full moon) night.
Mar Masi Magam attracts large crowds of pilgrims.
Apr-May Brahmotsava lasts for 10 days.
Oct-Nov The Palanquin Festival is held at the Stalasayana Perumal Temple.

Kanchipuram *p61, map p62*
Mar-Apr The Panguni Uthiram Festival is the largest of Kanchipuram's festivals, very atmospheric. Celebrated all over Tamil Nadu.

◎ Shopping

Mahabalipuram *p57, map p57*
Hidesign, 138 East Raja St. Excellent Western-style leather goods, very reasonable. Recommended.
Himalayan Handicrafts, 21 East Raja St, also has 900 books for exchange.
JK Books, off the beach on Othavadai St. Books and newspapers.
Silver Star, 51 East Raja St, good tailor.

Kanchipuram *p61, map p62*
Silk and cotton fabrics with designs of birds, animals and temples or in plain beautiful colours, sometimes 'shot', are sold by the metre in addition to saris. It's best to buy from government shops or Co-operative Society stores.
AS Babu Shah, along Gandhi Rd. High-quality silks.
BM Silks, 23G Yadothagari, Sannathi St. Worth a look.
Murugan Silk Weavers' Co-operative, 79 Gandhi Rd.
Sreenivas, 135 Thirukatchi Nambi St (Gandhi Rd).

⚙ What to do

Mahabalipuram *p57, map p57*
Tour operators
Hi Tours, 123 East Raja St, T044-2744 3360, www.hi-tours.com. Train/air tickets, tours, foreign exchange, Kerala house boats.
Tamil Nadu Tourism runs a hop-on-hop-off bus service from Chennai, departing the Tourism Complex (2 Wallajah Rd) at 0900, 0930, 1000, 1100, returning from Mahabalipuram at 1600, 1700, 1730 and 1800; stops include the Crocodile Bank and Dakshina Chitra; tickets Rs 250. Also day tours to Kanchipuram and Mahabalipuram. 0630-1900. Tiring, but good value if you don't mind being rushed. It also includes a stop at the appallingly garish Indian kitsch, VGP Beach Resort.

⊖ Transport

Mahabalipuram *p57, map p57*
Bicycle/car hire Bicycle hire from tourist office and shops in East Raja St and hotels, Rs 40-50 per day. Recommended for **Tirukkalukundram** – from Dec to Feb a comfortable and very attractive ride. The same shops also hire out mopeds and motorbikes at around Rs 200-300. Car hire from the tourist office.

Bus The bus stand in the centre has buses to **Tirukkalukundram**, and further afield to **Chennai**, **Puducherry** and **Tiruvannamalai**.

Taxi Taxis charge Rs 1000-1200 for a 1-day excursion from Chennai, around Rs 1000 from Mahabalipuram to the airport.

Train The nearest train station is Chengalpattu, 29 km away, which has express trains to **Chennai** and south Tamil Nadu; buses from here to Mahabalipuram take an hour.

Kanchipuram *p61, map p62*
Auto-rickshaws Available for visiting temples. Also cycle rickshaws.

Bicycle hire The town is flat and easy to negotiate so the best and cheapest way to get about is by hiring a bike from near the bus stand or off East Raja St.

Bus The bus station in the middle of town with direct Govt Express to **Chennai** (*No 828*) 2½ hrs, **Bengaluru (Bangalore)** (*No 828*), **Kaniyakumari** (*No 193*), **Puducherry** (*No 804*, 109 km) 3½ hrs, and **Tiruchirappalli** (*No 122*). For **Mahabalipuram** (65 km) 2 hrs, direct bus or take a bus to Chengalpattu (35 km) and catch one from there. Frequent buses to **Vellore**, other buses go to **Tirupati**, **Tiruttani** and **Tiruvannamalai**.

Train The train station, on a branch line, is under 1 km to the northeast of the bus stand. There are 3 direct passenger trains to **Chennai** (**Egmore**), at 0715, 1750 and 1900, 2 hrs; for long-distance trains, it's better to go by bus to **Arakkonam**, 28 km to the north, which is on the main Chennai–Bengaluru line.

Around Kanchipuram *p63*
Vedanthangal Bird Sanctuary is best accessed by car; an overnight taxi from Chennai will cost around Rs 2500, less from Mahabalipuram. The closest major town and railway station is Chengalpattu, which has several daily buses to the sanctuary and frequent connections to Chennai and Mahabalipuram.

⏰ Directory

Mahabalipuram *p57, map p57*
Banks Cherry, Beach St, for exchange. LKP, 130 East Raja St. Good rate, speedy. Prithvi Securities, opposite **Mamalla Heritage**, no commission, transfers money. **Libraries** English-language dailies. Book exchange at **Himalayan Handicrafts**. **Post** Post office on a back street off Kovalam Rd.

Kanchipuram *p61, map p62*
Banks State Bank of India, Gandhi Rd, with ATM. Amex TCs not accepted; Indian Overseas Bank, Gandhi Rd. **Post** Head Post Office, 27 Gandhi Rd.

Puducherry and Auroville

Pretty little Puducherry (still widely known by its old name of Pondicherry) has all the lazy charm of a former French colony: its stately whitewashed 18th-century homes froth with bright pink bougainvillea and its kitchens still smack gloriously of Gaul – excellent French breads, hard cheese and ratatouilles that run with olive oil, accompanied by real French wines. The primly residential French quarter contrasts wonderfully with the dog-eared heritage houses of the Tamil districts, whose streets were built to tilt towards Mecca, while the scores of pristine grey mansions indicate the offices of the Sri Aurobindo Ashram, headquarters of one of India's liveliest spiritual schools of thought.

Up the road is the 1960s Westernized branch of Sri Aurobindo's legacy, Auroville, the 'City of Dawn', which was conceived as "a place where human beings could live freely as citizens obeying one single authority, that of the supreme Truth". This is the industrious fulcrum of people seeking an alternative lifestyle – a place of spirulina, incense and white cotton weeds – and while many tourists visit Auroville on a rushed day trip from Puducherry, if you're of a meditative mindset and can forgo your fix of Gallic good cheer, it can be far more interesting to do it the other way round.

Puducherry (Pondicherry) → *For listings, see pages 72-77.*

Puducherry is the archetypal ambling town: cleaved in two with the **French quarter** along the beach, boasting pretty high-ceilinged wood-slatted residential houses with walled gardens and bougainvillea, and with the markets, mess, businesses and 'talking streets' of the **Tamil** ('black') town to its west. While the French area, with 300 heritage buildings, is well maintained (the majority owned by the ashram), the Tamil area, despite its 1000 homes now classified as heritage, is dangerously dilapidated. The European Commission has funded the restoration of Calve Subraya Chettiar (Vysial) street (between Mission and Gandhi streets), while Muslim domestic architecture is clearly visible in the streets of Kazy, Mulla and Tippu Sultan, in the southern part of the Tamil quarter.

Many people come to Puducherry to visit the campus-like ashram of **Sri Aurobindo Ghosh** and his chief disciple Mirra Alfassa ('The Mother'). Ghosh was an early 20th-century Bengali nationalist and philosopher who struggled for freedom from British colonial power and wrote prodigiously on a huge variety of subjects, particularly Integral Yoga and education. In his aim to create an ashram utopia he found a lifelong *compadre* in the charismatic Frenchwoman Alfassa, who continued as his spiritual successor after his death in 1950. It was Alfassa who pushed into practice Sri Aurobindo's ideas on integral schooling, the aim of which is to develop all aspects of the student's being – "mind, life, body, soul and spirit". In the ashram school, class sizes are limited to eight students, and both pupils and teachers enjoy an extraordinary freedom to alter classes according to individual needs. Alfassa died in 1973 at the age of 93. Both Sri Aurobindo and Alfassa live on as icons, their images gazing down from the walls of almost every building in Puducherry.

Arriving in Puducherry → *Phone code: 0413. Population: 220,700.*

Getting there Buses take under four hours from Chennai on the East Coast Road. The well-organized bus stand is just west of the town, within walking distance, or a short auto-ride from the centre (expect the usual hassle from rickshaw-wallahs). The train station, on a branch line from Villupuram which has trains to major destinations, is a few minutes' walk south of the centre.

Getting around Puducherry is lovely to explore on foot, but hiring a bike or moped will give you the freedom to venture further along the coast. ▸▸ *See Transport, page 76.*

Tourist information Puducherry Tourism ① *40 Goubert Salai, T0413-233 9497, http:// tourism.puducherry.gov.in, 0845-1300, 1400-1700.* Well run with maps, brochures and tours. The **Indian National Trust for Art and Cultural Heritage (INTACH)** ① *62 rue Aurobindo St, T0413-222 5991, http://intachpuducherry.org,* is particularly active in Puducherry and runs heritage walks from its offices. **La Boutique d'Auroville** ① *38 JL Nehru St, T0413-233 7264.* Provides information on visiting Auroville.

Background

Ancient Vedapuri was where the sage **Agastya Muni** had his hermitage in 1500 BC and in the first century AD Romans traded from nearby Arikamedu. The French renamed the area Puducherry in 1673. In 1742, Dupleix, newly named Governor of the French India Company, took up residence. In 1746 the British lost Fort St George in Madras to Dupleix but in 1751 Clive counter-attacked by capturing Puducherry in 1761. Puducherry was voluntarily handed over to the Indian government in 1954 and became the Union Territory of Puducherry.

Places in Puducherry

The **French Quarter**, which extends from the seafront promenade inland to the canal, contains most of Puducherry's sights, and wandering the quiet streets, stopping into antique shops and colonial mansions, is a pleasure in itself.

The **Sri Aurobindo Ashram** ① *rue de la Marine, 800-1200, 1400-1800, free, meditation Mon-Wed, Fri 1925-1950,* has its main centre in rue de la Marine. Painted in neat grey and white like most of the ashram's buildings, it contains the flower-bedecked marble Samadhi (resting place and memorial) of both Sri Aurobindo and the Mother.

The **French Institute** ① *rue St Louis,* was set up in 1955 for the study of Indian culture and the 'Scientific and Technical Section' for ecological studies. There's a French and English library looking over the sea, and the colonial building is an architectural treat in its own right.

Puducherry Museum ① *next to the library, rue St Louis, Tue-Sun 0940-1300 and 1400-1720, closed public holidays, free,* has a good sculpture gallery and an archaeological

Puducherry

Where to stay 🛏
Ajantha Sea View 1 *F5*
Aurodhan 5 *A5*
Balan Guest House 2 *C2*
De l'Orient 3 *E4*
De Pondicherry and Le Club 4 *F4*
Executive Inn 6 *B4*
Family Guest House 7 *E2*
International Guest House 9 *C4*
Mother Guest House 10 *C4*
Mother Sea View Residency 15 *F5*
Park Guest House 11 *F5*
Ram Guest House 12 *D2*
Sea Side Guest House 13 *C5*
Surguru 14 *A3*
Villa Helena 16 *E4*
Youth Hostel 19 *A2*

Restaurants 🍴
Ananda Bhavan 7 *C4*
Ashram Dining Hall 1 *C4*
Au Feu de Bois 2 *E4*
Baker Street 8 *E3*
Blue Dragon 3 *F5*
Café des Arts 16 *D5*
Hot Breads 4 *C4*
Indian Coffee House 5 *C3*
La Terrasse 6 *F4*
Le Café 9 *D5*
Le Club 7 *F5*
Lighthouse 10 *D5*
Rendezvous 13 *E4*
Satsanga 14 *F4*

Bars & clubs 🍸
Asian House 11 *F4*
Le Space 12 *E4*
Seagulls 15 *F5*

section with finds discovered at the Roman settlement at Arikamedu. The French gallery charts the history of the colony and includes Dupleix's four-poster bed.

Another place worth seeking out is the grand whitewashed **Lycée Français** ⓘ *rue Victor Simonel*, with its lovely shady courtyard and balconies.

The French Catholic influence is evident in a number of churches, notably the **Jesuit Cathedral** (Notre Dame de la Conception, 1691-1765). The attractive amber and pink **Church of Our Lady of Angels** (1855) holds an oil painting of Our Lady of Assumption given to the church by King Louis Napoleon III.

The **Government (Puducherry) Park**, laid out with lawns, flower beds and fountains (one at the centre is of the Napoleon III period), lies in front of the Raj Niwas, the residence of the lieutenant governor. This was the original site of the first French garrison, Fort Louis, which was destroyed in Clive's raid of 1761.

Auroville → *For listings, see pages 72-77.*
Phone code: 0413. Population 1700.

ⓘ *Visitor centre, International Zone, T0413-262 2239, www.auroville.org, Mon-Sat 0900-1300 and 1400-1730, Sun 1000-1200 and 1400-1730. All visitors are expected to report here first. Passes for visits to Matrimandir gardens and Amphitheatre are issued here (Mon-Sat 0930-1230 and 1400-1600, Sun 0930-1230; gardens open daily 1000-1250 and 1400-1630), and a 5-min video about the Matrimandir is shown according to demand. Visitors may enter the Inner Chamber for 10 mins' silent 'concentration' with at least 1 day's notice; apply in person at the Visitor Centre 1000-1100 or 1400-1500 any day except Tue. A useful information booklet, The Auroville Handbook, is available here and at La Boutique d'Auroville, 38 JL Nehru St, Puducherry.*

Futuristic Auroville, 'City of Dawn', was founded in 1968 by 'The Mother' (Mirra Alfassa) as a tribute to Sri Aurobindo, and remains a fascinating experiment in communal living and spiritual evolution. The founding charter reads: "To live in Auroville one must be a willing servitor of the Divine Consciousness," and describes it as belonging "to humanity as a whole ... the place of an unending education, of constant progress ... a bridge between the past and the future ... a site of material and spiritual researches for a living embodiment of actual human unity".

A baked and desolate plateau when the first residents moved here, Auroville has been transformed into a lush forest, among which are scattered 100 distinct hamlets, housing a permanent population of 2200 people plus a regular throughflow of international eco-warriors, holistic therapists and spiritually inclined intellectuals. It's a place where concepts that would be deemed too flakey to fly in the outside world are given free rein: the town plan is based on the shape of a spiralling galaxy, with the Matrimandir – an extraordinary 30-m-high globe-shaped meditation chamber clad in shimmering discs of gold leaf, with a lotus bud shaped foundation urn and a centrepiece crystal said to be the largest in the world – at its spiritual and geographic fulcrum. The main buildings are based on principles espoused in Sri Aurobindo's philosophical tracts. And a town that can't provide enough housing to accommodate all its would-be residents has found the money to build a gleaming pavilion dedicated to study of Aurobindo's epic poem Savitri. Yet there's a great deal of serious and earnest work going on here, in the fields of sustainable architecture, reforestation, education, organic agriculture, renewable energy and self-development.

Residents are quick to point out that Auroville is not a tourist attraction, and a casual day trip here can be as much an exercise in frustration as inspiration. Tours from Puducherry visit the Matrimandir gardens for a view of the dome, but to experience the unforgettable womb-like interior and spend 10 minutes in silent 'concentration' you have to request permission in person at the Matrimandir office, at least 24 hours in advance.

On the other hand, the community welcomes visitors who have a genuine interest in its philosophy – all the more so if you can find a project you'd like to work on – and an extended stay here makes a very pleasant retreat. An ideal way to get to know the place is to take the three-day orientation tour, which guides you around many of Auroville's 'villages' by bike and provides a good opportunity to interact with Aurovilians.

Puducherry and Auroville listings

For hotel and restaurant price codes and other relevant information, see pages 14-18.

Where to stay

Puducherry *p68, map p70*

$$$$-$$$ The Dune, 15 km from Puducherry, T0413-265 5751, www.thedune hotel.com. Funky beachside eco-hotel with 36 themed villas and 15 colourful, clean and comfortable rooms spread amongst 12 ha of landscaped grounds. Yoga, reflexology, Ayurvedic massage, organic food and optional detox programmes are on offer, along with a pool, tennis and free bike hire.

$$$ Ajantha Sea View, 1C 50 Goubert Salai, T0413-234 9032, www.ajanthasea viewhotel.com. The best-value sea views in town (other than the ashram guesthouses, see below). Not the most modern rooms, but they're clean, bright and have huge balconies gazing straight out into the Bay of Bengal.

$$$ Aurodhan, 33 rue François Martin, T0413-222 2795, www.aurodhan.com. 16 superb rooms stuffed with top-quality art and quirky antique furniture in an otherwise undistinguished building, with art galleries on the lower floors, Wi-Fi, a kitchen for home cooking and great views from the rooftop.

$$$-$$ Hotel de l'Orient, 17 Romain Rolland St, T0413-234 3067, www.neemrana hotels.com. Beautifully renovated 19th-century school now a small exclusive hotel, with 16 tastefully decorated rooms in colonial style with objets d'art. Mixed reviews of the restaurant (French/Creole) and service, but achingly beautiful location. Recommended.

$$ Hotel de Pondichery, 38 rue Dumas, T0413-222 7409, www.hoteldepondichery. com. Simple, clean, tastefully decorated 10 rooms (some with no windows but private courtyard), in the same colonial-style building as the popular French bistro Le Club (so can get noisy). Very friendly and efficient staff. A/c. Babysitting service available.

$$ Mother Sea View Residency, 1-C rue Bazar St Laurent, T0413-222 5999, mother_residency@yahoo.co.in. A handful of spacious, airy, marble-floored rooms with balconies pointing seawards.

$$ Villa Helena, 14 Suffren St, T0413-222 6789, www.villa-helena-pondicherry.com. 5 comfortable rooms with antique furniture set around large shady courtyard, suite on the 1st floor, includes breakfast.

$$-$ Executive Inn, 1a Perumal Koil St, T0413-233 0929, www.executiveinn.biz. 11 a/c suites, TV, restaurant, internet, no smoking, no alcohol, quiet yet short walk from the beachfront and bazar, good value. Recommended.

$$-$ Surguru, 104 Sardar Patel Rd, T0413-233 9022. Good, clean rooms, some a/c, excellent South Indian restaurant, bit noisy.

$ Balan Guest House, 20 Vellaja St, T0413-233 0634. 17 immaculate rooms with bath, clean linen.

$ Family Guest House, 526 MG Rd, T0413-222 8346, fghpondy@yahoo.co.in. 4 rooms, TV, hot water, bit cramped but very clean, roof terrace, hall, dining area, friendly.

$ Mother Guest House, 36 Ambur Salai, T0413-233 7165. Well-located cheap dive just off the JL Nehru shopping strip, with dark but clean enough rooms squirrelled

away along labyrinthine corridors above a clothes shop.

$ Ram Guest House, 546 MG Rd, 278 Avvai Shanmugham (Lloyds) Rd, T0413-222 0072, ramguest@hotmail.com. 20 excellent rooms set back from the main road, maintained to European standards, spotless, good breakfast from clean kitchen. Recommended.

$ Youth Hostel, Solaithandavan Kuppam, T0413-222 3495, north of town. Dorm beds (Rs 30), close to the sea among fishermen's huts. Bicycle or transport essential.

Ashram guesthouses

Though these are mainly for official visitors and guests associated with the ashram, they are open to the public. Gates close by 2230 (late-comers may be locked out) and alcohol and smoking are prohibited. Book well in advance.

$ International Guest House, Gingee Salai, T0413-233 6699, ingh@aurosociety.org. 57 very clean and airy rooms, some a/c, huge for the price, very popular so often full.

$ Park Guest House, near Children's Park, T0413-222 4644. 93 excellent sea-facing rooms, breakfasts, clean, quiet, great garden, reading room, ideal for long stays. Recommended.

$ Sea Side Guest House, 14 Goubert Salai, T0413-223 1700, seaside@aurosociety.org. 25 excellent, large rooms, hot showers, breakfast, spotless, sea views. Recommended.

Auroville *p71*

For details of the 20-odd guesthouses scattered around Auroville, see www. aurovilleguesthouses.com. Accommodation ranges from basic thatched huts with shared toilets to self-contained studios, with rooms available in 4 distinct zones: Centre (close to the Matrimandir, theatres and cafés), Residential, Forest and Beach. The Auroville Guest Service, T0413-262 2704, can also help with finding a room. Costs vary from **$$-$**, though some operate a kibbutz-type arrangement.

$ Centre Guest House, T0413-262 2155. Most short-stay visitors are accommodated here ("welcomes those who wish to see and be in Auroville, but not to work there"), lovely setting under a huge banyan treee. Bikes and scooters for rent, famous weekly pizza.

🍴 Restaurants

Puducherry *p68, map p70*
$$$ Le Club, 38 rue Dumas, T0413-233 9745. Tue-Sun 0830-1830. French and Continental. Smart, excellent cuisine (Rs 400 for a splurge), French wine (Rs 1000). Mixed reviews: "we could have been in a French Bistro!" to "dearest but not the best".
$$$ Lighthouse, on the roof of **Promenade Hotel**, 23 Goubert Salai, T0413-222 7750. Superb barbecue fare, including some quite adventurous veg options alongside the expected seafood and meat options, served on a glassed-in terrace with front-row sea views. Good cocktails, too.
$$ Blue Dragon, 30 rue Dumas near New Pier (south end of Goubert Salai). Chinese. Excellent food, antique furniture.
$$ Café des Arts, 1 rue Labourdonnais. Very pleasant courtyard café serving good coffees and sandwiches, attached to an art gallery. Also has free Wi-Fi and clean toilets.
$$ La Terrasse, 5 Subbaiyah Salai, T0413-222 7677. Open 0830-2000, closed Tue. Excellent Continental. Good value, huge salads, no alcohol.
$$ Rendezvous, 30 Suffren St. French and Continental. Attractive, modern, reasonable food but overpriced wine, nice roof terrace, pleasant atmosphere: the owner worked for a wealthy American family for 20 years and so his continental grub is first rate.
$$ Salad Bar, 13 rue Surcouf. Delivers what it promises: fresh, hygienic and delicious salads, as well as falafel wraps, burgers and crepes. There's free Wi-Fi too.
$$ Satsanga, 32 rue Mahe de Labourdonnais, T0413-222 5867. Closed Thu. Continental (quite expensive wine), friendly,

French atmosphere with art 'gallery'. Garden setting and staff make up for mediocre food.
$ Ananda Bhavan, 15 Nehru St. Big, buzzy and modern pure veg place, excellent for sweets and *thalis*, and good fun if you don't mind elbowing your way to the front of the queue.
$ Ashram Dining Hall, north of Government Place. Indian vegetarian. Simple, filling, meals (Rs 30 per day) in an unusual setting, seating on cushions at low tables, farm-grown produce, non-spicy and non-greasy. Buy a ticket (from ashram guesthouses or Central Bureau), then turn up at 0640, 1115, 1745 or 2000. Recommended, though non-ashramites can expect a grilling before being sold a ticket.
$ Au Feu de Bois, rue Bussy. Pizzas, salads, crêpes at lunchtime.
$ Baker Street, 123 rue Bussy. Closed Mon. Excellent new French sandwich shop and patisserie, with good but pricey coffee and handmade chocolates.
$ Hot Breads, Ambur Salai. Open 0700-2100. Good burgers, chicken puffs, pizzas, pastries, sandwiches and shakes.
$ Indian Coffee House, 41 Nehru St. Real local vegetarian fare from 0700.
$ Le Café, Goubert Salai, by Gandhi statue. Cute beachside pavilion in a grassy garden, great for hanging out with a milkshake or ice cream, though service is stretched and you'll be in for a long wait if it's busy.

🍸 Bars and clubs

Puducherry *p68, map p70*
Asian House, 7 Beach Blvd. Slick Bali-themed disco-pub, with a Buddha presiding over the bartenders and a DJ playing Euro house until the lights come on at 2300.
Le Space, 2 rue de la Bourdonnais. Sociable hippy-chic roof terrace hideaway strung with lanterns, with cheap drinks and music that's not too loud to talk over. Draws a mixed crowd of backpackers, Chennai hipsters and Pondy's young and beautiful.

Seagulls, near Children's Park. Recently renovated, but the old formula of cheap beer and sea views remains unchanged.

✪ Festivals

Puducherry *p68, map p70*
4-7 Jan International Yoga Festival held at Kamban Kalairangam, contact Puducherry Tourism for full details.
Jan Pongal is a 3-day harvest, earth and sun festival, popular in rural areas.
Feb/Mar Masi Magam on the full moon day of the Tamil month of Masi, pilgrims bathe in the sea when deities from about 40 temples from the surrounding area are taken in colourful procession for a ceremonial immersion. 'Fire walking' sometimes accompanies the festival.
14 Jul Bastille Day.
Aug Fete de Puducherry cultural programme.

✪ Shopping

Puducherry *p68, map p70*
The shopping areas are along Nehru St and Mahatma Gandhi Rd. *Experience! Puducherry* booklet has a good shopping guide.

Dolls of papier mâché, terracotta and plaster are made and sold at Kosapalayam. Local grass is woven into *korai* mats. Craftsmen at the Ashram produce marbled silk, hand-dyed cloths, rugs, perfumes and incense sticks.

Antiques
Geethanjali, 20 rue Bussy. Pricey but well selected and restored pieces. **Heritage Art Gallery**, rue Romain Rolland.

Books
Focus, 204 Mission St. Good selection of Indian writing in English, cards, stationery, CDs, very helpful. **Kailash French Bookshop**, 87 Lal Bahadur Shastri St. Large stock.

Clothes and crafts
Several Ashram outlets on Nehru St. **Aurosarjan**, rue Bussy. Auroville clothes and crafts. **Cluny Centre**, 46 Romain Rolland St, T0413-233 5668. This is run by a French order in a lovely colonial house where nuns both design and oversee high quality embroidery. **Curio Centre**, 40 Romain Rolland St. Some fine antiques and good reproduction colonial furniture. **Kalki**, 134 Mission St, T0413-233 9166. Produces exceptional printed and painted silk scarves, hangings, etc. **Pondy Cre'Art**, 53B Suffren St. Intriguing variety of locally handmade products, from pencil cases and notebooks to pottery, cushion covers and bespoke bamboo fountains. Also some fantastic clothes. Highly recommended. **Red Courtyard**, 4 Chetty St. Floaty, feminine, boho clothing in silks, linens and cottons by local designer Virginie Malé, plus artworks, bags and jewellery by other local creators. **Sri Aurobindo Handmade Paper Factory**, 44 Sardar Patel Rd. Shop sells attractive products.

Auroville *p71*
Shops at the visitor centre sell products made in the hive of industry that is Auroville, including handmade paper, incense, wind chimes and the like. **La Boutique d'Auroville** has excellent clothes and accessories, cut to suit Western tastes.

✪ What to do

Puducherry *p68, map p70*
Swimming
Pools in **Hotel Blue Star** and **Calve Bungalow**, Kamaraj Salai open to non-residents for a fee.

Tours and tour operators
Auro Travels, Karikar Building, Nehru St, T0413-233 5560. Efficient, quick service. **PTDC**, T0413-233 9497. Full-day sightseeing, 0930-1730, Rs 200 including lunch: Ashram, Govt Museum, Botanic Gardens, Sacred Heart church, Auroville and Matrimandir.

Half day covers ashram, museum and Auroville, 1430-1730, Rs 100. Departs from tourist office on Goubert Salai.

Yoga

Ananda Ashram, on Yoga Sadhana Beach, 16 Mettu St, Chinna Mudaliarchavadi, Kottakuppam, T0413-224 1561. It runs 1-, 3- and 6-month courses starting in Jan, Apr, Jul and Oct; or book through **Puducherry Tourism**, Rs 1500 for 10 lecture modules.

Auroville *p71*
Body and soul

With a guest pass to Auroville you can participate in retreat activities from Indian dance to ashtanga yoga. There's also a Quiet Healing Centre on the nearby beach, well known for its underwater body treatments. The hydrotherapy treatment tank is a little public so it may be best to stick to the good Ayurvedic massages.

Tours

Available 0830-1100 from **Ashram**, Puducherry, autocare@auroville.org.in; 1430-1745 from **Cottage Complex**, Ambur Salai, includes Auroville Visitor Centre and Matrimandir. Visitors recommend going independently. A 5-day residential introduction to Auroville is available through the **Guest Service**, T0413-262 2704, www.aurovilleguestservice.org.

⊖ Transport

Puducherry *p68, map p70*
Bicycle/scooter hire Bike hire is well worthwhile as the streets are broad, flat and quiet. The best choice of mopeds and bikes is on Mission St between Amballattadavar Madam St and Caltisvaran Koil St. Day rates start from Rs 30 for a bike, Rs 100 for a scooter, Rs 200 for a motorbike, plus photo ID (some places ask to keep it) and Rs 500 deposit.

Bus Local bus stand: T0413-233 6919, 0430-1230, 1330-2130. **Main bus stand:** a few hundred metres west of the junction of Anna Salai and Lal Bahadur Shastri, T0413-233 7464, serves all State bus companies. Computerized Reservations: 0700-2100 (helpful staff). **Puducherry Tourism Corporation (PTC)**, T0413-233 7008, 0600-2200, also runs long-distance services. Left luggage, Rs 20 per 24 hrs, at cloakroom on Platform 5. Auto-rickshaw to town Rs 30-40.

Bengaluru (Bangalore): 7½ hrs, overnight Volvo service with PTC; **Chennai**: frequent express buses via East Coast Rd, 3 hrs; **Chidambaram**: frequent, 1½ hrs; **Coimbatore** via **Salem** and **Erode**: 8½-9½ hrs; **Kanniyakumari**: overnight service; **Kannur** and **Mahé**: 15 hrs; **Karaikal**: 4 hrs; **Madurai** via **Tiruchirappalli**: 6½-8 hrs overnight; **Mahabalipuram**: several, 4 hrs; **Tirupati**: 6½-7 hrs; **Tiruvannamalai** (via **Villupuram** or **Tindivanam**, 1 hr, and **Gingee**, 2 hrs): regular buses between 0600-2000, 3½-4 hrs; **Kottakarai**, frequent service from **Town Bus Stand**.

Car hire One-way and round trips to many destinations can be arranged at roughly Rs 10 per km (though be aware that even if you travel only one way you'll be charged the cost of returning to Puducherry) eg **Bengaluru (Bangalore)** (310 km) Rs 5500; **Chidambaram** (74 km), Rs 3300; **Chennai** (166 km), Rs 3500; **Mahabalipuram** (130 km), Rs 2600; **Tiruvannamalai**, Rs 2400. Also available for multi-day trips, eg **Madurai**, 2 days, Rs 3500; **Ooty**, 3 days, Rs 5300; **Cochin**, 4 days, Rs 6000. Add 20% for a/c, plus extra charges for driver (Rs 200 per day), hill driving (Rs 350), tolls and parking.

Companies include: Siva Sakthi, 66 Perumal Koil St, T0413-222 1992, www.sivasakthitravels.com, helpful but with limited English. Praveen Cabs, 63 Laporte St, T0413-222 9955.

Taxi Easiest to find along the canal. For local sightseeing, expect to pay around Rs 400 for 4 hrs (40 km), Rs 800 for 8 hrs (80 km).

Train Reservations: T0413-233 6684, Mon-Sat 0800-1400 and 1500-1900, Sun 0800-1400. Pondy has virtually no direct express trains, but is connected by branch line to Villupuram, which has good connections towards Chennai and Madurai.

Direct express trains: to **Chennai**, *Auroville Exp 16116*, 0535; *Chennai Pass 56038*, 1435, 5 hrs. To **Villapuram**: 6 trains daily at 0535, 0805, 1325 (continues to Tirupati, 9 hrs), 1515, 1600 and 1935; 45 mins. Also frequent buses, which drop off at the bus stop 100 m from Villlupuram station.

Express trains from Villupuram: **Chennai** several daily; **Madurai**: *Vaigai Exp 12635*, 1550, 6 hrs, via **Trichy**, 3 hrs, and **Kodaikanal Rd**, 5½ hrs. It's possible to make computerized reservations from Pondy station to any other station, and there is a quota on major trains leaving from Chennai Central.

Auroville *p71*
Bicycle hire Rent a bicycle (Rs 25 per day, though at some guesthouses they are free) and take advantage of the many cycle paths. Centre Guest House is one of several places renting bikes/mopeds.

Rickshaw/taxi Either of the 2 roads north from Puducherry towards Chennai leads to Auroville. A rickshaw from **Puducherry** will cost around Rs 200, a taxi costs around Rs 500 return.

Directory

Puducherry *p68, map p70*
Banks Many ATMS along Nehru St, Mission St and MG Rd. **Andhra Bank**, 105 Easwaran Koil St, offers cash against Visa. **State Bank of India**, 5 Suffren St, changes cash and TCs (Amex, Thomas Cook), 24-hr ATM. LKP, 185 Mission St. No commission. **Cultural centres** French Institute, rue St Louis, close to the north end of Goubert Salai. **Alliance Française**, southern end of Goubert Salai for cultural programmes, Mon-Fri 0800-1230, 1500-1900, Sat 0830-1200.
Embassies and consulates French Consulate, 2 Marine St. **Internet** Coffee. com, 236 Mission St, plays DVDs, great coffee and real Italian pasta, but service and connection are equally slow. Shreenet, 54 Mission St. High speed, good computers, scanning. **Medical services** General Hospital, rue Victor Simone, T0413-233 6050; JIPMER, T0413-227 2381. Ashram Dispensary, Depuis St, near seaside.
Post Head Post Office, northwest corner of Govt Place, T0413-233 3051. CTO, Rangapillai St. **Useful contacts** Foreigners' Regional Registration Office, Goubert Salai.

Palar Valley

Running between the steep-sided northern Tamilnad hill range is the broad, flat bed of the River Palar, an intensively irrigated, fertile and densely populated valley cutting through the much poorer and sometimes wooded high land on either side. The whole valley became the scene of an Anglo-French-Indian contest at the end of the 18th century. Today it is the centre of South India's vitally important leather industry and intensive agricultural development.

Vellore → *For listings, see pages 82-84. Phone code: 0416. Population: 177,400.*

The once strategically important centre of Vellore, pleasantly ringed by hills, is in the process of converting itself from the dusty market town of old into an unmissable stop on the Tamil Nadu temple circuit, complete with its own airport. The reason for this transformation is the glittering new **Sripuram Temple** ① *12 km south of town at the base of the Thirumalaikodi hills, www.sripuram.org, 0700-2000, free entry*, which opened in late 2007 with funding from the local Sri Narayani Peedam trust, headed by Sri Sakthi Amma. The central temple building is covered in 1.5 tonnes of gold leaf – more than adorns the Golden Temple in Amritsar – which is laid over sheets of copper embossed with figures of gods. The temple has attracted no small measure of controversy, largely because of the huge sum of money ploughed into its construction – an estimated 600 million rupees – which some feel would have been better spent on poverty alleviation programs. Sri Sakthi Amma has defended the temple on the basis that it will serve as an attraction to people from all over the world, with lasting financial benefits to the area's people – from increased tourism spending as well as from donations to the trust's various beneficent activities – and spiritual benefits to visitors. To reach the temple you have to negotiate a 2-km-long covered walkway, modelled after the star-shaped Sri Chakra and festooned with quotes from the Vedas, Bible and Koran. The inner sanctum contains a granite idol of Mahalaxmi, the goddess of wealth, draped in golden adornments.

Before Sripuram, Vellore was best known for its **Christian Medical College Hospital**, founded by the American missionary Ida Scudder in 1900. Started as a one-room dispensary, it extended to a small hospital through American support. Today it is one of the country's largest hospitals with over 1200 beds and large outpatients' department which caters for over 2000 patients daily. The college has built a reputation for research in a wide range of tropical diseases. One of its earliest and most lasting programmes has been concerned with leprosy and there is a rehabilitation centre attached. In recent years it has undertaken a wide-ranging programme of social and development work in villages outside the town to back up its medical programmes.

Vijayanagar architecture is beautifully illustrated in the temple at **Vellore Fort**, a perfect example of military architecture and a *jala durga* (water fort). Believed to have been built by the Vijayanagara kings and dating from the 14th century, the fort has round towers and huge gateways along its double wall. The moat, still filled with water by a subterranean drain, followed ancient principles of defence: it was home to a colony of crocodiles. A wooden drawbridge crosses the moat to the southeast. In 1768 Vellore came under the control of the British, who defended it against Haidar Ali. After the victory in Seringapatnam in 1799, Tipu Sultan's family was imprisoned here and a mutiny of 1806, in which many British and Indian mutineers were killed, left many scars. In the fort is a parade ground, the CSI church, the temple and two-storeyed *mahals*, which are used as government offices.

Jalakantesvara Temple ① *bathing Rs 2*, with a 30-m-high seven-storeyed granite *gopuram*, has undergone considerable restoration. Enter from the south and inside on the left, the *kalyana mandapa* (wedding hall), one of the most beautiful structures of its kind, has vivid sculptures of dragons and 'hippogryphs' on its pillars. The temple consists of a shrine to Nataraja in the north and a lingam shrine in the west.

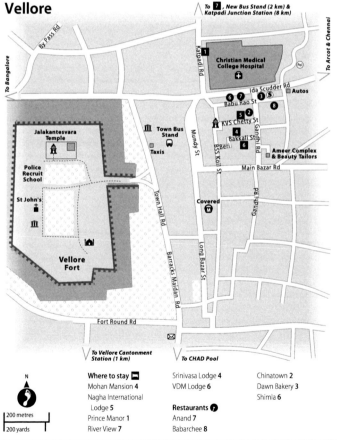

Vellore

Where to stay
Mohan Mansion **4**
Nagha International
  Lodge **5**
Prince Manor **1**
River View **7**
Srinivasa Lodge **4**
VDM Lodge **6**

Restaurants
Anand **7**
Babarchee **8**
Chinatown **2**
Dawn Bakery **3**
Shimla **6**

Gingee → *For listings, see pages 82-84. Phone code: 04145.*

Gingee (pronounced *Senjee*), just off the NH45, situated between Chennai and Tiruvannamalai, has a remarkable 15th-century Vijayanagar fort with much to explore. It is well off the beaten track, very peaceful and in beautiful surroundings. Spend the night here if you can. Lovers come here at the weekends; it's on the domestic tourist map because it is often used as a film location. The landscape is made up of man-sized boulders, like Hampi, piled on top of each other to make mounds the texture of cottage cheese.

The fort ① *0900-1700, allow 2½ hrs for Rajagiri, and 2 hrs for Krishnagiri (if you have time), foreigners Rs 100, Indians Rs 20, camera Rs 50, video Rs 250, includes both forts,* was intensely contested by successive powers before being captured by an East India Company force in 1762, by the end of the century, however, it had lost its importance. Although it had Chola foundations, the 'most famous fort in the Carnatic' was almost entirely rebuilt in 1442. It is set on three strongly fortified Charnockite hills: Krishnagiri, Chakklidrug and Rajagiri. In places the hills on which the fort stands are sheer cliffs over 150 m high. The highest, Rajagiri ('King's Hill'), has a south-facing overhanging cliff face, on top of which is the citadel. The inner fort contains two temples and the Kalyana Mahal, a square court with a 27-m breezy tower topped by pyramidal roof, surrounded by apartments for the women of the governor's household. On top of the citadel is a huge cannon and a smooth granite slab known as the Raja's bathing stone. An extraordinary stone about 7 m high and balanced precariously on a rock, surrounded by a low circular brick wall, it is referred to as the Prisoner's Well. There are fine Vijaynagara temples, granary, barracks and stables and an 'elephant tank'. A caretaker may unlock a temple and then expect a tip.

The Archaeological Survey of India Office is just off the main road towards the fort. They may have guides to accompany you to the fort. Carry provisions, especially plenty of drinks; a few refreshments are sold, but only at the bottom of the hill. The climb is only for the fit and healthy; it's cooler in the morning and the views are less hazy.

Tiruvannamalai → *For listings, see pages 82-84. Phone code: 04175. Population: 130,300.*

At the foot of rocky Arunachala Hill, revered by Hindus across South India as the physical manifestation of Siva, Tiruvannamalai is one of Tamil Nadu's holiest towns. It is a major pilgrimage centre, focused around the enormous and fascinating Arunachaleshwar Temple whose tall *gopurams* stand dazzling white against the blue sky, and for the first half of the 20th century was home to one of India's most beloved saints, the clear-eyed Sri Ramana Maharishi.

One of the largest temples in South India, the 16th- and 17th-century **Arunachala Temple** was built mainly under the patronage of the Vijayanagar kings and is dedicated to Siva as God incarnate of Fire. Its massive bright white *gopurams*, the tallest of which is 66 m high, dominate the centre of the town. The temple has three sets of walls forming nested rectangles. Built at different periods they illustrate the way in which many Dravidian temples grew by accretion. The east end of each is extended to make a court, and the main entrance is at the east end of the temple. The lower parts of the *gopurams*, built of granite, date from the late Vijayanagar period but have been added to subsequently. The upper 10 storeys and the decoration are of brick and plaster. There are some remarkable carvings on the *gopurams*. On the outer wall of the east *gopuram*, for example, Siva is shown in the south corner dancing, with an elephant's skin. Inside the east doorway of the first courtyard is the 1000-pillared *mandapa* (hall, portico) built in the late Vijayanagar period. To the south of the court is a small shrine dedicated to Subrahmanya. To the south again is a large tank. The pillars in the *mandapa* are typically carved vigorous horses, riders and lion-like *yalis*. The middle court has four much earlier *gopurams* (mid-14th century), a large columned *mandapa* and a tank. The innermost court may date from as early as the 11th century and the main sanctuary with carvings of deities is certainly of Chola origin. In the south is Dakshinamurti, the west shows Siva appearing out of a lingam and the north has Brahma. The outer porch has small shrines to Ganesh and Subrahmanya. In front of the main shrine are a brass column lamp and the *Nandi* bull.

Some 2 km southwest of the centre, the **Sri Ramanasramam** ① *T04175-237292, www.sriramanamaharshi.org*, was founded by Sri Ramana Maharishi, the Sage of Arunachala (1879-1950). Aged 16, he achieved spontaneous self-realization and left his family to immerse himself in *samadhi* at the foot of the holy mountain. He spent 20 years in caves, steadily accumulating followers, one of whom was his own mother, who died at the base of the mountain in 1922. Recognized as a saint herself, Sri Ramana chose his mother's shrine as the site for his ashram.

The peacock-filled ashram grounds, which attract a sizeable community of Westerners between December and April, contain a library with 30,000 spiritual books and many photos of Maharishi, the last of which were taken by Henri Cartier-Bresson, who photographed him when he was alive and also the morning after his death in April 1950. Apart from the two daily *pujas* (1000 and 1815) the ashram organizes few daily programs; the focus here is on quiet self-enquiry and meditation. Foreigners wishing to stay need to write to the ashram president with proposed dates.

A gate at the back of the ashram gives access to the hillside, from where you can begin the 14-km *pradakshina* (circuit) of Arunachala. The hike is done barefoot – no shoes should be worn on the holy mountain – and takes four to five hours; on full moon nights, particularly during the annual **Karthikai Deepam** festival (November-December), the trail fills with crowds of pilgrims who chant the name of Siva and make offerings at the many small temples along the way. Another track, branching off to the right shortly after the ashram gate, climbs to Skandasramam, a shady hermitage dug into the rock at which Sri Ramana lived from 1916 to 1922. From here there's a wonderful view over the town, best at sunrise when the temples rise out of the haze like a lost Mayan city. The challenging trek to the summit of Arunachala continues beyond Skandasramam (allow six hours up and down).

Tiruvannamalai

To Katpadi Junction
To Vellore
Main **3**
Folur Rd
Muthuvinayagar Kovil St
Arunachala Hill
Subrahmanya Temple
Chinnakadai Vith
Mathlanguam St
Kosamadam St
Tindivanam Rd
Durga Temple
Big St
Gandhi Statue
A Car St
Arunachala Temple
Sannidhi St
K Mudali St
Indra Tirtha Tank
Kilathur Rd
To Gingee, Tindivanam & Chennai

N

400 metres
400 yards

To **2 4 3**, Sri Ramana Maharishi Ashram (2 km) & Salem

Where to stay
Arunachala **1**

Arunachala Ramana Home **2**
Ramakrishna **3**
Siva Sannidhi **4**

Restaurants ❼
Brindavan **1**
Manna **2**
Pumpernickel Bakery **3**

Palar Valley listings

For hotel and restaurant price codes and other relevant information, see pages 14-18.

🛏 Where to stay

Vellore *p78, map p79*
$ Mohan Mansion, 12 Beri Bakkali St, T0416-222 7083, 15 mins' walk from bus stand. Small, basic and clean, quieter than others.
$ Nagha International Lodge, 13/A KVS Chetty St, T0416-222 6338. Some a/c rooms.
$ Prince Manor, 41 Katpadi Rd, T0416-222 7106. Comfortable rooms, excellent restaurant.
$ River View, New Katpadi Rd, T0416-222 5251, 1 km north of town. 31 rooms, some a/c (best on tank side), modern, pleasant courtyard with mature palms, 3 good restaurants.
$ Srinivasa Lodge, Beri Bakkali St, T0416-222 6389. Simple and clean.
$ VDM Lodge, T0416-222 4008. Very cheap, pleasant, helpful staff.

Gingee *p80*
Avoid **Aruna Lodge**, near bus stand.
$ Shivasand, M Gandhi Rd, opposite bus stand, T04145-222218. Good views of fort from roof, 21 clean rooms with bath, some a/c, veg restaurant, a/c bar, helpful manager.

Tiruvannamalai *p80, map p81*
The best areas to stay are around the temple and in the streets opposite the ashram; hotels opposite the bus stand are uniformly grim. At full moon pilgrims arrive to walk around Arunachala Hill and hotels are overbooked.
$ Arunachala, 5 Vadasannathi St, T04175-228300. 32 clean, rooms, 16 a/c, TV, hot water, best away from temple, can get noisy during festivals, great vegetarian food downstairs.
$ Arunachala Ramana Home, 70 Ramana Nagar, off Chengam Rd, near ashram, T04175-236120. Friendly place with clean, good-value rooms. The owners can arrange bike hire and taxis, and also hand out a home-made map of the ashram area and mountain circuit.
$ Ramakrishna, 34F Polur Rd, T04175-250005, info@hotelramakrishna.com. Modern, 42 rooms, 21 a/c, TV, hot water, excellent vegetarian tandoori restaurant, parking, helpful and friendly staff. Recommended.
$ Siva Sannidhi, Siva Sannidhi St, opposite ashram, T04175-236972. Spacious, simple and clean rooms, some with balconies overlooking Arunachala, slightly institutional feel of this large complex. Free veg meals.

🍴 Restaurants

Vellore *p78, map p79*
$ Anand, Ida Scudder Rd. Excellent breakfasts.
$ Babarchee, Babu Rao St. Good fast food and pizzas.
$ Best, Ida Scudder Rd. Some meals very spicy, nice parathas, 0600 for excellent breakfast.
$ Chinatown, Gandhi Rd. Small, friendly, a/c. Good food and service.
$ Dawn Bakery, Gandhi Rd. Fresh bread and biscuits, cakes, also sardines, fruit juices.
$ Geetha and **$ Susil**, Ida Scudder Rd. Rooftop or inside, good service and food.
$ Shimla, Ida Scudder Rd. Tandoori, naan very good.

Tiruvannamalai *p80, map p81*
This town is a *thali* lover's paradise with plenty of 'meals' restaurants.
$ Brindavan, 57 A Car St. Great *thali*.
$ Manna, next to Arunachala Ramana Home (see Where to stay). Super-relaxed place for salads and snacks, with free Wi-Fi and a noticeboard listing upcoming events.
$ Pumpernickel Bakery, Agni Nilam St, near ashram. Western-orientated place split between 2 neighbouring rooftops, serving good breakfasts, soups and fantastic pastries.

❀ Festivals

Tiruvannamalai *p80, map p81*
Nov-Dec Karthikai Deepam, full moon day.
A huge beacon is lit on top of the hill behind
the temple. The flames, which can be seen
for miles around, are thought of as Siva's
lingam of fire, joining the immeasurable
depths to the limitless skies. A cattle market
is also held.

◯ Shopping

Vellore *p78, map p79*
Most shops are along Main Bazar Rd
and Long Bazar St. Vellore specializes in
making 'Karigari' glazed pottery in a range
of traditional and modern designs. Vases,
water jugs, ashtrays and dishes are usually
coloured blue, green and yellow.
Beauty, Ameer Complex, Gandhi Rd.
Cheapest good-quality tailoring.
Mr Kanappan, Gandhi Rd. Very friendly,
good-quality tailors, bit pricier.

◐ What to do

Vellore *p78, map p79*
Hillside Resort, CHAD (Community Health
and Development), south of town. Open early
morning to late evening, closed Mon and
1200-1500. Excellent pool, Rs 250 per day.

◒ Transport

Vellore *p78, map p79*
Bus The new long-distance bus stand
is 2 km north of the town centre, which
can be reached by local buses 1 and 2 or
auto-rickshaw. Buses to **Tiruchirappalli**,
Tiruvannamalai, **Bengaluru (Bangalore)**,
Chennai, **Ooty**, **Thanjavur** and **Tirupathi**.
The regional state bus company PATC
runs frequent services to **Kanchipuram**
and **Bengaluru** from 0500 (2½ hrs) and
Chennai. From the Town Bus Stand, off
Long Bazar Rd near the fort, buses 8 and
8A go to the Sripuram temple.

Train Vellore Town station has daily
passenger trains to **Tirupati** at 1015 and
1800. The main station, **Katpadi Junction**,
8 km north of town, is on the broad gauge
line between **Chennai** and **Bengaluru**.
Buses and rickshaws (Rs 35) into Vellore.
Chennai (C): dozens of trains a day; *West
Coast Exp 16628*, 1245, 2½ hrs. **Bengaluru
(C)**: *Brindavan Exp 12639*, 0903, 4¼ hrs;
Lalbagh Exp 12607, 1745, 4 hrs. **Tirupati**:
Seshadri Exp 17209, 1755, 2 hrs; also
unreserved passenger trains at 0610, 1030,
1415, 1820 and 2100. It is also on the metre
gauge line to **Villupuram** to the south, with
1 or 2 trains per week to **Puducherry** mostly
at inconvenient hours of the night.

Gingee *p80*
Bicycles There are bicycles for hire next to
the bus station.

Bus Buses to/from **Puducherry**, infrequent
direct buses (2 hrs); better via Tindivanam
(45 mins). To/from **Tiruvannamalai**, 39 km:
several buses (1 hr), Rs 13; Express buses
will not stop at the fort. TPTC bus *122* to/
from **Chennai**.

Rickshaw To visit the fort take a cycle-
rickshaw from the bus stand to the hills;
Rs 30 for the round trip, including a 2-hr
wait. There are bicycles for hire next to the
bus station.

Tiruvannamalai *p80, map p81*
Bicycle Cycling can be hazardous in this
very busy small town, but it's a practical
way to get around the ashram area.
Bikes for hire from a stand just east of
the Amman Rooftop Café, Rs 20 per day.

Bus Buses to major cities in **Tamil Nadu**,
Kerala and **Karnataka**. Local people will
point out your bus at the bus stand; you
can usually get a seat although they do
get crowded. To **Gingee**, frequent, 1 hr;
Chennai, 5 hrs, Rs 30, including 4 non-stop
a/c buses per day; **Puducherry**, 3-3½ hrs.

Train At present there are no trains to Tiruvannamalai. The closest useful stations are Tindivanam, on the Chennai–Trichy line, and Katpadi on the Chennai–Bengaluru line. Frequent buses to both.

O Directory

Vellore *p78, map p79*
Banks Central Bank, Ida Scudder Rd, east of hospital exit, is at least 10 mins faster at changing TCs than the State Bank of India.

Internet Net Paradise, north of bus stand.
Medical services CMC Hospital, Ida Scudder Rd, T0416-228 2066. **Post** CMC Hospital has PO, stamps, takes parcels.

Tiruvannamalai *p80, map p81*
Bank ATM on South Sannadhi St. Vysya Bank, Sannathi St. Quick for cash and TCs.
Internet Sri Bhagavan Net Park, 18/7 Manakkula Vinayagar St (near ashram), good connection, Wi-Fi, cold drinks.
Post A Car St.

Chola Heartland and the Kaveri Delta

Chidambaram, Trichy and Tanjore together represent the apotheosis of Tamilian temple architecture: the great temples here act as *thirthas*, or gateways, linking the profane to the sacred. This pilgrim's road boasts the bare granite Big Temple in the charming agricultural town of Tanjore, which was for 300 years the capital of the Cholas; Trichy's 21-*gopuram*, seven-walled island city of Srirangam, a patchwork quilt of a temple built by successive dynastic waves of Cholas, Cheras, Pandyas, Hoysalas, Vijayanagars and Madurai Nayaks; and the beautiful Nataraja Temple at Chidambaram, with its two towers given over to bas reliefs of the 108 *mudras*, or gestures, of classical dance.

Chidambaram → *For listings, see pages 96-101. Phone code: 04144.*

The capital of the Cholas from AD 907 to 1310, the temple town of Chidambaram is one of Tamil Nadu's most important holy towns. The town (population 59,000) has lots of character and is rarely visited by foreigners. Its main attraction is the temple, one of the only ones to have Siva in the cosmic dance position. It is an enormously holy temple with a feeling all its own.

The **Nataraja Temple** ① *0400-1200, 1630-2200, visitors may be asked for donations, entrance into the inner sanctum Rs 50, men must remove their shirts*, was the subject of a supreme court battle that ended in Delhi, where it was decided that it should remain as a private enterprise. All others fall under the state, with the Archeological Survey of India's sometimes questionable mandate to restore and maintain them. The unique brahmin community, with their right forehead shaved to indicate Siva, the left grown long and tied in a front top knot to denote his wife Parvati, will no doubt trot this out to you. As a private temple, it is unique in allowing non-Hindus to enter the sanctum (for a fee); however, the brahmins at other shrines will ask you to sign a book with other foreign names in it, supposedly having donated Rs 400. The lack of state support does make this temple poorer than its neighbours, but if you want to give a token rupee coinage instead then do so. The atmosphere of this temple more than compensates for any money-grabbing tactics, however. Temple lamps still hang from the hallways, the temple music is rousing and the *puja* has the statues coming alive in sudden illumination. The brahmins themselves have a unique, stately presence too. The evening *puja* at 1800 is particularly interesting. At each shrine the visitor will be daubed with *vibhuti* (sacred ash) and paste. It is not easy to see some of the sculptures in the interior gloom. You may need patience and persuasive powers if you want to take your own time but it is worth the effort.

There are records of the temple's existence before the 10th century and inscriptions from the 11th century. One legend surrounding its construction suggests that it was built by 'the golden-coloured emperor', Hiranya Varna Chakravarti, who suffered from leprosy. He came to Chidambaram on a pilgrimage from Kashmir in about AD 500. After bathing in the temple tank he was reputed to have recovered from the disease and in gratitude offered to rebuild and enlarge the temple.

On each side are four enormous *gopurams*, those on the north and south being about 45 m high. The east *gopuram* (AD 1250), through which you enter the temple, is the oldest. The north *gopuram* was built by the great Vijayanagar king **Krishna Deva Raya** (1509-1530). Immediately on entering the East Gate is the large **Sivaganga Tank**, and the **Raja Sabha**, a 1000-columned *mandapa* (1595-1685). In the northwest of the compound are temples dedicated to Subrahmanya (late 13th century), and to its south the 12th century shrine to Sivakumasundari or Parvati (circa 14th century). The ceiling paintings are 17th century. At the southern end of this outer compound is what is said to be the largest shrine to **Ganesh** in India. The next inner compound has been filled with colonnades and passageways. In the innermost shrine are two images of Siva, the Nataraja and the lingam. A later Vishnu shrine to Govindaraja was added by the Vijayanagar kings. The **inner enclosure**, the most sacred, contains four important *Sabhas* (halls), the **deva sabha**, where the temple managers hold their meetings; the **chit sabha** or *chit ambalam* (from which the temple and the town get their names), meaning the hall of wisdom; the **kanakha sabha**, or golden hall; and the

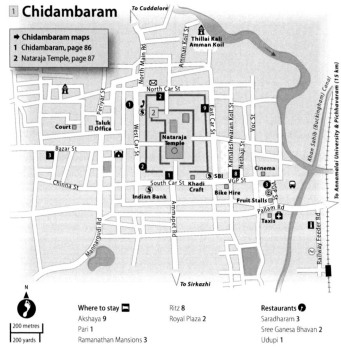

1 Chidambaram

➡ Chidambaram maps
1 Chidambaram, page 86
2 Nataraja Temple, page 87

To Cuddalore

Thillai Kali
Amman Koil

North Main Rd

Amman Koil St

North Car St

Periyar St

West Car St

Court

Taluk
Office

Bazar St

Chinna St

Nataraja
Temple

East Car St

Kamaleshwaran Koil St

Nethaji St

VOC St

Khan Sahib (Buckingham) Canal

To Annamalai University & Pichhavaram (15 km)

South Car St

Khadi
Craft

SBI

VGP St

Cinema

Indian Bank

Bike Hire

Fruit Stalls

Ammapet Rd

Pallam Rd

Taxis

Mannargudi Rd

Railway Feeder Rd

To Sirkazhi

N

200 metres
200 yards

Where to stay
Akshaya 9
Pari 1
Ramanathan Mansions 3

Ritz 8
Royal Plaza 2

Restaurants
Saradharam 3
Sree Ganesa Bhavan 2
Udupi 1

nritta sabha, or hall of dancing. Siva is worshipped in the *chit ambalam*, a plain wooden building standing on a stone base, in his form as Lord of the Dance, Nataraja. The area immediately over the deity's head is gold plated. Immediately behind the idol is the focus of the temple's power, the Akasa Lingam, representing the invisible element, 'space', and hence is itself invisible. It is known as the Chidambaram secret.

Around Chidambaram

The Danish king Christian IV received permission from Raghunath Nayak of Thanjavur to build a fort here at **Tranquebar** (Tharangampadi) in 1620. The Danish Tranquebar Mission was founded in 1706 and the Danesborg **fort** and the old **church** still survive. The Danes set up the first Tamil printing press, altering the script to make the casting of type easier and the Danish connection resulted in the National Museum of Copenhagen today possessing a remarkable collection of 17th-century Thanjavur paintings and Chola bronzes. There is a **museum** and a good beach, plus the evocatively ruined 14th-century Masilamani Nathar temple on the seashore. From Chidambaram most transport requires a change at Sirkazhi. From Thanjavur there are some direct buses; other buses involve a change at Mayiladuthurai (24 km).

2 Nataraja Temple, Chidambaram

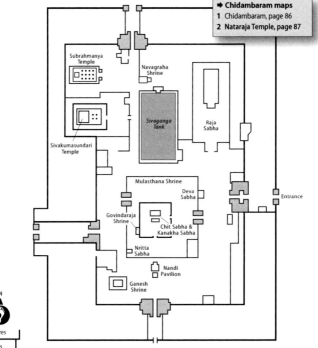

➡ **Chidambaram maps**
1 Chidambaram, page 86
2 **Nataraja Temple, page 87**

Gangaikondacholapuram → For listings, see pages 96-101.

Once the capital of the Chola king Rajendra (1012-1044), this town (whose name means 'The city of the Chola who conquered the Ganga') has now all but disappeared. The temple and the 5-km-long 11th-century reservoir embankment survive.

The **temple** ① *0700-1200, 1600-2100,* that Rajendra built was designed to rival the Brihadisvara temple built by Rajendra's father Rajaraja in Thanjavur. Unlike the *Nandi* in Thanjavur, the huge *Nandi* facing the *mandapa* and sanctuary inside the compound by the ruined east *gopuram* is not carved out of one block of stone. As in Thanjavur, the *mandapa* and sanctuary are raised on a high platform, orientated from west to east and climbed by steps. The whole building is over 100 m long and over 40 m wide. Two massive *dvarapalas* (doorkeepers) stand guard at the entrance to the long closed *mandapa* (the first of the many subsequent *mandapas* which expanded to 'halls of 1000 pillars'); the plinth is original. A *mukha-mandapa* (narrow colonnaded hall) links this hall to the shrine. On the east side of this hall are various carvings of Siva for example bestowing grace on Vishnu, who worships him with his lotus-eye. On the northeast is a large panel, a masterpiece of Chola art, showing Siva blessing Chandikesvara, the steward. At the centre of the shrine is a huge *lingam* on a round stand. As in Thanjavur there is a magnificent eight-tiered, pyramidal *vimana* (tower) above the sanctuary, nearly 55 m high. Unlike the austere straight line of the Thanjavur Temple, however, here gentle curves are introduced. Ask the custodian to allow you to look inside (best for light in the morning). Immediately to the north of the *mandapa* is an excellently carved shrine dedicated to Chandikesvara. To north and south are two shrines dedicated to Kailasanatha with excellent wall sculptures. The small shrine in the southwest corner is to Ganesh.

Kumbakonam → For listings, see pages 96-101. Phone code: 0435. Population: 140,000.

This very pleasant town, 54 km from Thanjavur, was named after the legend where Siva was said to have broken a *kumbh* (water pot) after it was brought here by a great flood. The water from the pot is reputed to have filled the Mahamakam Tank. High-quality betel vines, used for chewing paan, are grown here.

Places in Kumbakonam

The temples in this region contain some exceptional pieces of jewellery – seen on payment of a small fee. There are 18 **temples** ① *closed 1200-1630, no photography,* in the town centre and a monastery of the Kanchipuram Sankaracharya. The oldest is the **Nagesvara Swami Temple**, a Shaivite temple begun in AD 886. The small Nataraja shrine on the right before you reach the main sanctum is designed to look like a chariot being pulled by horses and elephants. Superb statues decorate the outside walls of the inner shrine; Dakshinamurti (exterior south wall), Ardinarisvara (west facing) and Brahma (north) are in the central panels, and described as being among the best works of sculpture of the Chola period. The temple has a special atmosphere and is definitely worth a visit.

Sarangapani is the largest of Kumbakonam's shrines. Dedicated to Vishnu (one of whose avatars is Krishna the cowherd), it is also one of the few temples in Tamil Nadu where you will see devotees actively paying reverence to cows. Beyond the 11-storey main *gopuram* that towers above the entrance lies a cattle shed, where visitors can offer gifts of leaves before tiptoeing in (barefoot, naturally) to touch the hindquarters of the closest cow. The Nayaka *mandapa*, with huge beams of beautifully carved stone, leads through a second, smaller *gopuram* to a further *mandapa* carved in the form of a chariot, towed by horses and elephants.

The **Kumbesvara Temple** dates mainly from the 17th century and is the largest Siva temple in the town. It has a long colonnaded *mandapa* and a magnificent collection of silver *vahanas* (vehicles) for carrying the deities during festivals. The **Ramasvami Temple** is another Nayaka period building, with beautiful carved rearing horses in its pillared *mandapa*. The frescoes on the walls depict events from the *Ramayana*. The **Navaratri Festival** is observed with great colour.

The **Mahamakam Tank** is visited for a bathe by huge numbers of pilgrims every 12 years, when 'Jupiter passes over the sign of Leo'. It is believed that on the day of the festival nine of India's holiest rivers manifest themselves in the tank, including the Ganga, Yamuna and Narmada.

Darasuram

About 5 km south of Kumbakonam is Darasuram with the **Airavatesvara Temple** ① *open 0600-1200, 1600-2000*, after Thanjavur and Gangaikondacholapuram, the third of the great Chola temples, built during the reign of **Rajaraja II** (1146-1172). The entrance is through two gateways. A small inner gateway leads to a court where the mainly granite temple stands in the centre. The *gopuram* is supported by beautifully carved *apsaras*. Inside, there are friezes of dancing figures and musicians. The *mandapa* is best entered from the south. Note the elephant, ridden by dwarfs, whose trunk is lost down the jaws of a crocodile. The pillars illustrate mythological stories for example 'the penance of Parvati'. The five gods Agni, Indra, Brahma, Vishnu and Vayu in the niches are all shown paying homage to Siva. The

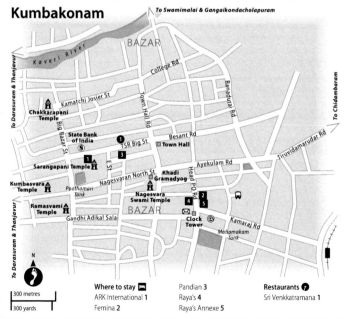

Kumbakonam

Where to stay 🛏
ARK International 1
Femina 2
Pandian 3
Raya's 4
Raya's Annexe 5

Restaurants 🍴
Sri Venkkatramana 1

The terrifying guardian deities

Many Hindu villagers in Tamil Nadu believe in guardian deities of the village – Ayyanar, Muneeswaram, Kaliamman, Mariamman and many more. Groups of larger-than-life images built of brick, wood or stone and covered in *chunam* (brightly painted lime plaster) guard the outskirts of several villages. They are deliberately terrifying, designed to frighten away evil spirits from village homes, but villagers themselves are also very frightened of these gods and try to keep away from them. The deities are supposed to prevent epidemics, but if an epidemic does strike, special sacrifices are offered, mainly of rice. Firewalking, often undertaken in fulfilment of a vow, is a feature of the special festivals at these shrines. Disease is also believed to be held at bay by other ceremonies, including piercing the cheeks and tongue with wire and the carrying of *kavadis* (special carriages or boxes, sometimes designed like a coffin).

main mandapa, completely enclosed and joined to the central shrine, has figures carved in black basalt on the outside. The ceilings are also richly decorated and the pillars have the same flower emblems as in the outer *mandapa*. The main shrine has some outstanding sculptures; the guardians on the north are particularly fine. Sculpted doorkeepers with massive clubs guard the entrance to the main shrine, which has a *Nandi* at the entrance. Some of the niches inside contain superb early Chola sculptures of polished black basalt, including a unique sculpture of Ardhanarisvara with three faces and eight arms, a four-armed Nagaraja and a very unusual sculpture of Siva destroying Narasimha. The **outer walls** are also highly decorative. Siva as Dakshinamurti on the south wall, Brahma on the north wall and Siva appearing out of the lingam on the west wall. The inner wall of the *prakara* (encircling walkway) is divided into cells, each originally to house a deity. The corners of the courtyard have been enlarged to make four *mandapas*, again with beautiful decoration.

Thanjavur (Tanjore) → *For listings, see pages 96-101.*

Thanjavur is a mathematically perfect Brihadisvara Temple. A World Heritage Site, it is one of the great monuments of South India, its huge Nandi bull washed each fortnight with water, milk, turmeric and gingelly in front of a rapt audience that packs out the whole temple compound. In the heart of the lush, rice-growing delta of the Kaveri, the upper echelons of Tanjore life are landowners, rather than industrialists, and the city itself is mellow in comparison with Trichy, especially in the old town surrounding the Royal Palace.

Arriving in Thanjavur → *Phone code: 04362. Population: 215,700.*
Getting there Most long-distance buses stop at the New Bus Stand 4 km southwest of the centre, from where there are frequent buses and autos (Rs 60) to town. There's a second, more central bus stand off South Rampart Street, close to several budget hotels, which has some direct buses to Chennai. The train station is at the south end of the town centre, about a 20-minute walk from the Brihadisvara Temple, with connections to Tiruchirappalli, Chennai and Bangalore.

Getting around Most hotels are within a 15-minute walk of the temple. Auto-rickshaws charge Rs 20-30 for trips around town. ›› *See Transport, page 100.*

Tourist information ① *In the grounds of Hotel Tamil Nadu, Railway Station Rd (aka Gandhiji Rd), T04362-230984.*

Places in Thanjavur

Brihadisvara Temple ① *0600-2030, inner sanctum closed 1230-1600,* known as the Big Temple, was the achievement of the Chola king Rajaraja I (ruled AD 985-1012). The magnificent main temple has a 62-m-high *vimana* (the tallest in India), topped by a dome carved from an 80-tonne block of granite, which needed a 6.5-km-long ramp to raise it to the top. The attractive gardens, the clean surroundings and well-lit sanctuaries make a visit doubly rewarding, especially in the evening. The entrance is from the east. After crossing the moat you enter through two *gopurams*, the second guarded by two *dvarapalas* typical

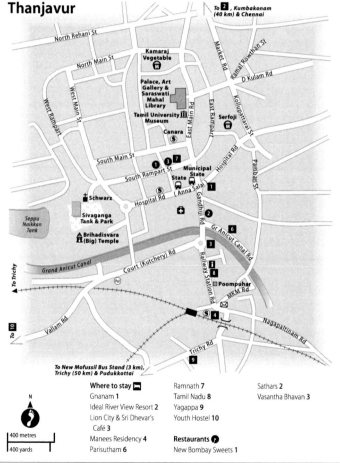

Thanjavur

Where to stay 🛏
Gnanam **1**
Ideal River View Resort **2**
Lion City & Sri Dhevar's Café **3**
Manees Residency **4**
Parisutham **6**

Ramnath **7**
Tamil Nadu **8**
Yagappa **9**
Youth Hostel **10**

Restaurants 🍴
New Bombay Sweets **1**

Sathars **2**
Vasantha Bhavan **3**

of the early Chola period, when the *gopurams* on the outer enclosure walls were dwarfed by the scale of the *vimana* over the main shrine. An enormous Nandi, carved out of a single block of granite 6 m long, guards the entrance to the sanctuary. According to one of the many myths that revolve around the image of a wounded Nandi, the Thanjavur Nandi was growing larger and larger, threatening the temple, until a nail was driven into its back. The temple, built mainly with large granite blocks, has superb inscriptions and sculptures of Siva, Vishnu and Durga on three sides of the massive plinth. Siva appears in three forms, the dancer with 10 arms, the seated figure with a sword and trident, and Siva bearing a spear. The carvings of dancers showing the 81 different Bharat Natyam poses are the first to record classical dance form in this manner. The main shrine has a large lingam. In the inner courtyard are Chola frescoes on walls prepared with lime plaster, smoothed and polished, then painted while the surface was wet. These were hidden under later Nayaka paintings. Since music and dance were a vital part of temple life and dancing in the temple would accompany the chanting of the holy scriptures which the community attended, Rajaraja also built two housing colonies nearby to accommodate 400 *devadasis* (temple dancers). Subsidiary shrines were added to the main temple at different periods. The Vijayanagara kings built the Amman shrine, the Nayakas the Subrahmanya shrine and the Marathas the Ganesh shrine.

The **palace** ① *1000-1700, foreigners Rs 50, Indians Rs 5, camera Rs 30*, built by the Nayakas in the mid-16th century and later completed by the Marathas, is now partly in ruins, its walls used as makeshift hoardings for the latest Tamil movie release or political campaign. Still, there's evidence of its original splendour in the ornate Durbar Hall. The towers are worth climbing for a good view; one tower has a whale skeleton which was washed up in Chennai. The **art gallery** ① *0900-1300, 1500-1800, foreigners Rs 20, Indians Rs 5, camera Rs 30*, with bronze and granite sculptures, **Sangeeta Mahal** (the Hall of Music, where musicians and dancers performed before the Chola kings) with excellent acoustics, and the **Tamil University Museum** are here, together with some government offices. The pokey **Saraswati Mahal Library** ① *Thu-Tue 1000-1300, 1330-1700*, is brilliant. Among its 40,000 rare books are texts from the medieval period, beautiful botanical pictures from the 18th century, palm leaf manuscripts of the *Ramayana*, intricate 250-year-old miniatures, and splendid examples of the gaudy Tanjore style of painting. It also has old samples of dhoti cloth design, and 22 engravings illustrating methods of torture from other oriental cultures in the 'Punishments of China'.

Around Thanjavur

A visit to **Thiruvaiyaru**, 13 km away, with the Panchanatheswara Siva temple, known for its **Thyagaraja Music Festival**, gives a glimpse of South Indian rural life. Hardly visited by tourists, music connoisseurs arrive in large numbers in January. Performances vary and the often subtle music is marred by loud amplification. There is a **Car Festival** in March. Catch one of the frequent, crowded buses from the old bus station in Thanjavur, taking 30 minutes.

Point Calimere (Kodikkarai) Wildlife and Bird Sanctuary ① *open throughout the year, best season mid-Dec to Feb, Rs 5, camera Rs 5, video Rs 50*, is 90 km southeast of Thanjavur. The coastal sanctuary, half of which is tidal swamp, is famous for its migratory water birds. The Great Vedaranayam Salt Swamp (or 'Great Swamp') attracts one of the largest colonies of flamingos in Asia (5000-10,000) especially in December and January. Some 243 different bird species have been spotted here. In the spring green pigeons, rosy pastors, koels, mynahs and barbets can be seen. In the winter vegetables and insects attract paradise flycatchers, Indian pittas, shrikes, swallows, drongos, minivets, blue jays, woodpeckers and robins among others. Spotted deer, black buck, feral horses and wild boar are also found, as well as reptiles. The swamp supports a major commercial fishing industry. Jeeps can be booked at reception. Exploring on foot is a pleasant alternative to being 'bussed'; ask at reception for a guide.

Tiruchirappalli (Trichy) → *For listings, see pages 96-101.*

Trichy, at the head of the fertile Kaveri Delta, is an industrial city and transport hub of some significance, with its own international airport connecting southern Tamil Nadu to Singapore and the Gulf. Land prices are high here, and houses, as you'll see if you climb up to its 84-m-high rock fort, are densely packed, outside the elegant doctors' suburbs. If you are taking public transport you will want to break here to visit the sacred Srirangam temple but if you have your own wheels you may prefer to bypass the city, which has little else to offer by way of easily accessed charms. Allow at least half a day to tour Srirangam, then stay in the more laid-back agricultural centre of Tanjore to the north or the more atmospheric temple madness of Madurai further south.

Arriving in Tiruchirappalli → *Phone code: 0431.*
Getting there Trichy airport, 8 km from the centre, has flights to Madurai and Chennai. With good transport connections to major towns, the Junction Railway Station and the two bus stations are in the centre of the main hotel area, all within walking distance.

Getting around Much of Trichy is quite easy to see on foot, but plenty of autos and local buses run to the Rock Fort and Srirangam. ►► *See Transport, page 100.*

Tourist information Tourist office ① *New Central Bus Stand, T0431-246 0136.* Also counters at the railway station and airport.

Background
Trichy was mentioned by Ptolemy in the second century BC. A Chola fortification from the second century, it came to prominence under the Nayakas from Madurai who built the fort and the town, capitalizing on its strategic position. In legend its name is traced to a three-headed demon, Trisiras, who terrorized both men and the gods until Siva overpowered him in the place called Tiruchi. Cigar making became important between the two world wars, while the indigenous *bidis* continue to be made, following a tradition started in the 18th century. Trichy is the country's largest artificial diamond manufacturing centre. Jaffersha Street is known as Diamond Bazar. The town is also noted for its high-quality string instruments, especially veenas and violins.

Places in Tiruchirappalli
Rock Fort (1660), stands on an 84-m-high rock. **Ucchi Pillayar Koil (Vinayaka Temple)** ① *Tue-Sun 0600-1200, 1600-2100, camera Rs 10, video Rs 50,* approached from Chinna Bazar, is worth climbing for the stunning panoramas but don't expect much from the temple. At the top of the first flight of steps lies the main 11th-century defence line and the remains of a thousand-pillared hall, destroyed in 1772. Further up is a hundred-pillared hall where civic receptions are held. At the end of the last flight is the **Tayumanasvami Temple**, dedicated to Siva, which has a golden *vimana* and a lingam carved from the rock itself. There are further seventh-century Pallava cave temples of beautiful carved pillars and panels.

Try to make time to explore the atmospheric old city, particularly **Big Bazar Street** and **Chinna Bazar**. The **Gandhi Market** is a colourful vegetable and fruit market.

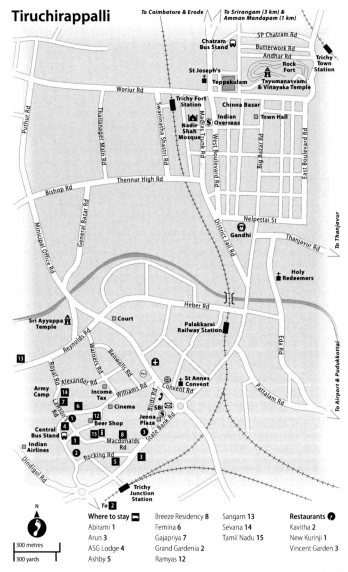

Tiruchirappalli

Where to stay 🛏
Abirami 1
Arun 3
ASG Lodge 4
Ashby 5
Breeze Residency 8
Femina 6
Gajapriya 7
Grand Gardenia 2
Ramyas 12
Sangam 13
Sevana 14
Tamil Nadu 15

Restaurants 🍴
Kavitha 2
New Kurinji 1
Vincent Garden 3

Among the dozen or so mosques in the town, the **Nadir Shah Mosque** near the city railway station stands out with its white dome and metal steeple, said to have been built with material taken from a Hindu temple. **St Joseph's College Church** (Church of our Lady of Lourdes), one of several Catholic churches here, was designed as a smaller version of the Basilica at Lourdes in France. It has an unusual sandalwood altar but is rather garish inside. The grounds are a peaceful spot. The 18th-century **Christ Church**, the first English church, is north of the Teppakulam, while the early 19th-century **St John's Church** has a memorial plaque to Bishop Heber, one of India's best known missionary bishops, who died in Trichy in 1826.

Around Tiruchirappalli → *For listings, see pages 96-101.*

Srirangam

The temple town on the **Kaveri**, just north of Trichy, is surrounded by seven concentric walled courtyards, with magnificent gateways and several shrines. On the way to Srirangam is an interesting river *ghat* where pilgrims take their ritual bath before entering the temple. The countryside to the west of the temple is an excellent place to sample rural Indian life and a good way to spend a couple of hours.

Sri Ranganathasvami Temple ① *0700-1300, 1400-1800, camera Rs 50, video Rs 100 (Rs 10 for the rooftop viewing tower), allow about 2 hrs, guides will greet you on arrival (their abilities are highly variable; some tell you that the staircase to the viewpoint will close shortly, which is usually a scam to encourage you to use their services),* is one of the largest in India and dedicated to Vishnu. It has some fine carvings and a good atmosphere. The fact that it faces south, unlike most other Hindu temples, is explained by the legend that Rama intended to present the image of Ranganatha to a temple in Sri Lanka but this was impossible since the deity became fixed here, but it still honours the original destination. The temple, where the Vaishnava reformer **Ramanuja** settled and worshipped, is famous for its superb sculpture, the 21 impressive *gopurams* and its rich collection of temple jewellery. The 'thousand' pillared hall (904 columns) stands beyond the fourth wall, and fifth enclosure there is the unusual shrine to Tulukka Nachiyar, the god's Muslim consort. Non-Hindus are not allowed into the sanctuary but can enter the fourth courtyard where the famous sculptures of *gopis* (*Radha's* milk maids) in the Venugopala shrine can be seen.

Nearby, on the north bank of the Kaveri, **Amma Mandapam** is a hive of activity. The *ghats*, where devotees wash, bathe, commit cremated ashes and pray, are interesting to visit, although some may find the dirt and smell overpowering.

So named because a legendary elephant worshipped the lingam, **Tiruvanaikkaval** is located 3 km east of Srirangam. It has the architecturally finer **Jambukesvara Temple** ① *200 m east off the main Tiruchi–Chennai road, a short stroll from Srirangam or easily reached by bus, officially 0600-2045, camera Rs 10, non-Hindus are not allowed into the sanctuary,* with its five walls and seven splendid *gopurams* and one of the oldest and largest Siva temples in Tamil Nadu. The unusual lingam under a *jambu* tree always remains under water.

Chola Heartland and the Kaveri Delta listings

For hotel and restaurant price codes and other relevant information, see pages 14-18.

📑 Where to stay

Chidambaram *p85, map p86*

The overall quality of hotels partly explains why most people visit the town on day trips, but there are plenty of lower-bracket choices around the temple, particularly on East Car St (also known as East Sannithi).

$ Akshaya, 17-18 East Car St, T04144-220191, www.hotelakshaya.com. Comfortable small hotel right in the centre (can be noisy) with 24 well-swept rooms and a rooftop overlooking the temple grounds.

$ Pari, 1 South Car St, T04144-220733. With a great atmospheric location near the temple's south gate and relatively grime-free rooms, this is the pick of the rock-bottom options. A/c available in 3- and 4-bed rooms.

$ Ramanathan Mansions, 127 Bazar St, T04144-222411. Away from busy temple area, quieter than most, 28 rooms with bath, spacious and airy (no power sockets), friendly.

$ Ritz, 2 VGP (Venugopal Pillai) St, T04144-223312, alritzhotel@gmail.com. Drab and decrepit-looking from the outside, but the all-a/c rooms and suites are cleaner than most in town, and service is enthusiastic – especially when tips might be in the offing.

$ Royal Plaza, North Car St, T04144-222179. Good and friendly cheapie, with most rooms boasting Indian toilets and no pretence of hot water, on the rarely tourist-trod northern edge of the temple.

Kumbakonam *p61, map p89*

Luxury Tax of 10-12.5% is always added. Most places offer 24-hr checkout.

$$-$ Raya's Annexe, 19 Head PO Rd, near Mahamaham tank, T0435-242 3270, www.hotelrayas.com. The shiny exterior conceals the best and cleanest rooms in town: 'Standard' rooms are a/c, light and spacious with good bathrooms; 'Elite' and 'Studio' rooms offer extra space and dining/sitting areas. Interesting views across temple roofs from upper floor lobbies.

$ ARK International, 21 TSR Big St, T0435-242 1234, www.hotelark.in. 50 good-size a/c rooms, some cleaner and brighter than others (some barely clean at all), all with bathroom and TV. Pure veg restaurant, room service meals.

$ Femina, 15/8 Head PO Rd, T0435-242 0369. Typically grim budget choice, with dank, grimy and musty rooms, but tolerable if you can snare one of the end rooms with outward-facing windows.

$ Pandian, 52 Sarangapani East Sannathi St, T0435-243 0397. The very cheap rooms here come with bath and TV, but little in the way of light and air. Chiefly popular with Tamil men, whose conversations echo along the corridor.

$ Raya's, 18 Head PO Rd, T0435-242 3170. Older and dingier than the annexe opposite, but OK at the price, and the otherwise uninspiring 'garden villas' are family-friendly with 1 double and 1 single bedroom. A/c restaurant downstairs, exchanges cash.

Thanjavur *p90, map p91*

Even modest hotels charge 20% Luxury Tax. Cheapies congregate near the railway station and opposite the Central Bus Stand on South Rampart Rd, but cleanliness standards are, with the odd notable exception, awful.

$$$$ Parisutham, 55 GA Canal Rd, T04362-231801, www.hotelparisutham.com. The poshest place in town, with 52 well-kept but wildly overpriced a/c rooms in a 1980s building. Passable restaurants, massages in cabin by pretty coconut-shaded pool, free internet (and claims of free Wi-Fi in rooms), relatively peaceful location, but derives most of its custom from package tours.

$$$ Ideal River View Resort, Vennar Bank, Palli Agraharam, 6 km north of centre, T04362-250533, www.idealresort.com. Clean, comfortable cottages (some a/c) in large grounds overlooking a branch of the Kaveri. A peaceful alternative to staying in Thanjavur, with boating, a big pool, restaurant and shuttles into town. Recommended.

$$ Gnanam, Anna Salai (Market Rd), T04362-278501, www.hotelgnanam.com. The mid-range sister hotel to **Parisutham** lacks the pool and top-end facilities, but offers much better value. 30 sparkling clean a/c rooms, some with balcony, vegetarian multi-cuisine restaurant, safety deposit lockers and travel desk, free Wi-Fi in lobby. Recommended.

$ Lion City, 130 Gandhiji Rd, T04362-275650, hotellioncity@hotmail.com. 25 well-appointed but unremarkable rooms in a fairly convenient but noisy location. TV, hot water, acceptably clean, spacious, good service.

$ Manees Residency, 2905 Srinivasam Pillai Rd (next to train station), T04362-271574, www.maneesresidency.com. The cleanest, newest and most pleasant in a row of similarly priced places on this street, with a veg restaurant downstairs.

$ Ramnath, 1335 South Rampart St, T04362-272567. Modern and friendly choice in the hectic bus stand area, with bright artworks adorning the corridors and pleasant, spacious, well-scrubbed rooms, plus a clean and popular restaurant downstairs.

$ Tamil Nadu I (TTDC), Gandhiji Rd, 5-min walk from railway station, T04362-231325. Pleasant setting around a cool inner courtyard, 32 moderately clean rooms with bath, some a/c, a bit mosquito-ridden, simple restaurant, bar, tourist office.

$ Yagappa, off Trichy Rd, south of station, T04362-230421. Good size, comfortable rooms with bath, restaurant, bar, good value.

$ Youth Hostel, Medical College Rd, T04362-235097. Dorm Rs 40.

Around Thanjavur *p92*
Nov-Dec are busy at Point Calimere (Kodikkarai) Wildlife Sanctuary, 3 Main St, Thanjavur.

$ Poonarai Illam, Point Calimere Sanctuary reservations via the Wildlife Warden, Collectorate, Nagapattinam, T04365-253092. 14 simple rooms with bath and balcony, caretaker may be able to arrange a meal with advance notice, intended for foreign visitors, rooms are often available.

$ PV Thevar Lodge, 40 North Main St, Vedaranyam, 50 m from bus station (English sign high up only visible in daylight), T04369-250330. Good value, 37 basic rooms with bath and fan, can be mosquito-proofed, fairly clean, very friendly owners. Indian vegetarian meals in the bazar near bus stand.

Tiruchirappalli *p93, map p94*
$$$$-$$$ Sangam, Collector's Office Rd, T0431-241 4480. Very friendly, 58 comfortable a/c rooms, restaurants (great tandoori), good breakfast in coffee shop, pleasant bar, exchange, pool, spacious lawns.

$$$ Breeze Residency, 3/14 Macdonalds Rd, T0431-241 4414, www.breezehotel.com. Pool (non-residents Rs 100), 93 a/c rooms, those in newer wing smaller but in better condition, good restaurants, excellent travel desk, exchange, beauty salon.

$$$ Grand Gardenia, Mannarpuram Junction (1 km south of station), T0431-404 5000, www.grandgardenia.com. Excellent new business hotel with spacious, sparkling clean rooms and good Chettinadu restaurant. Currently the best upscale deal in town.

$$$-$$ Femina, 14C Williams Rd, T0431-241 4501, www.feminahotels.in. 157 clean rooms, 140 a/c, vegetarian restaurants for great breakfasts, bar, pool in new block, good value, modern, comfortable 4-storey hotel.

$$-$ Kanchana Towers, 50 Williams Rd, 2-min walk from bus stand, T0431-420 0002. 90 spacious, comfortable rooms with bath,

26 a/c, restaurant, bar, travel agent, very quiet, new and clean.

$$-$ Ramyas, 13D/2 Williams Rd, T0431-400 0400, www.ramyas.com. 78 spotless rooms, 24 a/c, restaurants, bar.

$$-$ Tamil Nadu (TTDC), Macdonalds Rd, Cantt, T0431-241 4346. Run-down, 36 rooms, some a/c or bath, restaurant, bar, tourist office.

$ Abirami, 10 Macdonalds Rd, T0431-241 5001. Old fashioned, noisy location, 55 rooms, some a/c with bath, good busy a/c restaurant (vegetarian), exchange.

$ Arun, 24 State Bank Rd, T0431-241 5021. 40 rooms in garden setting, restaurant, bar, TV, excellent value.

$ ASG Lodge, opposite Arun. Very noisy but quite clean (from Rs 100).

$ Ashby, 17A Junction Rd, T0431-246 0652. Set around courtyard, 20 large a/c rooms with bath, good restaurants, bar. The oldest hotel in town, plenty of Raj character and a bit noisy and scruffy, but excellent friendly staff, good value.

$ Gajapriya, 5 Royal Rd, T0431-241 4411. 66 good-value rooms, 28 a/c (no twin beds), restaurant, bar, library, parking, spacious hotel, quieter than most.

$ Sevana, 5 Royal Rd, Cantt, T0431-241 5201. Quiet, friendly, 44 rooms, some a/c with bath, a/c restaurant (Indian), bar.

🍴 Restaurants

Chidambaram *p85, map p86*
$$ Hotel Saradharam, 10 VGP St. Popular, a/c. Excellent range of meals, pizzas and European dishes. Good variety and value.
$ Sree Ganesa Bhavan, West Car St. South Indian vegetarian. Friendly, helpful staff.
$ Udupi, West Car St. Good vegetarian, clean.

Kumbakonam *p61, map p89*
$$ Sri Venkkatramana Hotel, 40 Gandhi Park North St. Excellent vegetarian restaurant, with pure veg *thali*-style meals (complete with digestive *paan* package to

finish) served in Brahmnical cleanliness in a/c hall, and the usual gamut of snacks in the somewhat fly-blown main room.

Thanjavur *p90, map p91*
$$ Parisutham (see Where to stay). Good North Indian meat dishes, excellent vegetarian *thalis* ("best of 72 curries"), service can be slow.
$ New Bombay Sweets, South Rampart St. Tasty Indian snacks including pakora and kachori, and good sweets.
$ Sathars, Gandhiji Rd. Excellent for biryani and tandoori, both veg and meat variants.
$ Sri Dhevar's Café, Gandhiji Rd below Lion City Hotel. Widely recommended for pure veg meals.
$ Vasantha Bhavan, 1338 South Rampart Rd, near Hotel Ramnath. Wide range of South and North Indian and Chinese dishes, good juices bursting with sugar, very popular.

Tiruchirappalli *p93, map p94*
Good Indian vegetarian places in Chinna Bazar are: **$ New Kurinji**, below Hotel Guru Lawson's Rd, a/c vegetarian; and **$ Ragunath** and Vasantha Bhavan, *thalis*, good service.
$$ Abirami's (see Where to stay), T0431-246 0001. A/c, Vasantha Bhawan at the back, serves excellent vegetarian; front part is a meals-type eatery.
$$ Breeze Residency (see Where to stay). Good Chinese, extensive menu, attentive service but freezing a/c. Also Wild West bar.
$$ Kavitha, Lawson's Rd. A/c. Excellent breakfasts and generous vegetarian *thalis*.
$$ Sangam's, T0431-246 4480. Indian and continental.
$$ Vincent Garden, Dindigul Rd. Pleasant garden restaurant and pastry shop, lots of coloured lights but on a busy road.

⊕ Entertainment

Thanjavur *p90, map p91*
Bharat Natyam, 1/2378 Krishanayar Lane, Ellaiyamman Koil St, T04362-233759. Performances by Guru Herambanathan from a family of dancers.
South Zone Cultural Centre Palace, T04362-231272. Organizes programmes in the Big Temple, 2nd and 4th Sat; free.

⊕ Festivals

Chidambaram *p85, map p86*
Feb/Mar Natyanjali Dance Festival for 5 days starting with Maha Sivaratri.
Jun/Jul Ani Tirumanjanam Festival.
Dec/Jan Markazhi Tiruvathirai Festival.

Tiruchirappalli *p93, map p94*
Mar Festival of Floats on the Teppakulam when the temple deities are taken out onto the sacred lake on rafts.

Around Tiruchirappalli *p95*
Srirangam
Dec/Jan Vaikunta Ekadasi (bus No 1 (C or D) from Trichy or hire a rickshaw), and associated temple car festival, draws thousands of pilgrims who witness the transfer of the image of the deity from the inner sanctum under the golden *vimana* to the *mandapa*.

Tiruvanaikkaval *p95*
Special festivals in Jan and the spring.
Aug Pancha Piraharam is celebrated and in the month of **Panguni** the images of Siva and his consort Akhilandesvari exchange their dress.

⊕ Shopping

Kumbakonam *p61, map p89*
Kumbakonam and its surrounding villages are renowned centres of bronze sculpture, some still practicing the traditional '*pancha loha*' (5 metals – gold, silver, lead copper

and iron) technique reserved for casting temple idols. You can visit workshops in Kumbakaonam itself, and in Swamimalai to the west and Nachiyar Koil to the southeast.

Thanjavur *p90, map p91*
You may not export any object over 100 years old. Thanjavur is known for its decorative copper plates with silver and brass relief (*repoussé*) work, raised-glass painting, wood carving and bronze/brass casting. Granite carving is being revived through centres that produce superb sculpted images. Craft shops abound in Gandhiji Rd Bazar.
Govindarajan's, 31 Kuthirai Katti St, Karandhai (a few kilometres from town), T04362-230282. A treasure house of pricey old, and affordable new, pieces; artists and craftspeople at work.

⊕ What to do

Thanjavur *p90, map p91*
TTDC, enquire at tourist office. Mon-Fri 1000-1745. Temple tour of Thanjavur and surroundings by a/c coach.

Tiruchirappalli *p93, map p94*
Indian Panorama, 5 Anna Av, Srirangam, T0431-422 6122, www.indianpanorama.in. Tours from Chennai, Bengaluru (Bangalore), Kochi, Madurai and Thiruvananthapuram. Recommended for tours (good cars with drivers), ticketing, general advice.

⊖ Transport

Chidambaram *p85, map p86*
Bus The bus station is chaotic with daily services to **Chennai**, **Madurai**, **Thanjavur**, and to **Karaikal** (2 hrs), **Nagapattinam** and **Puducherry** (2 hrs).

Train Reservations T04144-222298, Mon-Sat 0800-1200, 1400-1700; Sun 0800-1400. **Chennai** (**E**) *Cholan Exp 16854*, 1200, 6 hrs. **Rameswaram**: *Rameshwaram*

Exp 16701, 0130, 10½ hrs, via **Chettinad** (6 hrs). **Tiruchirappali**: *Cholan Exp 16853*, 1255, 3½ hrs, via **Kumbakonam**, 1½ hrs, and **Thanjavur**, 2 hrs.

Gangaikondacholapuram *p88*
Bus Frequent buses shuttle back and forth from Kumbakonam, and a few buses between **Trichy** and **Chidambaram** also stop here.

Kumbakonam *p61, map p89*
Car hire Half day for excursions, Rs 400.

Bus TN Govt Express buses to **Chennai**, *No 305*, several daily (7½ hrs); half hourly to **Thanjavur**. The railway station is 2 km from town centre. Trains to **Chennai (Egmore)**, 1010-2110, change at Tambaram (8½-9 hrs), **Chidambaram** (2 hrs), **Thanjavur** (50 mins) and **Tiruchirappalli**, 0600-1555 (2½ hrs).

Thanjavur *p90, map p91*
Bus
Most long-distance buses use the **New Bus Stand**, T04362-230950, 4 km south of town off Trichy Rd. Daily services to **Chennai** (8 hrs), **Chidambaram** (4 hrs), **Kumbakonam** (1 hr), **Madurai** (3½ hrs), **Puducherry** (6 hrs), **Tirupathi**, **Tiruchirappalli** (1½ hrs). Also to **Vedaranyam** (100 km) for Point Calimere, about hourly, 4-4½ hrs. Buses to Kumbakonam, and the odd one to Chennai and Puducherry, also leave from the **State Bus Stand** on South Rampart St.

Taxi
Taxis wait at the railway station and along South Rampart St, but drivers quote high rates, eg **Puducherry** Rs 3500, **Madurai** Rs 2500, **Chidambaram** Rs 2000.

Train
Reservations, T04362-231131, Mon-Sat 0800-1400, 1500-1700; Sun 0800-1400. For **Madurai** and points south, it's better to go to Trichy and change. **Chennai**

(ME): *Rockfort Exp 16878*, 2030, 9 hrs. **Tiruchirappalli**: several fast passenger trains throughout the day.

Around Thanjavur *p92*
Point Calimere (Kodikkarai)
Bus Buses via Vedaranyam, which has services to/from **Thanjavur**, **Tiruchirappalli**, **Nagapattinam**, **Chennai**, etc. From Thanjavur buses leave the **New Bus Stand** for **Vedaranyam** (100 km) hourly (4-4½ hrs); buses and vans from there to **Kodikkarai** (11 km) which take about 30 mins. Avoid being dropped at 'Sri Rama's Feet' on the way, near a shrine that is of no special interest.

Tiruchirappalli *p93, map p94*
Air
The airport, T0431-234 0551, is 8 km from the centre (taxi Rs 100-150). **Air India**, Dindigul Rd, 2 km from Express Bus Stand, T0431-248 3800, airport T0431-234 1601; flies to **Chennai** daily except Mon and Fri. **Sri Lankan**, 14 Williams Rd, T0431-246 0844, (0900-1730) to **Colombo**. Air Asia, www.airasia.com, no-frills flights to **Kuala Lumpur**.

Bus
Local Good City Bus service. From airport, Nos 7, 63, 122, 128, take 30 mins. The **Central State Bus Stand** is across from the tourist office (Bus *No 1* passes all the sights); 20 mins to Chatram Bus Stand.
Long distance The bus stands are 1 km from the railway station and are chaotic; TN Govt Express, T0431-246 0992, Central, T0431-246 0425. Frequent buses to **Chennai** (6 hrs), **Coimbatore** 205 km (5½ hrs), **Kumbakonam** 92 km, **Madurai** 161 km (3 hrs), **Palani** 152 km (3½ hrs), **Thanjavur** (1½ hrs). Also 2 to **Kanniyakumari** (9 hrs).

Taxi
Unmetered taxis, and tourist taxis from Kavria Travels, Hotel Sangam, Collector's Office Rd, T0431-246 4480.

Train

Enquiries, T131. **Bengaluru (Bangalore)**: *Mayiladuturai Mysore Exp 16232*, 2040, 9½ hrs, continues to **Mysore**, 3¼ hrs. **Chennai**: several throughout the day, including *Pallavan Exp 12606*, 0630, 5½ hrs; *Vaigai Exp 12636*, 0850, 5¼ hrs; all go via Villupuram (for Puducherry), 3 hrs. **Kollam**: *Nagore-Quilon Exp 16361*, 1615, 12½ hrs. **Madurai**: *Vaigai Exp 12635*, 1745, 2¾ hrs.

Directory

Chidambaram *p85, map p86*
Banks Changing money can be difficult. City Union Bank, West Car St has exchange facilities. **Indian Bank**, 64 South Car St. **Post** Head Post Office, North Car St.

Kumbakonam *p61, map p89*
Banks Changing money is difficult. State Bank of India, TSR Big St. **Internet** End of Kamaraj Rd, close to clock tower. **Post** Near Mahamakam Tank.

Thanjavur *p90, map p91*
Banks ATMs at the station, along South Rampart St, and opposite the tourist office on Gandhiji Rd. **Canara Bank**, South Main St, changes TCs. **Medical services** Govt Hospital, Hospital Rd, south of the old town. **Post** Head Post and Telegraph Office are off the Railway Station Rd. **Useful contacts** Police, south of the Big Temple between the canal and the railway, T04362-232200.

Tiruchirappalli *p93, map p94*
Banks Lots of ATMs around the bus stands. Exchange is available at Western Union money transfer in Jenne Plaza, Cantonment. Mon-Sat 0900-1730. Quick; good rates. **Internet** Mas Media, Main Rd, 6 terminals; Central Telegraph Office, Permanent Rd.

The Tamil Hill Stations

The Tamil ghats were once shared between shola forest and tribal peoples. But the British, limp from the heat of the plains, invested in expeditions up the mountains and before long had planted eucalyptus, established elite members' clubs and substituted jackals for foxes in their pursuit of the hunt. Don't expect to find the sheer awe-inspiring grandeur of the Himalaya, but there is a charm to these hills where neatly pleated, green tea plantations run like contour lines about the ghats' girth, bringing the promise of a restorative chill and walking tracks where the air comes cut with the smell of eucalyptus.

Arriving in the Tamil Hill Stations

The northern Nilgiris or the more southerly Palani Hills offer rival opportunities for high-altitude stopovers on the route between Tamil Nadu, Karnataka and Kerala. The most visited towns of Ooty and Kodai both have their staunch fan bases – Ooty tends to attract nostalgic British and rail enthusiasts, while Kody gets the American vote, thanks in part to its international schools. Both are well connected by road: Kody is best approached from Madurai; Ooty makes a good bridge to Kerala from Mysore or Tamil Nadu's more northern temple towns. The famous narrow-gauge rack-and-pinion Nilgiri Mountain Railway is most dramatic between Coonoor and Mettupalayam, which in turn has trains from Coimbatore and Chennai. The roads worsen dramatically when you cross the Tamil border from Kerala, reflecting the different levels of affluence between the two states. ▸▸ *See Transport, page 117.*

Udhagamandalam (Ooty) → *For listings, see pages 110-120.*

Ooty has been celebrated for rolling hills covered in pine and eucalyptus forests and coffee and tea plantations since the first British planters arrived in 1818. A Government House was built, and the British lifestyle developed with cottages and clubs – tennis, golf, riding – and tea on the lawn. But the town is no longer the haven it once was; the centre is heavily built up and can be downright unpleasant in the holiday months of April to June, and again around October. It's best to stay either in the grand ruins of colonial quarters on the quiet outskirts where it's still possible to steal some serenity or opt instead for the far smaller tea garden town of Coonoor (see page 104), 19 km down the mountain. **Tamil Nadu Tourism** ① *Wenlock Rd, T0423-244 3977*, is not very efficient.

Places in Udhagamandalam → *Phone code: 0423. Population 93,900. Altitude: 2286 m.*
The **Botanical Gardens** ① *3 km northeast of railway station, 0800-1800, Rs 25, camera, Rs 50, video Rs 500*, house more than 1000 varieties of plant, shrub and tree including orchids, ferns, alpines and medicinal plants, but is most fun for watching giant family groups picnicking and gambolling together among beautiful lawns and glass houses. To the east

of the garden in a Toda *mund* is the Wood House made of logs. The **Annual Flower Show** is held in the third week of May. The **Rose Garden** ① *750 m from Charing Cross, 0830-1830*, has over 1500 varieties of roses.

Ooty Lake was built in 1825 as a vast irrigation tank and is now more than half overgrown with water hyacinth, though it is still used enthusiastically for boating and **pedalo hire** ① *0900-1800, Rs 60-110 per hr.*

Kandal Cross ① *3 km west of the railway station*, is a Roman Catholic shrine considered the 'Jerusalem of the East'. During the clearing of the area to make way for a graveyard in 1927, an enormous 4-m-high boulder was found and a cross was erected. Now a relic of the True Cross brought to India by an Apostolic delegate is shown to pilgrims every day. The annual feast is in May.

St Stephen's Church was Ooty's first church, built in the 1820s. Much of the wood is said to be from Tipu Sultan's Lal Bagh Palace in Srirangapatnam. The inside of the church and the graveyard at the rear are worth seeing.

Udhagamandalam (Ooty)

Where to stay 🛏	Tamil Nadu 12	Hot Breads 2
Fernhills Palace 20	YWCA Anandagiri 14	Sharma Bhojanalaya 4
Glyngarth Heritage 21		Shinkow's 5
Nilgiri Woodlands 19	**Restaurants** 🍴	Pavilion 3
Reflections Guest House 15	Blue Hills 1	
Regency Villa 18	Chandan Vegetarian 6	
Savoy (Taj) 9	Garden Café 6	

Dodabetta ① *1000-1500, buses from Ooty, autos and taxis (Rs 200 round trip) go to the summit*, is 10 km east of the railway station off the Kotagiri road. Reaching 2638 m, the 'big mountain' is the second highest in the Western Ghats, sheltering Coonoor from the southwest monsoons when Ooty gets heavy rains. The top is often shrouded in mist. There is a viewing platform at the summit. The telescope isn't worth even the nominal Rs 2 fee.

Walks and hikes around Ooty

Hiking or simply walking is excellent in the Nilgiris. It is undisturbed, quiet and interesting. Climbing Dodabetta or Mukurti is hardly a challenge but the longer walks through the *sholas* are best undertaken with a guide. It is possible to see characteristic features of Toda settlements such as *munds* and *boas*.

Dodabetta–Snowdon–Ooty walk starts at Dodabetta Junction directly opposite the 3 km road to the summit. It is a pleasant path that curves gently downhill through a variety of woodland (mainly eucalyptus and conifers) back to Ooty and doesn't take more than a couple of hours. For longer treks, contact **Nilgiris Trekking Association** ① *Kavitha Nilayam, 31-D Bank Rd, or R Seniappan, 137 Upper Bazar, T0423-244 4449, sehi appan@yahoo.com*.

Mukurti Peak ① *buses from Ooty every 30 mins from 0630 or you can take a tour (see page 117), book early as they are popular*, is 36 km away, off the Gudalur road. After 26 km you reach the 6-km-long Mukurti Lake. Mukurti Peak (the name suggests that someone thought it resembled a severed nose), not an easy climb, is to the west. The Todas believe that the souls of the dead and the sacrificed buffaloes leap to the next world from this sacred peak. It is an excellent place to escape for walking, to view the occasional wildlife, to go fishing at the lake or to go boating.

Avalanche ① *24 km from town, bus from Ooty at 1110*, a valley, is a beautiful part of the *shola*, with plenty of rhododendrons, magnolias and orchids and a trout stream running through it, and is excellent for walking. The **Forestry Department Guest House** is clean and has good food. Contact the **Wildlife Warden** ① *1st floor, Mahalingam Building, Ooty, T0423-244098*.

The **River Pykara** ① *19 km from Ooty, several buses 0630-2030, or take a car or bicycle*, has a dam and power plant. There is breathtaking scenery. The **waterfalls**, about 6 km from the bridge on the main road, are best in July though it is very wet then, but they are also worth visiting from August to December.

Coonoor → *For listings, see pages 110-120. Phone code: 0423. Altitude: 1800 m. Population 50,100.*

① *When you arrive by train or bus (which doesn't always stop at the main bus stand if going on to Ooty), the main town of Lower Coonoor will be to the east, across the river. Upper Coonoor, with the better hotels 2-3 km away, is further east.*

Smaller and much less developed than Ooty, Coonoor is an ideal starting point for nature walks and rambles through villages. There's no pollution, no noise and very few people. The covered market, as with many towns and cities in South India, is almost medieval and cobblers, jewellers, tailors, pawn brokers and merchants sell everything from jasmine to beetroot. The picturesque hills around the town are covered in coffee and tea plantations.

The real attraction here is the hiking, though there are a couple of sights in town. The large **Sim's Park** ① *0800-1830, Rs 5*, named after a secretary to the Madras Club, is a well-maintained botanical garden on the slopes of a ravine with over 330 varieties of rose but is only really worth the journey for passionate botanists. Contact the **United**

Blue Mountain Railway

Ever since 15 June 1899, the narrow gauge steam *Mountain Railway*, in its blue and cream livery, has chugged from Mettupalayam to Ooty via Coonoor, negotiating 16 tunnels and 31 major bridges and climbing from 326 m to 2193 m. This was the location for the railway scenes of the *Marabar Express* in the film *A Passage to India*.

It's a charming 4½-hour (46 km) journey through tea plantations and forest, but – outside first class – be prepared for an amiable Indian holiday-makers' scrum. There are rest stops at Hillgrove (17 km) and Coonoor (27 km).

For enthusiasts, the pricier and more spacious *Heritage Steam Chariot* runs between Ooty and Runneymede picnic area, 23 km away, at weekends (more often in high season). The drawback is that you can be stranded for hours when the engine breaks down; some decide to scramble to the nearest road to flag down a bus.

Planters' Association of South India (UPASI) ⓘ *Glenview House, Coonoor, T0423-223 0270, www.upasi.org*, to visit tea and coffee plantations.

The **Wellington Barracks**, 3 km northeast of Lower Coonoor, which are the raison d'être for the town, were built in 1852. They are now the headquarters of the Indian Defence Services Staff College and also of the Madras Regiment, which is over 250 years old, the oldest in the Indian Army.

Lamb's Rock, on a high precipice, 9 km away, has good views over the Coimbatore plains and coffee and tea estates on the slopes. At **Dolphin's Nose** (12 km away, several buses 0700-1615), you can see **Catherine Falls**, a further 10 km away (best in the early morning). **Droog** (13 km away, buses 0900, 1345) has ruins of a 16th-century fort used by Tipu Sultan, and requires a 3-km walk.

Kotagiri ⓘ *29 km from Ooty, frequent services from Coonoor, Mettupalayam Railway Station and Ooty*, has an altitude of 1980 m. It sits on the northeast crest of the plateau overlooking the plains. It has a milder climate than Ooty. The name comes from Kotar–Keri, the street of the *Kotas* who were one of the original hill tribes and who have a village to the west of the town. You can visit some scenic spots from here: **St Catherine Falls** (8 km) and **Elk Falls** (7 km), or one of the peaks, **Kodanad Viewpoint** (16 km) – reached through the tea estates or by taking one of the several buses that run from 0610 onwards – or **Rangaswamy Pillar**, an isolated rock, and the conical Rangaswamy Peak.

Mettupalayam and the Nilgiri Ghat Road → *For listings, see pages 110-120.*

The journey up to Coonoor from Mettupalayam is one of the most scenic in South India, affording superb views over the plains below. Between Mettupalayam and the start of the Ghat road, there are magnificent groves of tall, slender areca nut palms. Mettupalayam has become the centre for the areca nut trade as well as producing synthetic gems. The palms are immensely valuable trees: the nut is used across India wrapped in betel vine leaves – two of the essential ingredients of India's universal after-meal digestive, *paan*.

The town is the starting point of the ghat railway line up to Ooty (see box, above). If you take the early-morning train you can continue to Mysore by bus from Ooty on the same day, making a very pleasant trip.

Mudumalai Wildlife Sanctuary → *For listings, see pages 110-120.*

ⓘ *Minibus safaris 0630-0900, 1530-1800, Rs 45, still camera Rs 25, video Rs 150; Reception Range Office, Theppakadu, T0423-252 6235, open 0630-1800, is where buses between Mysore and Ooty stop. There is a Ranger Office at Kargudi. The best time to visit is Sep-Dec and Mar-May when the undergrowth dies down and it's easier to see animals, especially at dawn when they're on the move. Forest fires can close the park temporarily during Feb-Apr.*

The sanctuary adjoins Bandipur National Park beyond the Moyar River, its hills (885-1000 m), ravines, flats and valleys being an extension of the same environment. The park is one of the more popular and is now trying to limit numbers of visitors to reduce disturbance to the elephants.

There are large herds of elephant, gaur, sambar, barking deer, wild dog, Nilgiri langur, bonnet monkey, wild boar, four-horned antelope and the rarer tiger and leopard, as well as smaller mammals and many birds and reptiles. **Elephant Camp**, south of Theppakadu, open 0700-0800 and 1600-1700, tames wild elephants. Some are bred in captivity and trained to work for the timber industry. You can watch the elephants being fed in the late afternoon, learn about each individual elephant's diet and the specially prepared 'cakes' of food.

You can hire a jeep for about Rs 10 per km but must be accompanied by a guide. Most night safaris are best avoided. Elephant rides from 0700-0830 and 1530-1700 (Rs 50 per person for 30 minutes); check timing and book in advance in Theppakadu or with the **Wildlife Warden** ⓘ *Mount Stuart Hill, Ooty, T0423-244 4098*. They can be fun even though you may not see much wildlife. There are *machans* near waterholes and salt licks and along the Moyar River. With patience you can see a lot, especially rare and beautiful birds. Treks and jeep rides in the remoter parts of the forest with guides can be arranged from some lodges, including **Jungle Retreat** (see page 112). You can spend a day climbing the hill and bathe at the impressive waterfalls. The core area is not open to visitors.

Coimbatore and the Nilgiri Hills → *For listings, see pages 110-120.*

Coimbatore → *Phone code: 0422. Population: 923,000.*

As one of South India's most important industrial cities since the 1930s development of hydroelectricity from the Pykara Falls, Coimbatore holds scant charm to warrant more than a pit stop. It was once the fulcrum of tussles between Tamilian, Mysorean and Keralite coastal rulers (the word *palayam* crops up tellingly often in Coimbatore – its translation being 'encampment') and sadly violence continues today. You are likely to stay here only if fascinated by the cotton trade or stuck for an onward bus or train.

Salem → *Phone code: 0427. Population: 693,200.*

Salem, an important transport junction, is surrounded by hills: the Shevaroy and Nagaramalai Hills to the north and the Jarugumalai Hills to the southeast. It is a busy, rapidly growing industrial town – particularly for textiles and metal-based industries – with modern shopping centres. The old town is on the east bank of the River Manimutheru. Each evening around Bazar Street you can see cotton carpets being made. The **cemetery**, next to the Collector's office, has some interesting tombstones. To the southeast of the town on a ridge of the Jarugumalai Hills is a highly visible *Naman* painted in *chunam* and ochre. On the nearby hill the temple (1919) is particularly sacred to the weavers' community. Some 600 steps lead up to excellent views over the town.

Yercaud and the Shevaroy Hills → *Phone code: 04281. Altitude: 1515 m.*

The beautiful drive up the steep and sharply winding ghat road from Salem quickly brings a sharp freshness to the air as it climbs to over 1500 m. The minor resort has a small artificial lake and Anna Park nearby. Some attractive though unmarked walks start here. In May there is a special festival focused on the **Shevaroyan Temple**, on top of the third highest peak in the hill range. Many tribal people take part but access is only possible on foot. Ask for details in the **Tamil Nadu Tourist Office** in Chennai, see page 31. There's also a tourist information office in the Tamil Nadu hotel in town.

Just outside town is **Lady's Seat**, overlooking the ghat road, which has wonderful views across the Salem plains. Near the old Norton Bungalow on the Shevaroyan Temple Road is another well-known local spot, **Bear's Cave**. Formed by two huge boulders, it is occupied by huge colonies of bats. The whole area is full of botanical interest. There is an orchidarium and a horticultural research station.

Kodaikanal and the Palani Hills → *For listings, see pages 110-120.*

The climb up the Palanis starts 47 km before Kodaikanal (Kodi) and is one of the most rapid ascents anywhere across the ghats. The views are stunning. In the lower reaches of the climb you look down over the Kambam Valley, the Vaigai Lake and across to the Varushanad Hills beyond, while higher up the scene is dominated by the sawn-off pyramid of Perumal Malai. Set around a small artificial lake, the town has crisply fresh air, even at the height of summer, and the beautiful scent of pine and eucalyptus make it a popular retreat from the southern plains. Today Kodai is a fast growing resort, yet it retains a relatively low-key air that many feel gives it an edge over Ooty.

Arriving in Kodaikanal → *Phone code: 04542. Population: 32,900. Altitude: 2343 m.*

Buses make the long climb from Madurai and other cities to the Central Bus Stand, which is within easy walking distance from most hotels. The nearest train station is Kodai Road. Kodai is small enough to walk around, though for some of the sights it is worth getting an unmetered taxi. There's a **Tamil Nadu Tourist Office** ① *Hospital Rd next to bus stand, T04542-241675, 1000-1745 except holidays*, with helpful staff and maps available. ▶▶ *See Transport, page 119.*

Background

The Palani Hills were first surveyed by British administrators in 1821, but the surveyor's report was not published until 1837, 10 years after Ooty had become the official sanatorium for the British in South India. A proposal to build a sanatorium was made in 1861-1862 by Colonel Hamilton, who noted the extremely healthy climate and the lack of disease, but the sanatorium was never built because the site was so inaccessible. So it was that Kodaikanal became the first hill station in India to be set up not by heat-sick Britons but by American missionaries.

The American Mission in Madurai, established in 1834, had lost six of their early missionaries within a decade. The missionaries had been eyeing a site in the Sirumalai Hills, at around 1300 m, but while these were high enough to offer respite from the heat of the plains they were still prone to malaria. Isolated Kodai, almost 1000 m higher, proved to be the ticket, and the first two bungalows were built by June 1845. Kodai's big transformation came at the turn of the 20th century with the arrival of the car and the bus. In 1905 it was possible to do the whole journey from Kodai Road station to Kodai within the hours of daylight. The present road, up Law's Ghat, was opened to traffic in 1916.

Places in Kodaikanal

Star-shaped **Kodaikanal Lake** covers 24 ha and is surrounded by gentle wooded slopes. The walk around the lake takes about one hour; you can also hire pedal boats and go fishing (with permission from the Inspector of Fisheries), although the water is polluted. The International School, established in 1901, has a commanding position on the lakeside, and provides education for children from India and abroad between the ages of five and 18.

The view over the plains from **Coaker's Walk**, built by Lieutenant Coaker in the 1870s, can be magnificent; on a rare clear day you can see as far as Madurai. It is reached from a signposted path just above the bazar, 1 km from the bus stand.

Kurinji Andavar Temple, northeast of the town past Chettiar Park, is dedicated to Murugan and associated with the Neelakurinji flower that carpets the hills in purple flowers once every 12 years (the next mass flowering is due in 2018). There are excellent views of the north and southern plains, including Palani and Vaigai Dams.

Kodaikanal

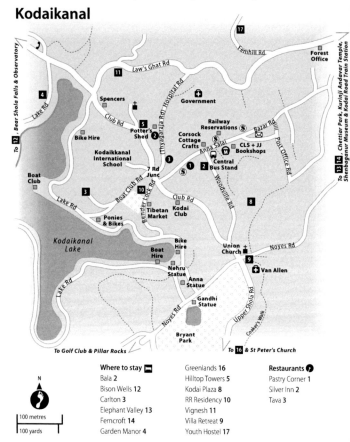

Where to stay 🛏		Greenlands 16	Restaurants 🍴
Bala **2**		Hilltop Towers **5**	Pastry Corner **1**
Bison Wells **12**		Kodai Plaza **8**	Silver Inn **2**
Carlton **3**		RR Residency **10**	Tava **3**
Elephant Valley **13**		Vignesh **11**	
Ferncroft **14**		Villa Retreat **9**	
Garden Manor **4**		Youth Hostel **17**	

The small but interesting **Shenbaganur Museum** ⓘ *5 km down Law's Ghat road, open 1000-1130, 1500-1700*, at the Sacred Heart College seminary, is the local flora and fauna museum, exhibiting 300 orchid species as well as some archaeological remains. It's an attractive walk downhill from the town passing a number of small waterfalls. Some 4 km west of the bus stand at a height of 2347 m, the **Solar Physical Observatory** ⓘ *T04542-240588, open Fri 1000-1230, 1900-2100*, is one of the oldest in the world, established in 1899.

Bear Shola Falls, named because it once attracted bears, is a favourite picnic spot about 2 km from the bus stand. The falls, like most others around Kodai, have been reduced to a trickle outside monsoon season. A pleasant walk or bike/scooter ride leads southwest from the lake along leafy avenues, past the golf course where wild deer and gaur are sometimes seen, to the striking viewpoint at Valley View; a further 3 km away are Pillar Rocks, a trio of impressive granite formations over 120 m high.

Around Kodaikanal → *For listings, see pages 110-120.*

If you're in the mood for an adventure there's a popular semi-official trekking route that links Kodaikanal to Munnar, roughly following the now-overgrown Escape Road built by the British Army in anticipation of a Japanese invasion in 1942. The route follows the Pillar Rocks road, then descends to beautiful Berijam Lake, 21 km southwest of Kodaikanal, where there's an adequate Forest Rest House. You can visit the lake on a day trip with permission from the **Forestry Department Office** ⓘ *Law's Ghat Rd, Kodaikkanal, T04542-240287; only 10 permits are granted a day so arrive at the office before 1000*. The next day you continue through pine and eucalypt plantations, patches of shola forest and the occasional village to Top Station in Kerala (five to six hours), where there is a Forest Hut and shops and tea stalls selling snacks. From here you can catch a bus or jeep to Munnar, 41 km away. You'll need permission from the Forestry Department in both Kodai and Munnar to complete the trek, and cross-border bureaucratic wrangling can make this hard to come by. Local guides can help with permits and transport at a charge: try **Raja** ⓘ *T(0)9842-188893*, or the semi-legendary **Kodai Mani** ⓘ *T(0)9894-048493*, who knows the trails well and charges accordingly.

The ghat road running north from Kodaikanal to **Palani** passes through smallholdings of coffee, oranges and bananas. Inter-planting of crops such as pepper is further increasing the yields from what can be highly productive land, even on steep slopes. The shrine to **Murugan** (Subrahmanya) on top of Palani (or Sivagiri) Hill is a very important site of pilgrimage. At full moon in January to February pilgrims walk from as far afield as Chettinad and Munnar to climb the 659 steps to the shrine. Many carry shoulder poles with elaborate bamboo or wooden structures on each end, living out the myth of Idumban, who carried the twin hills of Sivagiri and Shaktigiri from Mount Kailash to their present locations on either end of a bamboo *kavadi*. Around the temple, Palani presents a chaotic but compelling pastiche of pilgrim fervour, religious souvenir shopping and decaying flower garlands.

Pollachi, in a key strategic position on the east to west crossing of the ghats through the Palakkad Gap, has been an important trading centre for over 2000 years, as witnessed by the finds of Roman silver coins bearing the heads of the emperors Augustus and Tiberias. Today its main appeal is as the gateway to the small but very attractive Anamalai (Indira Gandhi) National Park (see below).

Anamalai (Indira Gandhi) Wildlife Sanctuary

① *0600-1800, Rs 15, camera Rs 25, video Rs 150; best time to visit Dec-Jun, closed mid-Feb to mid-Apr, avoid Sun. Reception and Information Centre at Top Slip organizes bus rides, elephant safaris and trekking guides. Day permits from entrance gate at Sethumadai; for overnight stays advance written permission is needed from Wildlife Warden (1176 Meenakalai Salai, Pollachi, 1.5 km out of town on road towards Top Slip, T04259-225356).*

This beautiful, unspoilt park covering 960 sq km of grassland, rainforest and mountain shola forest, is rarely visited except by Indian day trippers. Wildlife includes Nilgiri langur, lion-tailed macaque, elephant, gaur, tiger, panther, sloth, wild boar, birds – including pied hornbill, drongo, red whiskered bulbul, black-headed oriole – and a large number of crocodiles in the Amaravathi reservoir. There is an elephant camp, claimed to be the largest in Asia, reached by a two- to three-hour minibus ride through the forest (0615, 1130 and 1515, Rs 25), and short elephant rides can be arranged. Birdwatching is good from Kariam Shola watchtower, 2 km from Topslip.

There are some **trekking** routes that vary from easy treks to Pandaravara (8 km), Kozhikamuthi (12 km) and Perunkundru peak (32 km), which is demanding. Permits can be obtained from the **Range Officer** ① *Top Slip, Rs 150-300 per person.* Private guides charge upwards of Rs 100 for a three-hour trek.

Dindigul → *For listings, see pages 110-120.*

Now a large market town, Dindigul, north of Madurai, commands a strategic gap between the Sirumalai Hills to its east and the Palani Hills to the west. The market handles the produce of the Sirumalai Hills, including a renowned local variety of banana. Dindigul is particularly known for its cheroots.

The massive granite rock and **fort** ① *2 km west of the bus stand, 0730-1730, foreigners Rs 100, Indians Rs 5, autos Rs 20,* towers over 90 m above the plain. The Mysore army captured it in 1745 and Haidar Ali was appointed governor in 1755. It was ceded to the British under the Treaty of Seringapatam. There are magnificent views of the town, valley and hills on either side from the top of the rock fort. **Our Lady of Dolours Church,** one of several churches in the town, is over 250 years old and was rebuilt in 1970. The Old City is interesting to walk around; you can walk up to the fort from there. The station is 2 km south of the bus stand that has cheap lodges nearby.

The Tamil Hill Stations listings

For hotel and restaurant price codes and other relevant information, see pages 14-18.

🛏 Where to stay

Udhagamandalam (Ooty) *p102, map p103*
Rates quoted are for the high season. Good discounts Jul-Mar except during *puja* and Christmas (add 30% tax in upper categories). Winter nights can be bitterly cold and hotel fireplaces are often inadequate. Avoid the

budget accommodation round Commercial Rd and Ettines Rd, particularly if you are a woman travelling alone.

$$$$ Fernhills Palace, Fernhill Post, T0423-244 3910, www.fernhillspalace.co.in. After years of stop-start renovation, Wadiyar, the current Mysore maharaja has opened his ancestral palace as a luxury heritage hotel. It offers 30 suites, with teak furniture, wooden panelling, fireplaces and jacuzzis. Spa, gym, plus correspondingly high price tags.

$$$$ Savoy (Taj), 77 Sylkes Rd, T0423 222 5500. 40 well-maintained cottage rooms with huge wooden doors, open fires and separate dressing areas. Even if you're not staying it's worth a teatime visit for the building's interesting history and lovely gardens, and the wood-panelled dining room serves excellent takes on traditional Tamil food.

$$ Glyngarth, Golf Club Rd, Fingerpost (2 km from centre), T0423-244 5754, www.glyngarthvilla.com. Just 5 huge double rooms with period furniture plus original fittings including all-teak floors and fireplaces in a Raj building – complete with metal roof – dating from 1853. Modern bathrooms, meals made from fresh garden produce, large grounds, clean, excellent service, tremendously characterful (too much for some) good value. Walking distance to golf course. Recommended.

$$ Regency Villas, Fernhill Post, T0423-244 2555, regency@sancharnet.in. The maharaja of Mysore's staff had some of the best sunset views of the blue hills from their bungalows. The 19 villas here were under much-needed renovation at time of updating – hopefully not at the risk of the appealing air of ramshackle and rows of dog-eared colonial photos.

$$-$ The Nilgiri Woodlands, Race Course Rd, T0423-244 2551, nilgiris_woodlands@yahoo.com. 22 rooms ranging from paint-peeling doubles to spacious cottages. Shared veranda outside racecourse-facing rooms that give onto a garden and the pink/green/blue bungalows of Ooty central. Quiet and spacious rooms tucked round the back (without views) are best value.

$ Reflections Guest House, North Lake Rd, T0423-244 3834, www.reflectionsguesthouseooty.com. Clean, homely, quiet, with good views of the lake, 9 rooms (cheaper dorm beds), pleasant dining and sitting room serving good food, friendly owners. Rs 50 for wood for the fire or to use the stove for your own cooking, dodgy plumbing, can get chilly, restricted hot water.

$ Tamil Nadu (TTDC), Charing Cross, up the steps by the tourist office, T0423-244 4370. Spotless rooms and penthouse with good views, restaurant, bar, exchange, pleasant hotel tucked away. Avoid the food.

$ YWCA Anandagiri, Ettines Rd, T0423-244 2218, www.ywcaagooty.com. It's basic and a little institutional, and the hot water can be iffy, but this is the most atmospheric budget accommodation in Ooty, with high-ceilinged 1920s cottages in an extensive garden complex surrounded by tall pines and superb views.

Coonoor *p104*

Most hotels are 3-5 km from the station and bus stand.

$$$$-$$$ Gateway Hotel, Church Rd, Upper Coonoor, T0423-223 0021, www.tajhotels.com. This wonderful quiet place offers spectacular mountain views and a wide choice of rooms, including cool stone-walled cottages with private terraces, romantic open-sided treehouses, simple bamboo huts and a well-swept dorm (Rs 700). The friendly owners keep high standards and can arrange safaris, good treks with local guides and elephant rides. There's an excellent swimming pool, and somewhat pricey food.

$$$ The Tryst, Carolina Tea Estate, T0423-220 7057, www.trystindia.com. The shelves at this homestay groan under years of hoarding. 5 double rooms with well-stocked library, snooker table, games galore and gym, plus a huge cottage that sleeps 10. Unexpected and in an outstanding location away from all other accommodation cradled in the nape of a rolling tea estate. Excellent walking. Book in advance.

$ Blue Star, Kotagiri, next to bus station, T04266-274454. Rooms with shower and toilet in modern building.

$ Tamil Nadu (TTDC), Ooty Rd, Mt Pleasant (1 km north of station), T0423-223 2813. Simple rooms, TV, restaurant, bar and dorm.

$ 'Wyoming' Holiday Home (YWCA), near Hospital, Upper Coonoor (auto from bus stand Rs 25), T0423-223 4426. Set in a house with character and idyllic views, 8 large rooms and 2 dorms (8-bedded), excellent food (no alcohol) but some warn you should check bill and watch out for the neurotic labrador who is known to bark through the night. Garden, friendly, helpful, popular. Manager qualified in alternative therapies (runs clinic and courses). Book ahead.

Mettupalayam *p105*
$ EMS Mayura, 212 Coimbatore Main Rd, T04254-227936. Set back from the main road a 5-min walk from the station, this makes a decent overnight choice with clean rooms, a decent restaurant and bar.
$ Surya International, 345 Ooty Main Rd, T04254-223502, fairly clean rooms (Rs 150), rooftop restaurant, often empty, quiet, but characterless.

Mudumalai Wildlife Sanctuary *p106*
Advance booking is essential especially during the season and at weekends. Accommodation is better near Masinagudi which also has restaurants and shops but there is some in Bokkapuram, 3 km further south. Ask private lodges for pick-up if arriving by bus at Theppakadu.
$$$ Bamboo Banks Farm Guest House, Masinagudi, T09443-373201, www.bamboo banks.in. 6 clean rooms, 4 in cottages in a fine setting, attractive garden, good food, birdwatching, riding, jeep.
$$$-$$ Jungle Hut, near Bokkapuram, T0423-252 6463, www.junglehut.in. In valley, 12 clean, simple rooms with bath in 3 stone cottages plus a few small tents, good food ("lovely home cooking"), pool, jeep hire, game viewing and treks, very friendly welcome. Recommended.
$$$-$ Jungle Retreat, Bokkapuram, T0423-252 6469, www.jungleretreat.com. This wonderful, quiet place offers spectacular mountain views and a wide choice of rooms, including cool stone-walled cottages with private terraces, romantic

open-sided treehouses, simple bamboo huts and a well-swept dorm (Rs 700). The friendly owners keep high standards and can arrange safaris, good treks with local guides and elephant rides. There's an excellent swimming pool, and somewhat pricey food.
$$ New Mountania, Masinagudi, T0423-252 6267, www.newmountania.com. Rooms in cottages (prices vary), "nice but a bit overpriced", restaurant, jeep tour to waterfalls, easy animal spotting (evening better than morning).
$$-$ Monarch Safari Park, Bokkapuram, on a hill side, T0423-252 6250. Large grounds, with 14 rooms in twin *machan* huts on stilts with bath (but rats may enter at night), open-sided restaurant, cycles, birdwatching, good riding (Rs 150 per hr), some sports facilities, meditation centre, "lovely spot", management a bit slack but friendly, if slow, service.
$ Forest Department Huts, reserve in advance through Wildlife Warden, Mudumalai WLS, Mt Stuart Hill, Ooty, T0423-244 4098, or Reception Range Officer, Theppakadu, T0423-252 6235. Most have caretakers who can arrange food.
$ Forest Hills Farm, 300 m from Jungle Hut, T0423-252 6216, www.foresthillsindia. com. Friendly, 6 modern rooms with bath. Good views, good food, game viewing. Recommended.
$ Tamil Nadu (TTDC hostel), Theppakadu, T0423-252 6249. 3 rooms, 24 beds in dorm (Rs 45), restaurant, van for viewing.
Abhayaranyam Rest House, Kargudi. 2 rooms.
Abhayaranyam Annexe, Kargudi. 2 rooms. Recommended.
Minivet and **Morgan**, Kargudi. Dorm, 8 and 12 beds.
Peacock, Kargudi. 50-bed dorm, excellent food.
Rest House and **Annexe**, Kargudi. Ask for deluxe rooms.
Log House, Masinagudi, 5 rooms.
Rest House, Masinagudi, 3 rooms.

Coimbatore p106

$$$ Heritage Inn, 38 Sivaswamy Rd, T0422-223 1451, www.hotelheritageinn.in. Standard hotel with good restaurants, internet, excellent service, 63 modern, a/c rooms, good value.

$$ City Tower, Sivaswamy Rd (just off Dr Nanjappa Rd), Gandhipuram, near bus stand, T0422-223 0681, www.hotelcitytower.com. 91 excellent redecorated rooms, some a/c, small balconies, 2 restaurants (rooftop tandoori), no alcohol, superb service. Recommended.

$$ Sabari Nest, 739-A Avanashi Rd, 2 km from railway, T0422-450 5500, www.sabarihotels.com. 38 a/c rooms, some small, restaurant, bar, amazing supermarket downstairs (for Western snacks and last stop for supplies), business facilities, roof garden. Recommended.

$ Channma International, 18/109 Big Bazar St, T0422-239 6631. Oldish art deco-style hotel, 36 spacious clean rooms, tiny windows, restaurant, internet, health club and pool next door.

$ KK Residency, 7 Shastri Rd, by Central Bus Stand, Ramnagar, T0422-430 0200. 42 smallish but clean rooms, 6 a/c, good condition, restaurant, friendly service. Recommended.

$ Meena, 109 Kalingarayar St, T0422-223 5420. Small family hotel with 30 clean and pleasant rooms, vegetarian restaurant.

Salem p106

Choose a room away from the road if possible.

$$ Salem Castle, A-4 Bharati St, Swarnapuri, 4 km from railway station, T0427-244 8702. Rather brash modern hotel with 64 comfortable, very clean a/c rooms. Restaurants (good Chinese but expensive, the rest are Indian-style), coffee shop, bar, exchange, pool.

$ City View, Omalur Main Rd, T0427-233 4232. Rooms with bath, some clean, strong a/c, meals, travel. **Shree Saravanabhavan** in the same block does good south Indian veg.

$ Ganesh Mahal, 323 Omalur Rd, T0427-233 2820, www.ganeshmahal.com. Modern and comfortable, 45 pleasant rooms, TV, good restaurant, bar.

$ Railway Retiring Rooms. Battered but with olde-worlde feel.

$ Raj Castle, 320 Omalur Rd, T0427-233 3532. 21 nicely fitted rooms, 4 a/c, some with balcony, TV, hot water mornings, tourist car.

$ Selvam, T0427-233 4491. Clean rooms with bath, some a/c, good restaurant.

Yercaud p107

Most hotels offer off-season discounts Jan-Mar, Aug-Dec.

$$ Sterling Resort, near Lady's Seat, T04281-222444. 59 rooms, modern, excellent views.

$ Shevaroys, Main (Hospital) Rd, near lake, T04281-222288. 32 rooms, 11 **$$** cottages with baths, restaurant, bar, good views.

$ Tamil Nadu (TTDC), Salem-Yercaud Ghat Rd, near lake, behind Panchayat Office, T04281-222273. 12 rooms, restaurant, garden.

Kodaikanal p107, map p108

Room rates are high in Kody compared to the rest of Tamil Nadu, but so are standards of cleanliness, in every price category. Off-season rates are given here: prices rise by 30-100% Apr-Jun and 12.5% tax is charged everywhere. On Anna Salai cheap basic lodges, mostly with shared bathroom, can charge Rs 800 in season

$$$ Carlton, Boat Club Rd, T04542-248555, www.carlton-kodaikanal.com. Fully modernized but colonial-style hotel with 91 excellent rooms, many with private terraces overlooking the lake. Excellent restaurant, billiards, tennis, golf and boating, often full in season. Recommended.

$$$ Elephant Valley, Ganesh Puram village (20 km from Kodai off Palani road), T0413-265 5751. This tranquil eco-resort comprises 13 cute rustic stone cottages (some in converted village houses) dotted across a 30-ha organic farm on either side of a rocky river, visited by wild boar, gaur and elephants (best sightings Apr-Jun). Restaurant serves good food based on home-grown veg and herbs, fantastic salads, plus superb coffee which is grown, roasted and ground entirely on-site. Highly recommended.

$$-$ Villa Retreat, Coaker's Walk, T04542-240940, www.villaretreat.com. 8 deluxe rooms in an old house, 3 cottages (open fireplace), rustic, good service. Garden setting, excellent views, clean but overpriced.

$$ Bison Wells Jungle Lodge, Camp George Observatory, T04542-240566, www.wilderness-explorer.in. A cottage for the nature purist, with no electricity and space for only 3, a whole mountain range away from the rest of the hill station. Jeep transport from Kody arranged on request at extra cost.

$$ Ferncroft, 17 km from town on Palani Rd, T04542-230242, jfmfernando33@ yahoo.com. Simple, rustic lodgings on the ground floor of Tamil-Scots couple Jo and Maureen Fernando's stone built house, set among trees heavy with peaches, passion fruit and avocado. There's a small but comfortable bedroom, a kitchenette and living room with wicker chairs, plus a parcel of lush lawn with beautiful views down the valley. Far from town, but hard to beat for peace and quiet.

$$ RR Residency, Boathouse Rd, T04542-244300, residency@rediffmail.com. 7 well-furnished, top-quality rooms in newish hotel, though views are lacking and there's potential olfactory disturbance from adjacent petrol pump. Vegetarian restaurant next door.

$$-$ Garden Manor, Lake Rd (10-min walk from bus station), T04542-240461. Good location in pleasant gardens overlooking lake, with 7 rooms (including a 4-bed), restaurant with outdoor tables.

$ Bala, 11/49 Woodville Rd, opposite the bus station (entrance tucked away in private courtyard), T04542-241214, www.balagroups.com. Friendly and well-

kept hotel, with 57 rooms (ask for one on 2nd or 3rd floor as lower rooms look out on neighbouring walls), good vegetarian restaurant, friendly staff.

$ Greenlands, St Mary's Rd, Coaker's Walk end, T04542-240899, www.greenlands kodaikanal.com. Clean, small and friendly budget traveller choice. 15 very basic, clean rooms (jug and bucket of hot water 0700-0900), amazing views. A few newish rooms are less atmospheric but have hot water on tap. Pleasant gardens, 62-bed dorm (Rs 55-65).

$ Hilltop Towers, Club Rd, T04542-240413, www.hilltopgroup.in. 26 modern, properly cleaned and comfortable rooms, some noise from passing buses and limited hours for hot water, but the management are very obliging and the complex contains a slew of good restaurants. Recommended.

$ Kodai Plaza, St Anthoia Koil St (walk uphill from bus stand and turn left down steep narrow lane), T04542-240423. The cheapest choice around the bus stand, rooms not the cleanest but survivable, and some have good views of distant peaks framed by fluttering prayer flags.

$ Vignesh, Laws Ghat Rd, near lake, T04542-244348. Old period-style house, 6 spacious rooms (can interconnect), good views, garden setting. Recommended.

$ Youth Hostel (TTDC), Fernhill Rd, T04542-241336. Rooms and dorm beds.

Anamalai (Indira Gandhi) Wildlife Sanctuary *p110*

There are several Forest Department rest houses scattered around Top Slip and other parts of the sanctuary including Mt Stuart, Varagaliar, Sethumadai and Amaravathinagar May allow only 1 night's stay. Reservations: District Forest Officer, Coimbatore S Div, 176 Meeanakalai Salai, Pollachi, T04259-225356. The friendly canteen in Top Slip serves good *dosa* and *thalis* for lunch.

$ Sakti, 144 Coimbatore Main Rd, T04259-223050, Pollachi. Newish, large and smart, rooms, vegetarian restaurant.

Dindigul p110

$$ Cardamom House, Athoor village, Kamarajar Lakeside, T0451-255 6765, www.cardamomhouse.com. This pretty home of a retired British doctor from Southsea introduces you to Tamil village life in Athoor and is a good bridge for journeys between either Kerala and Tamil Nadu or Trichy and Madurai. Tucked out of the way at the foothills of the Palani hills overlooking the lake, which is rich in birdlife, 7 rooms spread across 3 buildings all with lake views.

$$-$ Maha Jyothi, Spencer Compound, T0451-243 4313, hotelmahajyothi@ rediffmail.com. Range of rooms, a/c, clean, modern, 24-hr check out.

$ Prakash, 9 Thiruvalluvar Salai, T0451-242 3577. 42 clean, spacious rooms. Recommended.

$ Sukanya Lodge, 43 Thiruvallur Salai (by bus stand), T0451-242 8436. Small, rather dark a/c rooms, but very clean, friendly staff, good value.

$ Venkateshwar Lodge, near bus stand, T0451-242 5881. Very cheap, 50 rooms, basic, clean, vegetarian restaurant next door.

❼ Restaurants

Udhagamandalam (Ooty) p102, map p103

There are usually bars in larger hotels. Southern Star is recommended, but pricey.

$$$ Savoy (see Where to stay). Old-world wood-panelled dining hall serving up and good food. Also has bar, café, snooker and table tennis halls.

$$ Chandan Vegetarian, Nahar Nilgiris, Charing Cross, T0423-244 2173. 1230-1530, 1900-2230. Roomy restaurant inside the Nahar hotel complex serving up vegetarian North Indian and Chinese food.

$$ The Pavilion, Fortune Hotel, 500 m from town, Sullivan Court, 123 Shelbourne Rd, T0423-244 1415. In modern hotel, good multi-cuisine plus separate bar.

$ Blue Hills, Charing Cross. Good-value Indian and continental, non-vegetarian.

$ Garden Café, Nahar Nilgiris, Charing Cross. 0730-2130. Lawn-side coffee shop and snack bar with South Indian menu: *iddli*, *dosa* and *chats* from Rs 30.

$ Hot Breads, Charing Cross. Tasty hot dogs, pizzas, etc.

$ Hotel Ooty Saravanaa's, 302 Commercial Rd. 0730-1000, 1130-2230. The place for super-cheap south Indian breakfast: large mint green place that does a fast trade in *iddli*, *dosa* and meals.

$ Sharma Bhojanalaya 12C Lower Bazar Rd. Gujarati and North Indian food served upstairs in comfortable (padded banquettes) but not aesthetically pleasing venue, overlooks race course, good vegetarian lunch *thali* (Rs 40).

$ Shinkow's, 38/83 Commissioner's Rd (near Collector's Office) T0423-244 2811. 1200-1545, 1830-2145. Authentic Chinese, popular, especially late evening. Chicken chilli Rs 120. Tartan tablecloths and fish tank. Highly recommended.

Cafés

Try local institutions Sugar Daddy and King Star (established in 1942), 1130-2030, for brilliant home-made chocolates such as fruit'n'nut and fudges.

Coonoor p104

$$ Velan Hotel Ritz, Bedford, T0423-223 0632. 0730-1030, 1230-1530, 1930-2230. Good multi-cuisine restaurant overlooking the Ritz's lawns – don't expect speedy service, though.

$ The Only Place, Sim's Park Rd. Simple, homely, good food.

$ Sri Lakshmi, next to bus station. Freshly cooked, quality vegetarian; try paneer butter masala and Kashmiri naan.

Mettupalayam p105

Karna Hotel in the bus station is good for *dosas*.

Coimbatore p106

$$$ Cloud Nine, City Tower Hotel (see Where to stay). Excellent views from rooftop of one of city's tallest buildings, good international food (try asparagus soup), buzzing atmosphere especially when it's full of families on Sun evening, pleasant service but slightly puzzling menu.

$$ Dakshin, Shree Annapoorna Hotel Complex, 47 East Arokiasamy Rd, RS Puram. International. Very smart, serving good food.
$$ Solai Drive-in, Nehru Stadium, near VOC Park. Chinese, Indian food and good ice creams.
$ Indian Coffee House, Ramar Koil St. South Indian snacks.
$ Royal Hindu, opposite Junction station. Indian vegetarian.

Kodaikanal *p107, map p108*
$$$ Carlton Hotel, set in very pleasant grounds overlooking lake and Garden Manor. Good for tea and snacks.
$$ Royal Tibet Hotel, J's Heritage complex, PT Rd. Noodle soup and momos.
$$ Silver Inn, Hospital Rd. Travellers' breakfasts and Indian choices. Popular but slow service.
$$ Tava, Hospital Rd. Very good Indian.
$$ Tibetan Brothers Hotel, J's Heritage Complex. 1200-2200 (closed 1600-1730). Serves excellent Tibetan, homely atmosphere, good value. Highly recommended.

Bakeries and snacks

Eco-Nut, J's Heritage Complex. Good wholefoods, brown bread, jams, peanut butter, etc (cheese, yoghurts, better and cheaper in dairy across the road).
Hot Breads, J's Heritage Complex. For very good pastries.
Pastry Corner, Anna Salai Bazar. Brown bread, pastries and chocolate brownies, plus a couple of tables out the front.
Philco's Cold Storage, opposite Kodai International School. For home-made chocolate, cakes, frozen foods, delicatessen. Also internet.
Spencer's Supermarket, Club Rd. Wide range of local and foreign products (cheeses).

Dindigul *p110*
Cascade Roof Garden, at Sree Arya Bhavan, 19 KHF Building, near the bus stand. Serves very good vegetarian.
Janakikarm, near new Roman Catholic church. Don't miss their pizzas, sweets and snacks, surprisingly good value, "*channa samosa* to die for".

✹ Festivals

Udhagamandalam (Ooty) *p102, map p103*
Jan Pongal.
May The Annual Flower and Dog Shows in the Botanical Gardens. Summer Festival of cultural with stars from all over India.

Kodaikanal *p107, map p108*
May Summer Tourist Festival: boat race, flower show, dog show, etc.

○ Shopping

Udhagamandalam (Ooty) *p102, map p103*
Most shops open 0900-1200, 1500-2000. The smaller shops keep longer hours.
Higginbotham's, Commercial Rd, T0423-244 3736. 0930-1300, 1550-1930, closed Wed. Bookseller.
Toda Showroom, Charing Cross. Sells silver and tribal shawls.
Variety Hall, Silver Market. Old family firm (1890s) for good range of silk, helpful, accepts credit cards.

Kodaikanal *p107, map p108*
Belgian Convent Shop, east of town. Hand-embroidered linen.
Cottage Crafts Shop, Anna Salai (Council for Social Concerns in Kodai). Mon-Sat 0900-1230, 1400-1830. Volunteer-run.
Govt Sales Emporium, near Township Bus Stand. Only open in season.
Kashmir Handicrafts Centre, 2 North Shopping Complex, Anna Salai. Jewellery, brass, shawls, walnut wood crafts and Numdah rugs.

Potter's Shack, PT Rd. Lovely earthy cups and vases made by local potters Subramaniam and Prabhu under tutelage of Ray and Deborah Meeker of Puducherry. Visits to the workshop can be arranged, and proceeds go to help disadvantaged children.

🅾 What to do

Udhagamandalam (Ooty) *p102, map p103*
Horse riding
Gymkhana Club, T0423-244 2254. Big bar open 1130-1530 or 1830-2300. Temporary membership; beautifully situated amidst superbly maintained 18-hole golf course. Riding from Regency Villa: Rs 500 for 2 hrs with 'guide'; good fun but no helmets.

Tour operators
Tours can be booked through the **TTDC**, at Hotel Tamil Nadu, T0423-244 4370. Ooty and Mudumalai: Ooty Lake, Dodabetta Peak, Botanical Gardens, Mudumalai Wildlife Sanctuary. 0830-2000. Rs 150. Kotagiri and Coonoor: Kotagiri, Kodanad View Point, Lamb's Rock, Dolphin's Nose, Sim's Park. 0830-1830. Rs 130.
Blue Mountain, Nahar Complex, Charing Cross, T0423-244 3650. Luxury coach bookings to neighbouring states.
George Hawkes, 52C Nahar Complex, T0423-244 2756. For tourist taxis.
Sangeetha Travels, 13 Bharathiyar Complex, Charing Cross, T0432-244 4782. Steam train.
Woodlands Tourism, Race Course Rd, T0423-244 2551. Ooty and Coonoor. 0930-1730. Rs 130. Stunning views.

Yoga
Rajayoga Meditation Centre, 88 Victoria Hall, Ettines Rd.

Coonoor *p104*
TTDC from Ooty (reserve in Ooty Tourist Office). Coonoor–Kotagiri Rs 120, 6 hrs; visiting Valley View, Sim's Park, Lamb's Rock, Dolphin's Nose, Kodadu viewpoint.

Coimbatore *p106*
Alooha, corner near **Heritage Inn**. Helpful travel agency.

Kodaikanal *p107, map p108*
Boating
Boat Club, T04542-241315. Rents out pedal boats, 6-seater row boats and romantic Kashmir-style *shikaras*, Rs 40-160 per 30 mins plus boatman fees. The boatmen here are friendly and speak good English. 0900-1730.
TTDC Boat House, next door. Similar services and prices. 0900-1730.

Golf
Golf club, T04542-240323. Kodai's forest-swathed course is one of the most beautiful and (out of season) peaceful in the world, and the greens and fairways are maintained with minimal watering and no chemical pesticides. A round costs Rs 200-250, club hire Rs 200.

Horse riding
Ponies for hire near the Boat House, Rs 300 per hr.

Tour operators
Several tour operators around town book similar sightseeing tours, at around Rs 85 for a half day, Rs 150 full day.
Vijay Tours, Anna Salai, T04542-241137.

Trekking
A reputable local guide is **Vijay Kumar**, T(0)9994-277373.

⊖ Transport

Udhagamandalam (Ooty) *p102, map p103*
Arrive early for buses to ensure a seat. They often leave early if full. Ghat roads have numerous hairpin bends which can have fairly heavy traffic and very bad surfaces at times. The Gudalur road passes through Mudumalai and Bandipur sanctuaries. You might see an elephant herd and other wildlife, especially at night.

Air The nearest airport is at Coimbatore, 105 km away. Taxis available.

Bus State government and private Cheran buses (T0423-244 3970) pull in to the bus stand, just south of the railway station and a 10-min walk from the town centre. Frequent buses to **Coimbatore** (every 20 mins, 0530-2000, 3½ hrs), **Coonoor** (every 10 mins, 0530-2045), and **Mettupalayam** (0530-2100, 2 hrs). Daily buses to **Bengaluru (Bangalore)** (0630-2000), **Mysore** (0800-1530, 3½-5 hrs), **Kozhikode** (0630-1515), **Chennai** (1630-1830), **Palani** (0800-1800), **Kanniyakumari** (1745), **Kodaikanal** (0630, 9½ hrs via magnificent route through Palani); **Puducherry** (1700); **Salem** (1300). Check timings. Several on the short route (36 km) to **Masinagudi** in Mudumalai, 1½ hrs on a steep and bendy but interesting road.

Train Ooty is the terminus of the Nilgiri Mountain Railway . 4 diesel trains a day run from Ooty to **Coonoor**, at 0915, 1215, 1400 and 1800; the 1400 *Ooty-Mettupalayam Passenger 56137* swaps to a steam loco at Coonoor and continues down the wonderfully scenic track to **Mettupalayam**. This train connects with the *Nilgiri Exp* to **Chennai** (for trains to Ooty, see Mettupalayam transport below). Book tickets well in advance. Railway station, T0423-244 2246. From **Mettupalayam** *Blue Mountain* (steam to **Coonoor**; then diesel to Ooty), 1 return train daily, see Mettupalayam transport, below.

Coonoor *p104*

Bus Frequent buses to **Ooty** (every 10 mins from 0530) some via Sim's Park and many via Wellington. Also regular services to **Kotagiri** and **Coimbatore** (every 30 mins) through **Mettupalayam**. Direct bus to **Mysore** (or change at Ooty).

Train Coonoor sits at the top of the most scenic section of the Nilgiri Mountain Railway; steam locos from Mettupalayam

terminate here, switching to diesel for the run into Ooty. Trains leave to **Ooty** at 0745, 1040, 1235 and 1630 (1½ hrs); and to **Mettupalayam** at 1515 (2½ hrs).

Mettupalayam *p105*

Train The *Nilgiri Express* from Chennai Central arrives in Mettupalayam at 0615, triggering a mad dash for tickets and seats on the tiny 'toy train' of the Nilgiri Mountain Railway, which departs for **Ooty** at 0710 (5 hrs). Only 30 tickets are available for same-day purchase on the toy train, so book as far in advance as possible. Note that the line is subject to landslides and washouts that can close the route for some months; check before travelling. If you're coming from Coimbatore, it is better to arrive in advance at Mettupalayam by bus (quicker and more frequent than local trains). If you have time to spare the engine sheds are interesting to look around. For **Chennai**: *Nilgiri Exp 12672*, 1945, 10½ hrs.

Mudumalai Wildlife Sanctuary *p106*

Bus Theppakadu is on the main Mysore–Ooty bus route. From **Mysore**, services from 0615 (1½-2 hrs); last bus to Mysore around 2000. From **Ooty** via **Gudalur** on a very winding road (about 2½ hrs); direct 20 km steep road used by buses, under 1 hr. Few buses between Theppakadu and Masinagudi.

Jeeps are available at bus stands and from lodges.

Coimbatore *p106*

Air Peelamedu Airport, 12 km centre, runs airport coach into town, Rs 25; taxis Rs 150-200; auto-rickshaw Rs 85. On Trichy Rd: **Air India**, T0422-239 9833, airport T0422-257 4623, 1000-1300, 1345-1730, to **Bengaluru (Bangalore)**, **Chennai**, **Delhi**, **Kochi**, **Kozhikode**, **Mumbai**. Jet Airways: 1055/1 Gowtham Centre, Avinashi Rd, T0422-221 2034, airport T0422-257 5375, to **Bengaluru (Bangalore)**, **Chennai**, **Mumbai**.

Bus City buses run a good service: several connect the bus stations in Gandhipuram with the Junction Railway Station 2 km south. No 20 goes to the airport (Rs 20).

There are 4 long-distance bus stations, off Dr Nanjappa Rd.

City or 'Town' Bus Stand in Gandhipuram. **Thiruvallur Bus Stand**, Cross Cut Rd. Computerized reservations T0422-226700, 0700-2100. Frequent Government Express buses to **Madurai** (5 hrs), **Chennai** (12 hrs), **Mysore** (6 hrs), **Ooty** (3 hrs), **Tiruchirappalli** (5½ hrs).

'Central' Bus Stand is further south, on corner of Shastri Rd. State buses to **Bengaluru (Bangalore)** and **Mysore**; **Ooty** via **Mettupalayam** (see below for train connection) and **Coonoor** every 20 mins, 0400-2400, 5 hrs.

Ukkadam Bus Stand, south of the city, serves towns within the state (**Pollachi, Madurai**) and in north Kerala (**Pallakad, Thrissur, Munnar**).

Taxi Tourist taxis and yellow top taxis are available at the bus stations, railway station and taxi stands. Rs 2.5 per km; for out-station hill journeys, Rs 3 per km; minimum Rs 30.

Train Junction Station, enquiries, T132, reservations, T131, 0700-1300, 1400-2030. **Bengaluru (Bangalore)**: *Tilak Exp 11014*, 0800, 7¼ hrs; *Bangalore Exp 12678*, 1245, 7 hrs; **Kanniyakumari**: *Kanyakumari Exp 16381*, 0010, 9 hrs. **Chennai**: *West Coast Exp 16628*, 0630, 9 hrs; *Kovai Exp 12676*, 1420, 7½ hrs. **Kochi (HT)**: *Ernakulam Exp 12677*, 1310, 4hrs; *Hyderabad-Kochi Exp 17030*, 0935, daily, 5½ hrs.

For **Ooty** best to take the bus to Mettupalayam (see above).

Salem *p106*
Bus The New Bus Stand, north of the hospital, off Omalur Rd, T0427-226 5917, has buses to all major towns in Tamil Nadu, Kerala and South Karnataka.

Train Salem Junction is the main train station. Enquiries, T132. Reservations,

T131, 0700-1300, 1400-2030. **Bengaluru (Bangalore)**: *Tilak Exp 11014*, 1040, 4½ hrs; *Bangalore Exp 12678*, 1535, 4 hrs. **Chennai (C)**: *Coimbatore–Chennai Exp 12680*, 0835, 5 hrs. **Madurai**: *Tuticorin Exp 16732*, not Tue, Wed, Sun, 0200, 5 hrs. For **Ooty**, *Nilgiri Exp 12671*, 0135, connects with narrow-gauge steam train from Mettupalayam.

Yercaud *p107*
Bus There are no local buses but some from Salem (1 hr) continue to nearby villages.

Kodaikanal *p107*, *map p108*
Bicycle hire There are several bike hire stands around the lake, charging Rs 10 per hr, Rs 100 per day for good new bikes.

Bus Check timings; reservations possible. To **Bengaluru (Bangalore)**, overnight, 12 hrs; **Chennai** (497 km) 12 hrs; **Coimbatore** (171 km) 6 hrs; **Dindigul** (90 km) 3½ hrs, via Kodai Rd; **Madurai** (120 km), 0730-1830, 4 hrs; **Kumily** (for Periyar NP), 5½ hrs, change buses at Vatigundu; **Palani** (65 km) 3 hrs; **Tiruchirappalli** (197 km) 6 hrs. To **Munnar** by bus takes 8 hrs, changing at Palani and Udhamalpet.

Taxi Unmetered taxis available for sight-seeing. Tourist taxis from agencies including Raja's, near Pastry Corner on Anna Salai, T04542-242422. Taxi transfer to **Munnar** costs around Rs 2200, or Rs 450 for a seat in a shared taxi.

Train Reservations counter off Anna Salai behind **Anjay** hotel, 0800-1200, 1430-1700, Sun 0800-1200. No Foreign Tourist Quota bookings. The nearest station is Kodai Rd, 80 km away. Taxi drivers at the station quote Rs 1000 to drop you in Kodai, but this price drops if you cross the road and look determined to catch a bus. **Hotel Tamil Nadu**, just south of the station, has rooms if you get stuck.

Anamalai (Indira Gandhi) Wildlife Sanctuary *p110*

Bus 3 daily buses connect **Top Slip** with Pollachi, which has connections to **Coimbatore** and **Palani**. To Top Slip: 0600, 1100, 1500 (but check timings); from Top Slip: 0930, 1300, 1830.

Dindigul *p110*

Bus Good and frequent bus service to **Tiruchirappalli**, **Chennai**, **Salem** and **Coimbatore** and long-distance connections.

Train Train to **Chennai (ME)** *Vaigai Exp 12636 (AC/ CC)*, 0730, 6¾ hrs via **Tiruchirappalli** 1½ hrs. To **Madurai** *Vaigai Exp 12635 (AC/CC)*, 1905, 1¼ hrs.

❶ Directory

Udhagamandalam (Ooty) *p102, map p103*

Banks ATMs congregate along Bank Rd and Commercial Rd. State Bank of India, on Bank Rd, deals in foreign exchange. **Internet** Gateways, 8/9 Moosa Sait Complex, Commercial Rd. Excellent, fast, ISDN lines, Rs 30 per hr. **Medical services** Govt Hospital, Hospital Rd, T0423-244 2212. **Post** Head Post Office, Collectorate and Telegraph Office, Town W Circle. **Useful contacts** Police, T100. Wildlife Warden, 1st floor, Mahalingam Building, T0423-244098, 1000-1730. Closed 1300-1400.

Coonoor *p104*

Banks Travancore Bank, Upper Coonoor (Bedford Circle) changes cash. South Indian Bank, Mount Rd, 1000-1400 changes cash and TCs. **Medical services** Lawley Hospital, Mt Rd, T0423-223 1050.

Coimbatore *p106*

Banks Several on Oppankara St. State Bank of India (exchange upstairs), and Bank of Baroda are on Bank Rd. **Medical services** Government Hospital, Trichy Rd. **Post** Near flyover, Railway Feeder Rd. **Useful contacts** Automobile Association, 42 Trichy Rd, T0422-222 2994.

Yercaud *p107*

Banks Banks with foreign exchange are on Main Rd. **Medical services** Govt Hospital, 1 km from bus stand; Providence Hospital, on road to Lady's Seat. **Post** On Main Rd.

Kodaikanal *p107, map p108*

Banks Several branches with ATMs on Anna Salai. Indian Bank does foreign exchange Hotel Tamil Nadu, has a counter for foreign exchange counter. **Medical services** Van Allan Hospital, T04542-241273, is recommended. Consultations (non-emergency): Mon-Fri 0930-1200, 1530-1630. Sat 1000-1200. Clean and efficient, good doctors. Government Hospital, T04542-241292. **Post** Head Post Office on Post Office Rd.

Madurai and around

Madurai is a maddening whirl of a temple town: the red-and-white striped sanctuary of the 'fish-eyed goddess' is a towering edifice crested by elaborate gaudy stucco-work *gopurams*, soundtracked by tinny religious songs, peopled by 10,000 devoted pilgrims prostrating themselves at shrines, lighting candles and presenting flower garlands to idols, seeking blessings from the temple elephant or palmistry on the shores of the Golden Lotus Tank. Even the city's town planning reflects the sanctity of the spot: surrounding streets radiate like bicycle spokes from the temple in the mandala architectural style, a sacred form of geometry. The centre seems all dust and cycle-rickshaws, but Madurai, as the second biggest city in Tamil Nadu, is also a modern industrial place that never sleeps. Around the city the area of fertile agricultural land is dotted with exotically shaped granite mountain ranges such as Nagamalai (snake hills) and Yanaimalai (elephant hills).

Madurai → *For listings, see pages 131-137. Phone code: 0452. Population: 922,900.*

There is the usual combination of messy crumbling buildings harking back to times of greater architectural aspirations, modern glass-and-chrome palaces, internet cafés, flower sellers, tailors and tinkers and Kashmiri antique and shawl dealers. Further out, in the leafy suburbs to the west and north across the Vaigai River, are museums, lakes and temple tanks. Allow at least two days to explore everything.

Arriving in Madurai

Getting there The airport is 12 km from town and is linked by buses, taxis and autos to the city centre. The railway station is within easy walking distance of many budget hotels (predatory rickshaw drivers/hotel touts may tell you otherwise). Hire an auto to reach the few north of the river. Most intercity buses arrive at the Mattuthavani Bus Stand 6 km northeast of the centre; those from Kodaikanal and destinations to the northwest use the Arapalayam Bus Stand, 3 km northwest. Both are linked to the centre by bus and auto. ▸▸ *See Transport, page 135.*

Getting around The city centre is compact and the temple is within easy walking distance of most hotels. Prepare for hordes of touts. To visit the sights around the city, buses and taxis are available.

Tourist information ① *W Veli St, T0452-233 4757, Mon-Fri 1000-1745*, has useful maps, tours (arranged through agents), guides for hire. Also at **Madurai Junction Railway Station** ① *Main Hall, 0630-2030*, and the airport counter during flight times.

Background

According to legend, drops of nectar fell from Siva's locks on this site, so it was named Madhuram or Madurai, 'the Nectar City'. The city's history goes back to the sixth century BC. Ancient Madurai, which traded with Greece and Rome, was a centre of Tamil culture, famous for its writers and poets during the last period of the three *Sangam* (Tamil 'Academies') nearly 2000 years ago.

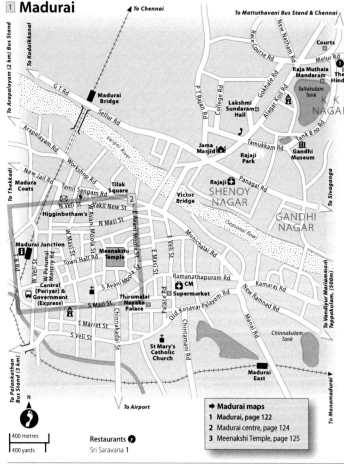

1 **Madurai**

→ **Madurai maps**
1 Madurai, page 122
2 Madurai centre, page 124
3 Meenakshi Temple, page 125

Restaurants 🍴
Sri Saravana 1

By the fourth century, Madurai, Tirunelveli and a part of southern Kerala were under the **Pandiyas**, a major power from the sixth to the early 10th century. The Pandiyas made Madurai their capital and remained here for 300 years, staying on even during the rule of the **Cholas**; after Chola power declined in the late 12th century the Pandiyas regained control of Madurai, and they presided over a period of flourishing international trade until Malik Kafur destroyed the city in 1310.

For a period Madurai became a sultanate, but Muslim rule in Tamil Nadu proved as short-lived as it was tenuous. In 1364 the city was recaptured by the Hindu Vijayanagar kings, who remained until 1565, when the defeat of the Vijayanagar Empire by a confederacy of Muslim states forced their leaders to take refuge in Madurai. As the **Nayaka** kings, they continued to rule well into the 17th century. The Nayakas have been seen essentially as warriors, given an official position by the Vijayanagar rulers, but in Sanskrit the term applied to someone of prominence and leadership. Burton Stein comments, "the history of the Vijayanagara is essentially the history of the great Telugu Nayakas" from Madurai.

The Vijayanagar had been great builders, preserving and enriching the architectural heritage of the town, and the Nayakas held true to their legacy. They laid out the old town in the pattern of a lotus, with narrow streets surrounding the Meenakshi Temple at the centre, and took up the Vijayanagar predilection for building temple complexes with tall *gopurams*. These increased in height to become dominating structures covered profusely with plaster decorations. The tall *gopurams* of Madurai were built by Thirumalai (ruled 1623-1655), the greatest of the Nayaka rulers, and may have served a strategic purpose as they moved away from the earlier Chola practice of giving the central shrine the tallest tower. The *kalyana mandapa* or marriage hall with a 'hundred' or 'thousand' pillars, and the temple tank with steps on all four sides, were introduced in some southern temples, along with the *Nandi* bull, Siva's vehicle, which occupies a prominent position at the entrance to the main Shaivite shrine.

In 1840, after the Carnatic Wars, the British destroyed the fort, filling in the surrounding moat; its original course is now followed by the four Veli streets. The inner streets encircling the central temple are named after the festivals which take place in them and give their relative direction: South 'Chitrai Street, East 'Avani Moola' Street and West 'Masi Street'.

Places in Madurai

Meenakshi Temple ① *Inner Temple 0500-1230, 1600-2130, foreigners Rs 50, camera Rs 50, tickets from counters near South Entrance and Thousand-Pillared Hall (valid for multiple entries on same day); art museum 0600-2030, Rs 5, camera fee Rs 50. Metal detectors and body searches at entrance gates. Sanctuaries of Meenakshi and Sundareswarar are open only to Hindus. Offers of good viewpoints made by helpful bystanders will invariably turn out to be from the roofs of nearby shops.* This is an outstanding example of Vijayanagar temple architecture and an exact contemporary of the Taj Mahal in Agra. Meenakshi, the 'fish-eyed goddess' and the consort of Siva, has a temple to the south, and Sundareswarar (Siva), a temple to the west. Since she is the presiding deity the daily ceremonies are first performed in her shrine and, unlike the practice at other temples, Sundareswarar plays a secondary role. The temple's nine towering *gopurams* stand out with their colourful stucco images of gods, goddesses and animals which are renewed and painted every 12 years – the most recent touch-up having been completed in February 2009. There are about 4000 granite sculptures on the lower levels. In addition to the Golden Lotus tank and various pillared halls there are five *vimanas* over the sanctuaries.

The temple is a hive of activity, with a colourful temple elephant, flower sellers and **musical performances** ① *1800-1930, 2100-2130*. There is an evening ceremony (arrive by 2100), when an image of Sundareswarar is carried in procession, to a heady accompaniment of whirling pipe and drum music and clouds of incense, from the shrine near the east *gopuram* to Meenakshi, to 'sleep' by her side; he is returned first thing the next morning. The procession around the temple is occasionally led by the elephant and a cow. During the day the elephant is on continual duty, 'blessing' visitors with its trunk and then collecting a small offering.

The main entrance is through a small door of the **Ashta Sakthi Mandapa (1)** (Porch of the Eight Goddesses) which projects from the wall, south of the eastern *gopuram*. Inside to the left is the sacred **Tank of the Golden Lotus (2)**, with a lamp in the centre, surrounded by pillared cloisters and steps down to the waters. The Sangam legend speaks of the test that ancient manuscripts had to undergo: they were thrown into the sacred tank, and only if they floated were they considered worthy of further study. The north gallery has murals (under restoration at the time of writing) relating 64 miracles said to have been performed by Siva, and the southern has marble inscriptions of the 1330 couplets of the *Tamil Book of Ethics*. To the west of the tank is the **Oonjal Mandapa (3)**, the pavilion leading to the Meenakshi shrine. Here the pillars are carved in the form of the mythical beast *yali* which recurs in temples throughout the region. Golden images of Meenakshi and Sundareswarar are brought to the *oonjal* or swing each Friday evening where they are worshipped.

② Madurai centre

Madurai maps
1 Madurai, page 122
2 Madurai centre, page 124
3 Meenakshi Temple, page 125

Where to stay 🛏
Gateway **14**
Germanus **3**
International **4**
Madurai Residency **5**
Park Plaza **6**
Royal Court **7**
Sulochna Palace **8**
Tamil Nadu **10**
TM Lodge **11**
Visakam Lodge **12**
YMCA **13**

Restaurants 🍴
Delhiwala Sweets **1**
Jayaram Sweets **2**
Sri Sabarees **4**

200 metres
200 yards

Cages with parrots, Meenakshi's green bird that brings luck, hang from the ceiling of the neighbouring **Kilikootu Mandapam (4)**, which is flanked by finely carved columns. The **Meenakshi shrine (5)** with the principal image of the goddess, stands in its own enclosure with smaller shrines around it.

To the north of the tank is another enclosure with smaller *gopurams* on four sides within which is the **Sundareswarar shrine (6)** guarded by two tall *dwarapalas*. In the northeast corner, the superb sculptures of the divine marriage of Meenakshi and Sundareswarar being blessed by Vishnu and Brahma, and Siva in his 24 forms are in the 19th-century **Kambathadi Mandapa (7)**, around the golden flagstaff.

The mid-16th century Thousand-pillared Hall (8) is in the northeast corner of the complex. The 985 exquisitely carved columns include a lady playing the *vina*, a dancing Ganesh, and a gypsy leading a monkey. The art museum here exhibits temple art and architecture, fine brass and stone images, friezes and photos (the labelling could be improved). Just inside the museum to the right is a cluster of five **musical pillars (9)** carved out of a single stone. Each pillar produces a different note which vibrates when tapped. Nayaka musicians could play these as an instrument.

The **Nandi pavilion (10)** is to the east and is often packed with market stalls peddling flowers, trinkets and coconuts. The long *Pudu Mandapa* (New Mandapa), across the road

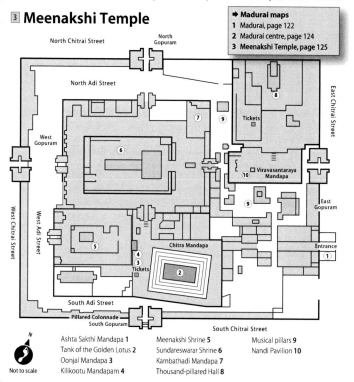

3 Meenakshi Temple

➡ **Madurai maps**
1 Madurai, page 122
2 Madurai centre, page 124
3 Meenakshi Temple, page 125

North Chitrai Street

North Gopuram

North Adi Street

East Chitrai Street

West Gopuram

8

7   9

Tickets

6

□ Viravasantaraya Mandapa

10

9

East Gopuram

West Chitrai Street

West Adi Street

5

4
3
Tickets

Chitra Mandapa

2

Entrance

1

South Adi Street

Pillared Colonnade
South Gopuram

South Chitrai Street

N

Not to scale

Ashta Sakthi Mandapa **1**
Tank of the Golden Lotus **2**
Oonjal Mandapa **3**
Kilikootu Mandapam **4**

Meenakshi Shrine **5**
Sundareswarar Shrine **6**
Kambathadi Mandapa **7**
Thousand-pillared Hall **8**

Musical pillars **9**
Nandi Pavilion **10**

from the East Tower, is lined with yet more beautiful sculptures of *yalis*, Nayaka rulers and elephants. Beyond lies the base of the unfinished *Raya Gopuram* which was planned to be the tallest in the country.

Northeast of the Meenakshi Temple, off N Avani Moola Street, is the **flower market**, a profusion of colour and activity at its best 0500-0730. It is a two-storey hall with piles of jasmine of all colours, lotuses, and huge jumbles of floral prettiness amid a sea of decomposing mulch of flowers trampled underfoot.

Thirumalai Nayaka Palace ① *0900-1300, 1400-1700, bus 17, 17A, 11, 11A*. Built in 1636 in the Indo-Mughal style, its 15 domes and arches are adorned with stucco work while some of its 240 columns rise to 12 m. Its *Swarga Vilasam* (Celestial Pavilion), an arcaded octagonal structure, is curiously constructed in brick and mortar without any supporting rafters. Special artisans skilled in the use of traditional lime plaster and powdered seashell and quartz have renovated parts. The original complex had a shrine, an armoury, a theatre, royal quarters, a royal bandstand, a harem, a pond and a garden but only about a quarter survives since Thirumalai's grandson removed sections to build another palace in Tiruchirappalli, and the original *Ranga* Vilasam was destroyed by Muslim invaders. It is a bit run down.

Vandiyur Mariammam Teppakulam ① *Buses 4 and 4A take 10 mins from the bus stand and railway station*. To the southeast of town, this has a small shrine in its centre where the annual **Float Festival** takes place in January/February.

Gandhi Museum ① *1000-1300, 1400-1730, free*. Located in the 300-year-old Rani Mangammal Palace, this is Madurai's best museum: informative, interesting and well laid out. It contains an art gallery, memorabilia (including the *dhoti* Gandhi was wearing when he was shot) and traces the history of the Independence struggle and the Quit India movement. It also has sections for Khadi and Village Industries and some stunning examples of South Indian handicrafts. Yoga classes are held daily (though only in Tamil) at 0630. Excellent bookshop.

Ramesvaram and around → *For listings, see pages 131-137.*

The conch-shaped island of Ramesvaram is normally lapped by the limpid blue waters of the Gulf of Mannar, but cyclones can whip the sea here into ferocious stormy waves. This is where Rama is believed to have worshipped Siva, making it sacred to both Shaivites and Vaishnavites, and so a pilgrim to Varanasi is expected to visit Ramesvaram next if he is to reach salvation. The great Ramalingesvara temple, which forms the core of the scrappy town, is one of India's most memorable, as much for the sight of priests spattering pilgrims with holy water from each of 22 sacred wells as for its cavernous, echoing corridors.

Arriving in Ramesvaram → *Phone code: 04573. Population: 38,000.*
Getting there Ramesvaram is connected to Madurai and other centres by regular bus and train services. The bus stand is 2 km from the centre, the railway station 1 km southwest of the great temple. There are also daily tours from Madurai.

Getting around Local buses and auto-rickshaws link the bus and train stations to the temple, where there are a few places to stay. ▶▶ *See Transport, page 136.*

Tourist information Tourist office ① *at bus stand, T04573-221371, 1000-1700. Also at* the **Railway Station** ① *T04573-221373, open (with some breaks) 0700-2030.* The **Temple Information** is on the east side of the temple.

Background

The *Ramayana* tells how the monkey king Hanuman built the bridges linking Ramnad to Pamban and Danushkodi (a spot where Rama is believed to have bathed) to help Rama rescue Sita from the demon king Ravana. When Rama returned he was told by the *rishis* that he must purify himself after committing the sin of murdering a Brahmin, for *Ravana* was the son of a Brahmin. To do this he was advised to set up a *lingam* and worship Siva. The red image of Hanuman north of the main East Gate illustrates this story.

The original shrine long predates the present great Ramesvaram temple. It is one of India's most sacred shrines and is visited by pilgrims from all over India. The temple benefited from huge donations from the 17th-century *Setupatis* (the so-called guardians of the causeway), who derived their wealth from the right to levy taxes on crossings to the island. The temple stands on slightly higher ground, surrounded by a freshwater lake.

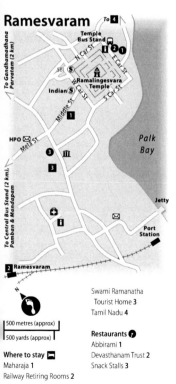

Ramesvaram

Swami Ramanatha
Tourist Home **3**
Tamil Nadu **4**

Restaurants ⊘
Abbirami **1**
Devasthanam Trust **2**
Snack Stalls **3**

Where to stay ⊟
Maharaja **1**
Railway Retiring Rooms **2**

To Ramesvaram and Adam's Bridge

Seen from the air the plains of the Vaigai River form one of the most remarkable landscapes in India, for there are over 5000 tanks, and irrigation has been so developed that barely a drop of water is wasted. The coastal districts of Ramnad have their own highly distinct economy and society. For the Hindus the sandbanks barely concealed in the Palk Strait are like giant stepping stones linking India and Sri Lanka: Adam's Bridge. Both Hindu and Muslim communities have long-established trading links across the Bay of Bengal, to Malaysia and Southeast Asia and to Sri Lanka. Small settlements along the coast like Kilakkarai have long been associated with smuggling. The civil war in Sri Lanka has made it a sensitive region.

Ramesvaram

The **Ramalingesvara** (or **Ramanathasvami**) **Temple** was founded by the Cholas but most of the temple was built in the Nayaka period (16th-17th centuries). It is a massive structure, enclosed by a huge rectangular wall with *gopurams* in the middle of three sides. Entrances through the east wall are approached through columned *mandapas* and the east *gopuram* is on the wall of the inner enclosure rather than the outer wall. Over 45 m high, it was begun in 1640 but

Holy dips

Having bathed in the Ganga at Varanasi, Hindu pilgrims head straight for Rameshvaram, where a bath in the 22 *theertham* (holy wells) dotted within and around the Ramalingesvara temple promise a final release from the chains of *karma*.

The *theertham* circuit is a festive event for the pilgrims, complete with much cheering and song as buckets are emptied over heads, and as a visitor it can offer one of the most atmospheric and memorable temple experiences in Tamil Nadu, especially if you can get yourself adopted by a group of Indian visitors. The locals tend to bring along a change of clothes and submit to a thorough drenching, but if you come overdressed it is possible to request a light sprinkle.

It's also traditional, but not obligatory, to taste of the waters; each apparently has a distinct flavour.

Brahmin priests wait at the train and bus stations and along the shoreline east of the temple to greet new arrivals, but he haggling of old has now been replaced by a standard charge of Rs 51 per person, which includes a dunking in each of the wells and access to the inner sanctum. Non-Hindus are traditionally prevented from entering the sanctum, but if you dress appropriately and arrive with a group (day tours from Madurai are an all-but-guaranteed way to join one) there's a good chance the priests will allow you in. If you do the circuit alone, it's best to leave valuables outside the temple: bystanders who offer to watch your bags are not all trustworthy.

left incomplete until recently. On entering, you see the statue of Hanuman, then the *Nandi* flanked by statues of the Nayaka kings of Madurai, Visvanatha and Krishnama. The north and south *gopurams* were built by Keerana Rayar of the Deccan in about AD 1420; the west *gopuram* is comparatively new.

The most remarkable feature of the temple is its pillared *mandapas*, the longest of which is over 200 m long. The pillars lining the four corridors, nearly 4 m tall, give an impression of almost unending perspective: those on the north and south sides are particularly striking. Tragically, however, the original stone pillars, decorated with scrollwork and lotus motifs, are being progressively phased out in favour of graceless grey concrete facsimiles. You're only likely to see the original versions lying on the ground in piles.

There are two gateways on the east side which give access to the Parvati and Ramalinga shrines at the centre; the masonry shrine is probably the oldest building on the site, going back to 1173. Non-Hindus are generally turned away, but you might be able to enter if you can tag along with a group of pilgrims doing the holy well circuit (see box, above).

Gandhamadana Parvatam

Gandhamadana Parvatam, 2 km north of Rameshvaram, takes its name from the Sanskrit words *gandha* (fragrance) and *mad* (intoxicate), 'highly fragrant hill'. Dedicated to Rama's feet, this is the spot from which Hanuman is believed to have surveyed the area before taking his leap across the narrow Palk strait to Sri Lanka. You can get an excellent view from the top of the *mandapa*.

Dhanuskodi

Dhanuskodi ('the end of the bow') is the island's toe-tip where the Bay of Bengal meets the Indian Ocean, so named because Rama, at the request of Vibishana, his friend, destroyed the bridge to Sri Lanka with the end of his bow. Some 20 km to the east of Ramesvaram island, it is considered particularly holy. There is a good beach, on which pilgrims will be making *puja*, and beautiful flat turquoise waters in which they take their holy bath, not to mention excellent views. A trip across the scrappy sand dunes is only recommended for the really hardy – get a local person to go with you. Travel by bus, and then join a pilgrim group on a jeep or lorry for the last desolate few miles (this should cost Rs 50 for a round trip but establish the price up front). Alternatively, take an auto to Adam's Bridge; insist on going as far as the radio mast for beach and fishing shack photos.

Cardamom Hills → *For listings, see pages 131-137.*

To the south of Madurai is a series of modest towns situated in the lee of the southern ranges of the Western Ghats. From Madurai to Thiruvanathapuram is a comfortable day's drive either via Tirunelveli or over the ghats, but there are several interesting places on the way if you wish to take your time.

Rajapalayam

ⓘ *To Sankaracoil, Rs 12, 30 mins; from there to Kalugumalai, Rs 8, 30 mins, buses to and from Tenkasi, Rs 30, 2 hrs.*

The town originated on the dispersal of the Vijayanagar families after 1565. The Sankarankovil temple is worth visiting. The Western Ghats rise to heights of over 1200 m immediately behind the town. Wild elephants still come down through the forests, devastating farmland.

Tenkasi

ⓘ *To Courtallam Falls frequent buses, Rs 8, to Courtallam Bus Stand, then walk through the grey arch to the 'Main Falls'. See Rajapalayam, above, for transport to Tenkasi.*

Literally the 'Kashi (Varanasi) of the South', Tenkasi is the nearest town to the Kuttalam (Courtallam) Falls, 6 km away. The impressive 16th-century Visvanatha temple dedicated to Siva has some fine carvings inside. The temple flagstaff is believed to be 400 years old. From Tenkasi the road goes through a low pass into the densely forested hills of Kerala.

Courtallam (Kuttalam)

With average temperatures of 22-23°C, Courtallam is a very popular health resort, especially during the monsoon. The impressive **Main Falls** is in town where the river Chittar cascades over 92 m. The approach is lined with spice, banana chips and knick-knack stalls and at the falls you'll find pilgrims washing themselves and their clothes. The waters, widely believed to have great curative powers, draw big crowds at the **Saral Festival** in July. The **Thirukutralanathar Temple** contains old inscriptions while the small **Chitra Sabha Temple** nearby contains religious murals.

Virudhunagar

The name Virudhupatti (Hamlet of Banners) was changed to Virudhunagar (City of Banners) in 1915, and was upgraded to a full municipality in 1957, reflecting the upwardly mobile social status of the town's dominant local caste, the Nadars. Originally low caste toddy tappers, they have established a wide reputation as a dynamic and enterprising group. The powerful Congress leader, Kamaraj Nadar, was chiefly responsible for Indira Gandhi's selection as prime minister.

Kalugumalai

Some 6 km south of Kovilpatti, Kalugumalai (Kazhugumalai) has a profusion of magnificent fifth-century bas-relief Jain figures on a huge rock which are well worth the detour. The Jain temple is to the north of the rock and is easily missed. There is also an unfinished monolithic cave temple to Siva (circa AD 950).

Chettinad → *For listings, see pages 131-137.*

The magnificent palaces of South India's old merchant and banking classes rise from the hot and dusty plains to stand as strong as fortresses and as gaudy as a packet of French Fancies. As the merchants, bankers and money-lenders of the British Empire, the Nattukottai Chettiars raked in enormous riches on their postings to places such as Burma, Sri Lanka, Indochina and South Africa, wealth they ploughed into these glorious architectural pastiches that explode in a profusion of colour in the arid desert-scape.

Now their monumental arches and long processional corridors open onto empty halls, the bats are more at home here than princes and shafts of light break on empty, cob-webbed dining rooms. The Nattukottai Chettiars saw their riches contract with the Second World War and the wanton palaces they built turned into tombstones, the series of south Indian villages they stand in left as virtual ghost towns. Architectural salvage merchants in the main town of Karaikkudi now sell off the portraits and granite pillars this proud caste have been forced to surrender to stave off financial hardship, while Bollywood crews make regular pilgrimages to the old mansions, propping up the owners with *lakhs* of studio rupees in return for the right to daub their chosen colour scheme across the walls.

Karaikkudi is in the heart of Chettinad, and has several typical mansions, particularly along the back lanes leading off busy Sekkalai Road (ask for the Thousand Window House, a well-known landmark). From here you can walk south to the local *santhai* (market), where you can find gold and silversmiths in their workshops, as well as antique and textile shops and several colourful temples.

Devakottai, 18 km south of Karaikkudi, is Chettinad's second largest town and offers similarly rich pickings in the way of old mansions and palaces: look out for the particularly grand Periya Minor's *veedu*.

Kanadukathan, 12 km north of Karaikkudi, has a number of magnificent mansions – some still inhabited by friendly owners (who'll let you have a look around for a Rs 100 donation), others are empty except for bats, monkeys and antique dealers. It has been estimated that the Burma teak and satinwood pillars in a single Chettiar house weighs 300 tonnes, often superbly carved. The plaster on the walls is made from a mixture of lime, egg white, powdered shells and myrobalan fruit (the astringent fruit of the tree *Phyllantles emblica*), mixed into a paste which, when dried, gives a gleaming finish. Most houses have the goddess of wealth, Lakshmi, made of stucco over the main arch.

The **Raja of Chettinad's Palace** ① *0930-1630, free, caretakers provide brief free tours*, is an amazing place overlooking the town's pond and full of sepia, larger-than-life-size portraits of stern family members, the frames garlanded with heavy yellow flowers. Next door is **Visalakshi Ramaswamy's house**, with a museum of local crafts, artefacts and handlooms upstairs. The raja's waiting room at the railway station is also pretty special.

Athangudi, 9 km away, is renowned for its tiles, which grace the floors of most Chettiar mansions; ask locally if you want to visit one of the 30-40 workshops in town. Nearby is Pillaiyarpatti, one of the most important temples in Chettinad, dedicated to Ganesh (known as Pillaiyaru in Tamil Nadu) and with an inner sanctum carved into a natural boulder.

At **Avudayarkoil**, 30 km northeast of Karaikkudi, the **Athmanathar Temple** has one of the most renowned sites in Tamil history. A legend tells that Manickavaskar, a Pandyan prime minister, redirected money intended for the purchase of horses to build the temple. However, his real fame lies as author of the *Thiruvasakam* ('Holy Outpourings'), one of the most revered Tamil poetic texts. Completely off the beaten track, the temple has superb sculptures, and is noted for the absence of any images of Siva or Parvati, the main deities, whose empty pedestals are worshipped. The woodcarvings on the temple car are notable too.

Pudukkottai and around

Pudukkottai, on the northern edge of Chettinad, 50 km south of Trichy, was the capital of the former princely state ruled by the Tondaiman Rajas, founded by Raghunatha Raya Tondaiman in 1686. At one entrance to the town is a ceremonial arch raised by the raja in honour of Queen Victoria's jubilee celebrations. The town's broad streets suggest a planned history; the temple is at the centre, with the old palace and a tank. The new palace is now the District Collector's office.

Thirukokarnam, 5 km north of the railway station, is the site of the rock-cut **Sri Kokarnesvarar Temple** ① *closed 1200-1600*, dates from the Pallava period. The natural rock shelters, caves, stone circles, dolmens and Neolithic burial sites show that there was very early human occupation. The local **museum** ① *Big St, open daily except except Fri, 2nd Sat of the month, public holidays, 0930-1700, free, allow 40 mins, recommended*, has a wide range of exhibits including sections on geology, zoology and the economy as well as sculptures and the arts. The archaeology section has some excellent sculptures from nearby temples. There is a notable carving of Siva as *Dakshinamurti* and some fine bronzes from Pudukkottai itself.

Sittannavasal, 13 km away, has a Jain cave temple (circa eighth century) with sculptures, where monks took shelter when they fled from persecution in North India. In a shrine and veranda there are some fine frescoes in the Ajanta-style and bas-relief carvings. You can also see rock-hewn beds of the monks. The *Brahmi* inscriptions date from the second century BC.

Madurai and around listings

For hotel and restaurant price codes and other relevant information, see pages 14-18.

⊙ Where to stay

Madurai *p131, maps p122 and p124*
Tax of up to 20% is added even by modest hotels. Cheap hotels line up along and around West Peramul Maistry St, 2 blocks east of the railway station, but rooms can be hard to find by late afternoon. Most offer 24-hr checkout. Although there are slick hotels across the Vaigai these are not good value as they lack character and are away from the town's atmosphere. It's best to visit Madurai either from the charming remove of the hilltop **Taj**, or abandon yourself to the throng and take a room near the temple.

$$$$ Gateway (Taj), Pasumalai Hills, 7 TPK Rd, 5 km southwest of centre on NH7, T0452 663 3000, www.thegatewayhotels.com. A real oasis, set on top of a hill with great views over surrounding country. The 30 rooms (some set in an old colonial house) set among shady gardens full of peacocks. There's a good bookshop and lovely pool.

$$$ Heritage Madurai, 11, Melakkal Main Road, Kochadai, T0452-238 5455, www. heritagemadurai.com. Stunning new resort set in the banyan-shaded refuge of the Madurai Club. Standard rooms are big and full of light, while the good value villas come with your own pool and personal chef. A spectacular step-well pool and good restaurants are well worth the 4-km trek to the temple.

$$$-$$ Germanus, 28 By-Pass Rd, T0452-435 6999, www.hotelgermanus.com. Functional and well-run though slightly dated business hotel with quiet, bright and well-equipped rooms. Excellent rooftop restaurant (1900-2300) serves Chettinad specialities. Choose rooms at the rear to save you from the busy roundabout in front.

$$$-$$ Park Plaza, 114 W Perumal Maistry St, T0452-301 1111. Some of the 56 smart, 60s-print, stylish a/c rooms offer temple views, breakfast included, excellent rooftop restaurant (1700-2300), bar, all facilities. Free pick-up from airport/railway station.

$$$-$$ Royal Court, 4 West Veli St, T0452-435 6666, www.royalcourtindia.com. 70 extremely clean a/c rooms with bath, satellite TV and great views from rooftop (open 1900-2300), good value.

$$ Supreme, 110 W Perumal Maistry St, T0452-234 3151, www.hotelsupreme.in. 69 slightly tatty but adequately clean rooms with marble and plastic furniture, 31 a/c, good rooftop restaurant, **Surya**, with temple views, bar, 24-hr travel desk, exchange, internet booths in the basement, a bit noisy and a mite overpriced. Security and service both wanting.

$$-$ The Madurai Residency, 14-15 West Marret St, T0452-438 0000, www.madurairesidency.com. Rather grand for Madurai: 75 rooms over 7 floors, glass lift. Economy rooms better than a/c due to musty smell.

$ Hotel Tamil Nadu, West Veli St, T0452-233 7471, htn-mdu1@ttdconline.com. Mint-coloured guesthouse dating from 1968 set around courtyard attached to the friendly TN tourist office. In bad need of a new lick of paint – it's pretty grubby – but there are TVs, huge rooms and the staff are charming.

$ International, 46 W Perumal Maistry St, T0452-437 7463. Friendly, 34 clean and tidy rooms with TV and views from upper floors. Tends to have rooms when others are full.

$ Sulochna Palace, 96 W Perumal Maistry St, T0452-234 1071. Good-value, clean rooms, and slightly more salubrious than the nearby bottom-bracket options. Avoid lower floors where generator noise is obtrusive.

$ TM Lodge, 50 W Perumal Maistry St, T0452-234 1651. 57 rooms (hot water), some a/c, some with TV, balcony, very clean, bookings for rail/bus journeys. Glowing reports.

$ YMCA International Guest House, Main Guard Sq, near temple, T0452-234 0861, www.ymcamadurai.com. A great option within spitting distance of the temple. The double rooms here are simple but spacious and clean, the staff are friendly, and profits go to worthwhile projects.

$ Visakam Lodge, 9 Kakathope St, T0452-234 1241. Good-value place with 18 clean rooms, very popular with Indian tourists.

Ramesvaram *p126, map p127*

$ Hotel Tamil Nadu (TTDC), 14 East Car St, T04573-221064. Sea-facing balconies, 53 rooms (2-6 beds), some a/c, close, grubby restaurant (breakfast from 0700), bar, sea bathing nearby, exchange. Very popular; book well in advance.

$ Maharaja, 7 Middle St, west of the Temple, T04573-221271. 30 rooms, some a/c with bath, exchange, temple music broadcast on loudspeakers, otherwise recommended.

$ Railway Retiring Rooms, T04573-221226. 9 rooms and dorm.

$ Swami Ramanatha Tourist Home, opposite museum, T04573-221217. Good clean rooms with bath, best budget option.

Chettinad *p130*

Chettinad is still largely uncharted territory, and the few really good places to stay are priced towards the higher end. A handful of cheaper options exist in Karaikkudi and other towns, but they do not have the guides on hand to gain access to the old private homes (without whose help the Raja of Chettinad's palace may be the only house you look inside).

$$$$ Visalam, Kanadukathan, T04565-273302, www.cghearth.com. Romantic and supremely comfortable high-celinged rooms, sparely furnished with Chettiar writing desks and 4-posters, in a beautifully restored art deco mansion – the only one in Chettinad built for a girl. The chef serves banana leaf lunches and does cooking demonstrations, good local guides are available for walking and bike tours, plus there's a huge pool and lawns.

$$$ The Bangala, Senjai, T04565-220221, www.thebangala.com. 8 bright and spacious a/c rooms with period colonial furniture, in restored 1916 bungalow, a heritage guesthouse of character set amidst orchards and palms, serves full-on, totally authentic Chettinad feasts for a fair whack at Rs 800 per meal (must be booked in advance, rest stop facilities for day visitors and a full-board option. The family here wrote the (coffee table) book on Chettinad architecture.

$$$ Chettinadu Mansion, behind the raja's palace, Kanadukathan, T04565-273080; book through **Deshadan Tours and Travels**, T0484-232 1518, www.chettinadumansion. com. Dating back to 1902, this stunning house takes up half the block, with courtyard after courtyard stretching back from the street. Huge rooms, with a quirky green-brown colour scheme, heavy painted shutters and private rooftop sit-outs, encircle the upper floor. Downstairs is still used for family *pujas* and storing the wedding dowry. Simple Chettinad-style meals, served in the colonnaded dining room or under stars in the courtyard, cost Rs 450, and the charming Mr Chandramouli, who was born in the house, is often on hand to share stories or sharp business advice.

$ Golden Singar, 100 Feet Rd, Karaikuddi, T04565-235521. Remarkably clean and good-value marble-floored rooms (fan-

cooled half the price of a/c), handy for bus stand though a bit distant from the market and temples. Clean restaurant downstairs and cheap internet cafés nearby.

$ Hotel Udhayam, A-333 Sekkalai Rd, Karaikuddi, T04565-234068. Another decent cheap option, similar to the **Golden Singar** but closer to the action.

$ Nivaas, Devakottai, 1st left from bus station coming from the north (no sign in English), T04561-272352. Basic (no electric sockets), no English spoken.

❼ Restaurants

Madurai *p131, maps p122 and p124*
$$ Surya, Supreme (see Where to stay). Open 1600-2400. 7th-floor rooftop restaurant with international as well as Indian menu. Excellent Andhra *thalis*, very busy Sun evenings.

$$ Temple View, Park Plaza (see Where to stay). Excellent rooftop venue.

$ Delhiwala Sweets, W Tower St. Delicious Indian sweets and snacks.

$ Jayaram Sweets, 6-7 Netaji Rd. Good salty namkeens and fantastic coconut buns.

$ Sri Sabarees, corner of W Perumal Maistry St and Town Hall Rd. Serves simple South Indian fare – *thalis* (lunchtime only), *pongal*, *iddli* and *dosai* – but the 2 dining halls are perpetually packed, as is the coffee stall out front.

$ Sri Saravana, 7 Melur Rd, opposite Court. Delicious sweets (try the spectacular milk *peda*) and decent meals, across the river from town. Worth a diversion if you're at the Gandhi Museum.

Rameswaram *p126, map p127*
Don't expect anything other than *thalis* here. There are several popular snack stands, with signs only in Tamil, on the road between Mela St and the museum.
Abbirami Hotel, off East Car St on road towards beach. Neat place churning out lunchtime meals and tiffin (*dosas, vada* and the like) after 1500.

Devasthanam Trust has a canteen opposite the east gate of the temple.

🎬 Entertainment

Madurai *p131, maps p122 and p124*
Folk performances, in the 4 'Chitrai' streets by the temple, every Sat 1700-1800, free.
Meenakshi Temple: 'Bedtime of the God' 2100, is not to be missed (see page 124).
Thirumalai Nayaka Palace: Sound and Light show: English 1845-1930; Rs 5 (take mosquito repellent), sadly, "poor, faded tape". During the day, dance drama and concerts are held in the courtyard.

🎉 Festivals

Madurai *p131, maps p122 and p124*
Jan Jallikattu Festival (Taming the Bull).
Jan/Feb The annual Float Festival marks the birth anniversary of Thirumalai Nayaka. Many temple deities in silks and jewels, including Meenakshi and Sundareswarar, are taken out on a full moon night on floats decorated with hundreds of oil lamps and flowers. The floats carry them to the central shrine to the accompaniment of music and chanting.
Apr/May The 10-day Chitrai Festival is the most important at the Meenakshi Temple, celebrating the marriage of Siva and Meenakshi.
Aug/Sep The Avanimoolam is the Coronation Festival of Siva when the image of Lord Sundareswarar is taken out to the river bank dressed as a worker.

Pudukkottai *p131*
Jan/Feb Bullock races (*manju virattu*) are held in the area.

🛍 Shopping

Madurai *p131, maps p122 and p124*
Kashmiri emporia pay 40-50% commission to touts who lure you into their shops with spurious promises of views into the temple. Best buys are textiles, wood and stone carvings, brass images, jewellery and appliqué work for temple chariots. Most shops are on South Avani Moola St (for jewellery), Town Hall Rd, Masi St and around the temple.

Books
Higginbotham's Book Exchange, near the temple.
New Century Book House, 79-80 West Tower St. Recommended.

Handicrafts
Handicrafts Emporium, 39-41 Town Hall Rd. Also try: **Khadi Gramodyog Bhandar** and **Surabhi** on W Veli St.

Textiles and tailors
The market near Pudu Mandapam, next to Meenakshi East Gate. Sells fabric and is a brilliant place to get clothes made.
Femina, 10 W Chitrai St. Similar to the market (you can take photos of the Meenakshi Temple from their rooftop).
Hajee Moosa, 18 E Chitrai St. Tailoring in 8 hrs; 'ready-mades' at **Shabnam**, at No 17.

Chettinad *p130*
Antiques
Muneesvaran Kovil St in Karaikkudi is lined with antiques shops selling old sepia photographs, temple lamps, old advertising posters, scrap book matter, religious paintings and Czech pewter jars.
Kattu Raja's, Palaniappa Chettiar St.
Old Chettinad Crafters, Murugen Complex, 37/6 Muneesvaran Kovil St, Karaikkudi, T(0)98428-223060, chettinaduantiques@yahoo.co.in. One of the best.
VJ Murugesan, sells old wooden furniture, household articles, wooden pillars, glass.
Venkateswara Furniture and Timber Merchant, No 8 Keela Oorani West, Karaikkudi, T(0)98424-232112. If you're in the market for bigger objects and weight is no object, this architectural salvage yard is a good starting point. Bargain hard.

Cotton and fabrics

MM Street and The Weavers' Lane beside the Bangala have Chettinad cotton for sale straight off the loom. Ask locally for the next *sandais*, the colourful local weekly markets.

⚙ What to do

Madurai *p131, maps p122 and p124*
Body and soul
Yoga classes at Gandhi Museum, T0452-248 1060. Daily at 0630.

Tour operators

Tours can be arranged with TTDC, via Hotel Tamil Nadu, West Veli St, T0452-233 7471, or through most hotel desks. Temple tour of Madurai and attractive surroundings by a/c coach; half day, 0700-1200, 1500-2000. Rs 125. Recommended for an overview. Apr-Jun: Courtallam, Rs 300; Kodaikanal, 0700-2100, Rs 300; Rameswaram, Rs 275. Ex-Serviceman Travels, 1 Koodalalagar, Perumal Kovil St, T0452-273 0571, City tour, half day, 0700, 1500, Rs 140; Kodaikanal or Rameswaram 0700-1900, Rs 275; overnight to Kanniyakumari, Rs 350.
Indian Panorama (Trichy), T0431-422 6122, www.indianpanorama.in. Tours from Madurai (and other towns). The Pandians are very helpful, efficient, South India tours, car with excellent driver. Highly recommended. Siraj, 28 T P K Rd, opposite Periyar Bus Stand, T097 8859 6388. Ticketing, good multilingual guides, cars.

⊖ Transport

Madurai *p131, maps p122 and p124*
Air
Madurai's small airport is 12 km south of the centre. There are daily direct flights from Chennai, Bengaluru and Hyderabad, with connecting flights from Mumbai and New Delhi; you can also fly cheaply to Colombo with Spicejet. The 10A bus runs from the airport to the central Periyar bus stand. Taxis to the centre charge around Rs 375; an auto should cost Rs 150-200.

Airport to city centre (12 km) by Pandiyan coach (calls at top hotels); taxi (Rs 375) or auto-rickshaw (Rs 150). Air India, 7A W Veli St, T0452-234 1234. 1000-1300, 1400-1700; Airport, T0452-269 0433. Jet Airways, T0452-252 6969; airport T0452-269 0771.

Bus
Local There is a good network within the city and the suburbs. Central (Periyar) Bus Stands, near W Veli St, are now used for buses around town and destinations nearby. Approaching on a bus from the south, to get to the centre, change to a city bus at Tirumangalam (15 km south).
Long distance Most intercity buses use the well-organized New Central Bus Stand (Mattuthavani Bus Terminal), 6 km northeast of town (continuation of Alagar Koil Rd), T0452-258 0680; Rs 100 by rickshaw, or catch city buses 3, 48 or 700. Buses leave from here for Bengaluru (Bangalore) (11 hrs), Ernakulam (Kochi), Chennai (10 hrs), Puducherry (9 hrs), Thiruvananthapuram (8 hrs), Kumbakonum, Rameswaram (under 4 hrs, every 15 mins), Thanjavur (4 hrs), Tiruchirappalli (2½ hrs), Tirunelveli (4 hrs, Rs 40). Buses for the west and northwest leave from the Arapalayam Bus Stand, 3 km northwest of centre (Bus route No 7A, auto-rickshaws Rs 40), T0452-236 1740. Destinations include Kodaikkanal (3½ hrs, buses crowded in peak season Apr-Jul), Coimbatore (5 hrs, change for Mettupalayam and Ooty, Periyar/Kumily (4 hrs), Salem (5½ hrs), Dindigul (2 hrs).

Rickshaw
Autorickshaw rates are theoretically Rs 10-15 per km, but drivers quote excessive rates for trips around town. A cycle rickshaw from the station area to temple should cost around Rs 30.

Taxi/car hire

Most taxis are unmetered. Local car hire rates begin at 4 hrs/40 km Rs 700, 8 hrs/80 km Rs 1200. **FastTrack** T0452-288 8999.

Train

Madurai Junction is the main station: enquiries, T131. 0700-1300, 1330-2000. New Computer Reservation Centre to south of main entrance. Left-luggage facilities. Pre-paid auto-rickshaw kiosk outside. **Chennai (ME)** via Villupuram for **Puducherry**: *Vaigai Exp 12636*, 0630, 8 hrs; *Pandiyan Exp 12638*, 2045, 10 hrs. **Coimbatore**: *Coimbatore Exp 16609*, 0040, 7 hrs. **Kanniyakumari**: *Chennai-Guruvayoor Exp 16127*, 1640, 5 hrs. **Rameswaram**: 3 unreserved passenger trains a day, at 0010, 0615 and 1815, 3-4 hrs. **Tiruchirappalli**: several, *Vaigai Exp 12636*, 0630, 2½ hrs (beautiful countryside); *Pandiyan Exp 12638*, 2045, 3½ hrs.

Rameswaram *p126, map p127*
Bicycle hire

Bike hire from West Car or East Car St.

Bus

Local Marudhu Pandiyan Transport Corporation (MPTC) covers the town and area around. Bus station is 2 km west of town. Take a bus from the train station to the Ramalingesvara Temple, to Pamban or to Dhanushkodi. From the temple's east gate to Dhanuskodi roadhead and to Gandhamadana Parvatam, both every 2 hrs. **Long distance** State, MPTC and private bus companies run regular services via **Mandapam** to several towns nearby. Govt Express Bus Reservations, North Car St, 0700-2100. Frequent buses to **Madurai**, 173 km (4½ hrs); tourist coaches (hotel-to-hotel) are better.

Taxi

A few cars and jeeps are available from the train station and hotels.

Train

Rameswaram Railway Station, enquiries and reservations, T226. 0800-1300, 1330-1730. **Chennai**: *Sethu Exp 16714*, 2000, 12½ hrs, via **Karaikkudi**, 4 hrs, and **Villupuram** (for Puducherry), 9 hrs. **Madurai**: 3 unreserved passenger trains a day, at 0005, 0525, 1735. **Tiruchirappalli**: *Chennai Egmore Exp 16702*, 1700, 5½ hrs.

Virudhunagar *p129*

Bus Leave Madurai early morning to catch the Kollam train; get off at police station and go to the end of the road opposite and turn left; the railway station is about 1 km on the right (take a rickshaw if carrying heavy luggage).

Train To **Kollam** and **Thiruvananthapuram**, Platform 3 across the bridge.

Chettinad *p130*

Bus Bus routes link **Karaikkudi** with every part of the state. Auto-rickshaws provide slow but relatively cheap transport between towns – Karaikkudi to Kanadukathan should cost around Rs 150.

Train **Chennai**: *Sethu Exp 16714*, 2340, 9 hrs; **Rameswaram**: *Boat Mail Express 16101*, 0715. **Tiruchirappali**: passenger trains at 0620, 0940, 1450, 1815, 2½ hrs.

Pudukkottai *p131*

Bus to **Tiruchirappalli**, **Thanjavur**, **Karaikkudi** via **Kanadukathan** (for Chettinad), **Madurai**, **Ramnad**, **Ramesvaram**, and to **Sittanavasal**.

Train Pudukkottai is 1 hr north of Karaikkudi on the Chennai-Rameswaram line. All trains listed for Karaikkudi stop here.

● Directory

Madurai *p131, maps p122 and p124*
Banks Several on East Avani Moola
St. **Alagendran Finance**, 182D N Veli St,
good rate for cash US$ but not for TCs.
Andhra Bank, W Chitrai St, accepts credit
cards; **Canara Bank**, W Veli St, cashes
Amex and sterling TCs. **Internet** Many
west of the temple and in the budget
hotel area charge Rs 20 per hr. **Medical
services** Christian Mission Hospital, East
Veli St; Grace Kennet Hospital, 34 Kennet
Rd. **Post** The town GPO is at the north end
of W Veli St (Scott Rd). In Tallakulam: Head
Post Office and Central Telegraph Office, on
Gokhale Rd.

Pudukkottai *p131*
Banks State Bank of India, East Main St.

Far South

India's southernmost point is a focus of pilgrimage that captures the imagination of millions of Hindus on a daily basis. Kanniyakumari occupies a beautiful headland site where the waters of the Bay of Bengal, the Indian Ocean and the Arabian Sea mingle together and crash upon the rocks. An hour further towards Kerala is Padmanabhapuram Palace, the painstakingly maintained ancient seat of the Travancore rulers. Tirunelveli, one-time capital of the Pandyas, is now a market and educational centre that is often passed over on the trail towards Madurai.

Tirunelveli and Palayamkottai → *For listings, see pages 142-144. Phone code: 0462. Population: 411,300.*

On the banks of the Tamraparni, the only perennial river of the south, **Tirunelveli** is an attractive town surrounded by a belt of rice fields (*nelveli* means 'paddy-hedge') irrigated from the river's waters. Rising only 60 km to the east, at an altitude of over 1700 m, the river benefits from both the southwest and southeast monsoons; it tumbles down to the plains where it is bordered by a narrow strip of rich paddy land. Tirunelveli is now joined with the twin settlement of Palayamkottai. It is a market town and one of the oldest Christian centres in Tamil Nadu. St Francis Xavier settled here to begin his ministry in India in the early 16th century, but it has also been a centre of Protestant missionary activity. In 1896 it became the head of an Anglican diocese, now Church of South India.

Tirunelveli

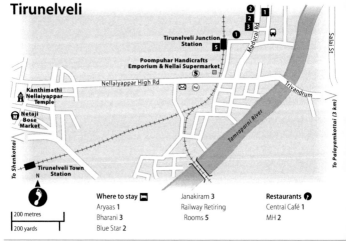

Where to stay
Aryaas 1
Bharani 3
Blue Star 2
Janakiram 3
Railway Retiring
Rooms 5

Restaurants
Central Café 1
MH 2

Places in Tirunelveli and Palayamkottai

Kanthimathi Nellaiyappar Temple ⓘ *closed 1230-1600, no photography*, is worth visiting; it is a twin temple, with the north dedicated to Siva (Nellaiyappar) and the south to Parvati (Kanthi). Each section has an enclosure over 150 m by 120 m. The temples have sculptures, musical pillars, valuable jewels, a golden lily tank and a 1000-pillared *mandapa*. There is a large white Nandi at the entrance. There is a **car festival** in June/July. The old town area around the temple is well worth a few hours of anyone's time, with the blue-painted houses reminiscent of Jodhpur (but without the tourist crowds). **Palayamkottai** has **St John's Church** (Church Missionary Society) with a spire 35 m high, a landmark for miles around. The town is known for its palm-leaf crafts.

Around Tirunelveli

Tiruchendur, 50 km east of Tirunelveli, has a famous **shore temple** ⓘ *Rs 50 for 'fast darshan', men must remove shirts*, dedicated to Subrahmanya, and considered to be one of his six 'abodes'. It is a hive of activity during festivals. There are caves with rock-cut sculptures along the shore.

Manapad, the predominantly Roman Catholic coastal village 18 km south of Tiruchendur, is where St Francis Xavier is said to have landed and lived in a cave near the headland. The **Holy Cross Church** (1581) close to the sea is believed to house a fragment of the True Cross from Jerusalem.

Kanniyakumari → *For listings, see pages 142-144.*

Kanniyakumari's grubby streets come alive in the hour before dawn, as thousands throng the shoreline to witness the sunrise over the southern tip of India. This important pilgrimage site is centred on worship of the Goddess Kumari, 'the protector of India's shores'. The new day is heralded in by the scent of jasmine garlands, the wail of temple music and the whoops and applause of excited children as the sun finally crawls its way over the sea. It's an early-morning party that everyone is invited to join. The view offshore is dominated by India's answer to the Statue of Liberty: a 133-ft sculpture of the Tamil poet Thiruvalluvar. Just behind is a memorial to the philosopher Swami Vivekananda, a spiritual leader inspired by the Devi. Both can be reached by a quick ferry ride. In April, at full moon, special *chithra pournami* celebrations are held at sunset and the town heaves with crowds who come to see the simultaneous setting and rising of the sun and moon.

Places in Kanniyakumari → *Phone code: 04652. Population: 19,700.*

The **Kanniyakumari Temple** ⓘ *0400-1200, 1600-2000, non-Hindus are not allowed into the sanctuary, shoes must be left outside and men must wear a dhoti to enter*, overlooks the shoreline. The Devi Kumari, an incarnation of Parvati, vowed to remain a virgin to her dying day after meddling gods prevented her marriage to Siva. Legend tells that the exceptionally brilliant diamond in the deity's nose ring is visible even from the sea, and the sea-facing temple door is kept closed to prevent ships being misguided by the gem's shimmer.

The **Vivekananda Memorial** ⓘ *0800-1600, Rs 10, ferry Rs 20, 15 mins (see page 143), allow 1 hr for the visit, smoking and eating prohibited, take off shoes before entering*, stands on one of two rocks, about 500 m from the mainland. The Bengali religious leader and philosopher Swami Vivekananda swam out here when a simple monk and devotee of the Devi, to sit in long meditation on this rock in 1892. He left convinced that religion could be a powerful instrument of social regeneration and individual development and was inspired to speak on Hinduism at the Parliament of Religions in Chicago, preaching that "the Lord is one, but the sages describe Him differently". On his return, he founded the Ramakrishna Mission in Chennai, which now has spread across the world. The rock was renamed Vivekananda Rock and a memorial was built in 1970. The design of the *mandapa* incorporates different styles of temple architecture from all over India and houses a statue of Vivekananda. People also come to see Sri Pada Parai, where the 'footprint' of the Devi has been enshrined on the rock.

The massive **Thiruvalluvar Statue** ① *0800-1600, free, ferry Rs 20, 15 mins,* immortalizes the writer of the Tamil classic, *Thirukkural*. The statue is exactly 133 ft (40 m) tall, to correspond with the 133 chapters of his most famous work. Stairs allow visitors to stand at his giant feet.

In 1948 some of Mahatma Gandhi's ashes were brought here for public display before being immersed in the sea. The **Ghandi Mandapam** ① *0700-1900, free,* was built as a memorial to this event. At midday on Gandhi's birthday, 2 October, the sun shines on the spot where his ashes were placed.

The **Wandering Monk Museum** ① *Main Rd, 0830-1200, 1600-2000, Rs 5,* has an informative exhibition on the life and work of Vivekananda. There is also a photo exhibition, in **Vivekanandapuram**, 1 km north, which can be reached by an easy walk along the beach though there is no access from the north side. The **Yoga Kendra** there runs courses from June to December. Further north there is a pleasant sandy beach, 3.5 km along Kovalam Road.

Kanniyakumari

Around Kanniyakumari

Suchindram Temple ① *open to non-Hindus, priests acting as guides may expect donations,* was founded during the Pandiyan period but was expanded under Thirumalai Nayaka in the 17th century. It was also used later as a sanctuary for the rulers of Travancore to the west and so contains treasures from many kingdoms. One of the few temples dedicated to the Hindu Trinity, Brahma, Vishnu and Siva, it is in a rectangular enclosure that you enter through the massive ornate seven-storeyed *gopuram*. North of the temple is a large tank with a small shelter in the middle while round the walls is the typically broad street used for car festivals. Leading to the entrance is a long colonnade with musical

400 metres
400 yards

Where to stay 🛏
Lakshmi **1**
Maadhini & Archana
  Restaurant **2**
Manickam **3**
Sankar's Guest House **7**

Saravana Lodge **6**
Seaview **5**
Singaar **9**
Sunrock **8**
Tamil Nadu & TTDC
  Restaurant **10**

Restaurants 🍴
Annapoorna **1**
Sangam **2**
Sravanas **3**

pillars and sculptures of Siva, Parvati, Ganesh and Subrahmanya on the front and a huge Hanuman statue inside. The main sanctuary, with a *lingam*, dates from the ninth century but many of the other structures and sculptures date from the 13th century and after. There are special temple ceremonies at sunset on Friday.

Nagercoil, 19 km from Kanniyakumari, is set with a stunning backcloth of the Western Ghats, reflected from place to place in the broad tanks dotted with lotuses. The landscape begins to feel more like Kerala than Tamil Nadu. It is an important railway junction and bus terminal. It is often a bottleneck filled with lorries so be prepared for delays. The old town of **Kottar**, now a suburb, was a centre of art, culture and pilgrimage. The **temple** ① *0630-0900, 1730-2000*, to Nagaraja, after which the town is named, is unique in that although the presiding deity is the serpent god Naga, there are also shrines to Siva and Vishnu as well as images of Jain Tirthankaras, Mahavira and Parsvanatha on the pillars. The temple is alive with snakes during some festivals. Christian missionaries played an important part in the town's development and left their mark in schools, colleges, hospitals and churches of different denominations. There is also a prominent Muslim community in Kottar, reflected in the shops closing on Fridays and remaining open on Sunday.

Padmanabhapuram → *For listings, see pages 142-144.*

① *Tue-Sun 0900-1300, 1400-1630 (last tickets 1600), Rs 200, child Rs 50 (accredited guide included, but expects a 'donation' after the tour), camera Rs 25, video Rs 1500. Best at 0900 before coach parties arrive.*

Padmanabhapuram, the old palace of the rajas of Travancore, contains some fascinating architecture and paintings but some of the methods employed during its restoration have been criticized. Although decaying somewhat, the Kuthiramalika Palace in Trivandrum – if you are venturing into Kerala – might be better worth looking round. The name Padmanabhapuram (*Padma*, lotus; *nabha*, navel; *puram*, town) refers to the lotus emerging from the navel of Vishnu. From the ninth century this part of Tamil Nadu and neighbouring Kerala were governed by the Ay Dynasty, patrons both of Jainism and Hinduism. However, the land was always contested by the Cholas, the Pandiyas and the Cheras. By the late 11th century the new Venadu Dynasty emerged from the Chera rulers of Kerala and took control of Kanniyakumari District in AD 1125 under Raja Kodai Kerala Varman. Never a stable kingdom, and with varying degrees of territorial control, Travancore State was governed from Padmanabhapuram between 1590-1790, when the capital was shifted to Thiruvananthapuram. Although the rajas of Travancore were Vaishnavite kings, they did not neglect Siva, as can be seen from various sculptures and paintings in the palace. The King never officially married and the heir to the throne was his eldest sister's oldest son. This form of matrilineal descent was characteristic of the earlier Chera Empire (who ruled for 200 years from the early 12th century). The palace shows the fine craftsmanship, especially in woodworking, characteristic of Kerala's art and architecture. There are also some superb frescoes and excellent stone-sculpted figures. The outer cyclopean stone wall is fitted together without mortar. It encloses a total area of 75 ha and the palace buildings 2 ha.

Far South listings

For hotel and restaurant price codes and other relevant information, see pages 14-18.

☕ Where to stay

Tirunelveli *p138, map p138*
Hotels are often full during the wedding season (Apr–Jun). Book ahead or arrive early. Several budget hotels are clustered near Junction Railway Station, most with Western toilet and shower.

$$-$ Aryaas, 67 Madurai Rd, T0462-233 9002. 69 rooms, 25 a/c, in dark bordello-style, non a/c better value, restaurants (separate vegetarian one, but it's also a mosquito's heaven), bar. Excellent internet café opposite.

$$-$ Bharani, 29 Madurai Rd, T0462-233 3234. 43 rooms, with hot shower, 10 a/c, clean, well maintained, vegetarian restaurant, in large modern block, lift, ample parking.

$$-$ Janakiram, 30 Madurai Rd, near bus stand, T0462-233 1941. 70 clean rooms, with hot shower, some a/c, lift, smart, brightly lit, outstanding vegetarian rooftop restaurant. Highly recommended.

$ Blue Star, 36 Madurai Rd, T0462-421 0501. 50 rooms with cold shower, 10 a/c, good veg restaurant, Indian style, modern. Good value.

$ Railway Retiring Rooms. Clean, secure rooms and dorm. Excellent value.

Kanniyakumari *p139, map p140*
Hotels are in heavy demand; book well ahead. Cheaper places may only offer squat toilets.

$$$ Seashore Hotel, East Car St, T04652-246704. Good rooms in a swish new hotel. The rooftop restaurant offers Indian and seafood dishes washed down with ocean views.

$$$ Seaview, East Car St, T04652-247841, www.hotelseaview.in. Plush, central hotel with spotlessly clean, a/c rooms. Helpful staff, restaurant, bar. Recommended.

$$ Hotel Singaar, Main Rd, 2 km from attractions, T04652-247992. Smart, popular hotel with comfortable rooms, many with balcony. Nice pool, decent restaurant. Breakfast included.

$$-$ Hotel Tamil Nadu (TTDC), Beach Rd, T04652-246257, www.ttdconline.com. Acceptably decrepit rooms in a superb location, with terraces looking out to sea and a nice garden setting, in a quiet spot away from the busy centre. Popular with Indian families.

$$-$ Maadhini, East Car St, T04652-246887. Wide variety of good value rooms. A/c rooms have balconies with sea views. Restaurant, bar, central location.

$ Lakshmi, East Car St, T04652-247203. Friendly, family-run hotel with clean rooms, some a/c. Can be noisy as guests arrive at 0500 to see sunrise from the roof. Excellent value.

$ Manickam, North Car St, T04652-246387. Under same management as **Maadhini**, this cheaper option has good-sized rooms but unfriendly staff. Overpriced a/c rooms.

$ Sankar's Guest House, Main Rd, T04652-246260. Best of the cheapies. Quiet and clean rooms all with TV and balcony. Very friendly management. Recommended.

$ Saravana Lodge, Sannathi St, T04652-246007. Moderately clean, basic rooms. Upstairs rooms open onto wide veranda with good sea view. The temple next door provides alarm clock services at 0500. Cheerful, helpful staff.

$ Sunrock, Pillyarkoil St, T04652-246167. Newish hotel tucked away down a back alley. Clean rooms, some a/c, all with terraces, but no views.

Around Kanniyakumari *p140*
$ Parvathi Residency, Nagercoil, T04652-233020. Clean good-sized rooms, some a/c.
$ Rajam, MS Rd, Vadasery, Nagercoil, T04652-276581. Good-value rooms, restaurant, roof garden.

🍴 Restaurants

Tirunelveli *p138, map p138*
$ Central Café, near station. Good vegetarian.
$ MH Restaurant, opposite Aryaas. Western fast food, pizzas. Modern.

Kanniyakumari *p139, map p140*
You'll find a dozen tiny restaurants serving cheap and tasty snacks of *dosai, vadai, bhaji* and *pakora* on Main Rd between Sth Car St and the Sangam Hotel.
$$ Archana, Maadhini (see Where to stay). Good mixed menu of Indian, Chinese and International options.
$ Annapoorna, Sannathi St. Excellent vegetarian food in clean, bright surroundings. Very popular with families.
$ Sangam, Sangam Hotel, Main Rd. Good *thalis*.
$ Sravanas, Sannathi St. Cheap and cheerful vegetarian meals. Recommended.
$ TTDC Restaurant, Hotel Tamil Nadu (see Where to stay). Looks like a barracks, but excellent non-vegetarian Indian meals.

❄ Festivals

Kanniyakumari *p139, map p140*
Apr Chithra Pournami is a special full moon celebration at the temple usually held in the 2nd week of Apr.
Oct Special **Navarathri** celebrations in 1st week of Oct.

⊖ Transport

Tirunelveli *p138, map p138*
Bus Good bus connections to **Kanniyakumari**, **Thiruvananthapuram**, and to **Madurai** (faster to change buses at Tirumangalam), **Tiruchirappalli** and **Chennai**. For **Courtallam**, go to Tenkasi (1½ hrs) and take bus to Courtallam (20 mins).

Train Train to **Chennai** (ME): *Nellai Exp 12632*, 1845, 12 hrs, via **Madurai** (2½ hrs).

Kanniyakumari: *Kanyakumari Exp 12633*, 0450, 2 hrs.

Kanniyakumari *p139, map p140*
Bus Long-distance buses leave from the station west of town on Kovalam Rd, 15 mins' walk from centre, T04652-271285. There are frequent services to **Nagercoil** (½ hr, Rs 10) and **Thiruvananthapuram** (2½ hrs, Rs 45). For **Kovalam** and **Varkala** change at **Thiruvananthapuram**. There are 4 daily departures to **Chennai** (16 hrs, Rs 390), via **Madurai** (6 hrs, Rs 145), at 0930, 1345, 1445 and 1630.

Ferry The ferry to **Vivekananda Rock** runs every 30 mins, 0700-1100, 1400-1700, Rs 20. Expect long queues during festivals.

Train The station is to the north, on Main Rd. Several important trains arrive and depart from Nagercoil, 15 mins away. **Chennai**, *Kanyakumari Exp 12634*, 1720, 13½ hrs, via **Madurai** (40½ hrs), **Trichy** (7 hrs) and **Villupuram** (for Puducherry, 11 hrs.

Around Kanniyakumari *p140*
Bus From **Nagercoil** there are frequent buses to **Thiruvananthapuram** (2 hrs); **Kanniyakumari** (30 mins); and **Madurai** (6½ hrs).

Train At **Nagercoil** the railway station is 3 km from the bus station. The daily *Kanniyakumari Mumbai Exp 16382*, and *Kanniyakumari Bengaluru Exp 16525* both stop here on their way to, and from **Kanniyakumari**. Frequent bus connections to **Thiruvananthapuram**, **Kanniyakumari** and **Madurai**.

Padmanabhapuram *p141*
Bus Regular buses to **Thiruvananthapuram** and **Kanniyakumari**. Less frequent buses to and from **Kovalam**. From Kovalam, depart approximately 0940 to **Thuckalai**. Return buses from Thuckalai depart 1445, 1530.

Taxi A taxi from Kovalam or Thiruvananthapuram costs Rs 800.

◐ Directory

Tirunelveli *p138, map p138*
Banks On Trivandrum High Rd.
Medical services Hospital in High Ground, Palayamkottai.
Post GPO, Trivandrum High Rd.

Kanniyakumari *p139, map p140*
Banks Canara Bank, State Bank of India and State Bank of Travancore, are all on Main Rd. All have ATMs. **Internet** There are several internet cafés on Main Rd. All charge around Rs 20 per hr. **Medical services** General Hospital, off Main Rd, T04652-248505. **Post** Head Post Office, Main Rd, 0800-1600, 1000-1400.

Contents

Footprint features

Background

Geography → *Population: 62.1 million. Area: 130,000 sq km.*

Tamil Nadu rises from the flat coastal plains in the east to the Western Ghats – the Nilgiris in the north and the Palani, Cardamom and Anamalai hills in the south. The Nilgiris ('blue mountains') rise like a wall above the haze of the plains to heights of over 2500 m. The plains are hot, dry and dusty, with isolated blocks of granite forming bizarre shapes on the ancient eroded surface. The coast itself is a flat alluvial plain, with deltas at the mouths of major rivers. The occasional medieval water tanks add beauty to the landscape.

Tamil Nadu's coast bore the brunt of India's casualties of the 2004 tsunami. Along 1000 km of shoreline, at least 8000 people died, and 470,000 were displaced. As well as loved ones, the wave washed away infrastructure: communities, homes, livelihoods, schools and health clinics.

History

Tamil Nadu's cultural identity has been shaped by the Dravidians, who have inhabited the south since at least the fourth millennium BC. Tamil, India's oldest living language, developed from the earlier languages of people who were probably displaced from the north by Aryan-based culture from 2000 BC to 1500 BC.

By the fourth century BC Tamil Nadu was under the rule of three dynasties: the **Cholas**, the **Pandiyas** and the **Cheras**. The **Pallavas** of Kanchi came to power in the fourth century AD and were dominant between AD 550 and AD 869. Possibly of northern origin, under their control Mahabalipuram (Mamallapuram) became an important port in the seventh century. The **Cholas** returned to power in AD 850 and were a dominant political force until 1173 before the resumption of Pandiya power for a further century. The defeat of the great Vijayanagar Empire by a confederacy of Muslim states in 1565 forced their leaders south. As the Nayaka kings they continued to rule from as far south as Madurai well into the 17th century. When Muslim political control finally reached Tamil Nadu it was as brief as it was tenuous.

It was more than 150 years after their founding of Fort St George at Madras in 1639 before the **East India Company** could claim political supremacy in South India. Haidar Ali, who mounted the throne of Mysore in 1761, and his son Tipu Sultan, allied with the French, won many battles against the English. When the Treaty of Versailles brought the French and English together in 1783 Tipu was forced to make peace. The English took Malabar (in Kerala) in 1792, and in 1801 Lord Wellesley brought together most of the south under the Madras Presidency. The **French** acquired land at Pondicherry in 1673. In 1742, Dupleix was named governor of the French India Company and took up residence there. He seized Madras within a few years but in 1751 Clive attacked Arcot. His victory was the beginning of the end of French ambitions in India. The Treaty of Paris brought their empire to a close in 1763, although they retained five counting houses.

Culture

The majority of Tamilians are Dravidians with Mediterranean ethnic origins, settled in Tamil Nadu for several thousand years. Tamil is spoken by over 85% of the population, which is 90% Hindu. Five per cent are Christian, a group especially strong in the south where Roman Catholic and Protestant missions have been active for over 500 years. There are small but significant minorities of Muslims, Jains and Parsis. There are isolated groups

The new organ grinders

While Karnataka, with its glut of world-class cardiac surgeons, pitches itself as the hot new 'health tourism' destination, neighbouring Tamil Nadu has drummed up its own less enviable reputation on the operating table. The state is at the centre of the Indian organs racket as its poor harvest their own kidneys as a lucrative cash crop. Around 60 to 70 transplants take place in the state each month.

A Journal of the American Medical Association investigation revealed that in 96% of cases those going under the knife did so to pay off debts. The fee? Not steep, by international standards: Indian donors typically receive around US$1070 (although most are initially promised more than double). Still, not bad for a state where the poverty line is US$538 a year per family.

Transplant tourism began in the subcontinent in the 1980s, but has since boomed, even though the success rate is pitifully low; as many as half of those kidneys bought abroad fail, and a third of patients die. But with almost a third of the 40,000 awaiting transplant in Europe dying in the queue for a legal donor, it's clearly a risk many feel is worth taking.

India outlawed the trade in 1995, when individual states set up medical authorization committees to determine the authenticity of relationships between donor and recipient – or to uncover evidence of financial inducements – but name changes and speedy weddings between Gulf men and Indian women (followed by equally swift post-operative divorces), make these committees easy to hoodwink.

Nor has South India's burgeoning medical industry done much to impede the trade; transplant operations bring in cash and confer prestige on institutions and surgeons.

And while the lure of short-term cash prizes will replenish the numbers in the donor queues, evidence shows that most quickly sink back to earlier levels of indebtedness, only now with the added handicap of one less kidney.

There has been little political will to end the trade, except for the storm triggered in early 2007 when a local NGO unearthed a high number of kidney donations among a small fishing community devastated by the 2004 tsunami. In one village just north of Chennai 150 women had sold a kidney. But Tamil Nadu's vulnerable are desperate to fight their common enemy, poverty, even at the cost of their health, with the only tool they have: their own organs.

of as many as 18 different types of **tribal people** in the Nilgiri Hills. Some of them are of aboriginal stock although local archaeological discoveries suggest that an extinct race preceded them. The **Todas** life and religion revolve around their long-horned buffalo which are a measure of wealth. Their small villages are called *munds* with around six igloo-like windowless bamboo and dried grass huts. Their chief goddess Tiekirzi, the creator of the indispensable buffalo, and her brother On rule the world of the dead and the living. There are only about 1000 Todas left. The **Badagas** are the main tribal group and probably came from Karnataka. They speak a mixture of Kannada and Tamil and their oral tradition is rich in folk tales, poetry, songs and chants. As agriculturalists their villages are mainly in the upper plateau, with rows of three-roomed houses. They worship Siva and observe special tribal festivals. Progressive and adaptable, they are being absorbed into the local community faster than others.

Screen gods

Tamil Nadu's lively temple society also keeps aflame sculpture and the arts, and makes for a people singularly receptive to iconography. Tamil film-making is every bit as prolific and profitable as its closest rival, Hindi-language Bollywood. The state's industry is famous for its dancing and choreography and the super-saturated colour of its film stock. Film stars, too, are massive here; worshipped like demigods, their careers often offering them a fast track into politics, where they are singularly well placed to establish personality cults. Two such figures who have hopped from the screen into the state's political driving seat as chief minister are the cherished MGR – MG Ramachandran, the film star and charismatic chief minister during the 1980s – and Jayalalitha, his one-time girlfriend and contentious successor, three times chief minister since 1991 despite being the figure of multiple corruption scandals.

Cuisine Many Tamilians are vegetarian and the strict Brahmins among them avoid the use of garlic and onion and in some cases even tomatoes. Favourites for breakfast or *tiffin* (snacks) include *dosa* (thin crisp pancakes, plain or stuffed with mildly spiced potato and onion as *masala dosa*), *iddli* (steamed, fermented rice cakes), delicious rice-based *pongal* (worth searching out) and *vadai* (savoury lentil doughnuts), all served with coconut chutney and *sambar* (a spicy lentil and vegetable broth). A *thali* here comes in the form of boiled rice with small steel containers of a variety of vegetables, pickles, *papadum*, *rasam* (a clear, peppery lentil 'soup') and plain curd. The most prized Tamil cuisine is that of the Chettinad region, which draws on unusual spices (including one derived from a tree-growing lichen) to create subtle blends of flavour; its reputation for relentless spiciness has come about only recently, and is the result of a crossover with Andhra cuisine. Dessert is usually the creamy rice pudding *payasam*. The drink of choice is coffee, which comes freshly ground, filtered and frothy, with hot milk and sugar.

Literature As the oldest living Indian language, Tamil has a literature stretching back to the early centuries before Christ. A second century AD poets' academy, the **Sangam** in Madurai, suggests that sages sat at the top of the Tamil social order, followed by peasants, hunters, artisans, soldiers, fishermen and scavengers – in marked contrast to the rest of the subcontinent's caste system. From the beginning of the Christian era Tamil religious thinkers began to transform the image of Krishna from the remote and heroic figure of the epics into the focus of a new and passionate devotional worship – *bhakti*. From the seventh to the 10th century there was a surge of writing new hymns of praise, sometimes referred to as the Tamil *Veda*.

Music Changes constantly occurred in different schools of music within the basic structure of **raga-tala-prabandha** which was well established by the seventh century. Differences between the *Hindustani* or the northern system (which included the western and eastern regions) and the *Carnatic* or the southern system became noticeable in the 13th century. The southern school has a more scale-based structure of *raga* whereas the northern school has greater flexibility and thus continued to develop through the centuries. The *tala* too is much more precise. It is nearly always devotional or didactic whereas the northern system also includes non-religious, every day themes and is occasionally sensuous. Telugu naturally lends itself to the southern system. The violin accompanies the vocal music – imported from the West but played rather differently.

Dance and drama Bharata Natyam may be India's oldest classical dance form: a highly stylized solo for a woman of movement, music, mime, *nritta* (pure dance) and *nritya* (expression). Its theme is usually spiritual love.

Modern Tamil Nadu

Tamil Nadu took its present form as a result of the States Reorganization Act of 1956. Until 1967 the Assembly was dominated by the Indian National Congress, but after an attempt by the central government to impose Hindi as the national language the Congress Party was routed in 1967 by a regional party, the Dravida Munnetra Kazhagam (DMK) under its leader CN Annadurai. After his death the party split and since then either the DMK, or the splinter party, the All India Anna DMK (AIADMK), has been in power in the state. Neither party has any constituency beyond Tamil Nadu and thus at the all India level each has been forced to seek alliances with national parties. From the late 1960s the AIADMK, which controlled the State Assembly for most of the time, has been led by two film stars. The first, MG Ramachandran, remained the chief minister until his death (even after suffering a stroke which left him paralysed). The record of Jayalalitha, his successor, one-time lover and fellow film star, has been less consistent, and her rule dogged by scandal. She and her party were ousted by the DMK in the May 1996 elections and she was temporarily jailed until, cleared of a wide range of criminal charges, she re-entered the Legislative Assembly in March 2002, taking over once more as chief minister after winning the state elections with an 80% margin (her administration then arrested the previous chief minister, senescent 83-year-old Karunanidhi, in a corruption case that some say was motivated by revenge). In the May 2004 national elections, though, the party, allied to the BJP and vocal in its opposition to Sonia Gandhi's foreign origin, failed to win a single seat. A coalition of opposition parties, arguing that she had lost her political mandate, demanded Jayalalitha's resignation, but she hung on to office, albeit swiftly reversing a raft of controversial policies – such as scrapping free electricity schemes, reducing rice rations, banning animal sacrifices – introduced during the earlier years of power. This wasn't enough to prevent a trouncing by the DMK and Karunanidhi, by now on his fifth term as Chief Minister. Nevertheless, Jayalalitha had the last laugh in the 2011 elections after Karunanidhi's government fell foul of allegations of nepotism and the arrest of his daughter MK Kaminozhi, an MP in the national Upper House, for her part in a scam to sell publicly owned 2G mobile spectrum to favoured companies.

The civil war in Sri Lanka caused tremendous stresses in Tamil politics on the mainland, neither the AIADMK nor the DMK wanting wither to alienate Tamil sentiment, nor wishing to back Sri Lanka's LTTE. Whether the ending of that conflict brings much needed relief will depend crucially on the political approach adopted by the Sri Lankan government to the Tamil populations in the island.

Contents

Footnotes

Language

Tamil words and phrases

Pronunciation
a as in *ah*   i as in *bee*
o as in *oh*   u as *oo* in book
nasalized vowels are shown as an *un*

Basics
Hello, good morning, goodbye   *vanakkam*
Thank you/no thank you   *nandri*
Excuse me, sorry   *manni kavum*
Yes/no   *aam / illai*
Never mind/that's all right   *kavalai padathe/ parava illai*

Questions
What is your name?   *ungal udaya peyar yenna?*
My name is ...   *en peyar...*
Pardon?   *Manni kavum?*
How are you?   *ninkal eppadi irukki riral?*
I am well, thanks, and you?   *naan nallai irkain, ninkal?*
Not very well   *naan nanraga illai*
Where is the...?   *...engai?*
Who is?   *idha yaar?*
What is this?   *idha enna?*

Shopping
How much?   *Evva lavu?*
That makes (20) rupees   *(eravadhu) ruba aayarka*
That is very expensive!   *romba adheegam!*
Make it a bit cheaper!   *konjam kamee mudiyuma!*

The hotel
What is the room charge?   *vaadagai evva lavu?*
Please show the room   *roomah katungo?*
Is there an air-conditioned room?   *ac room eru keradha?*
Is there hot water?   *sudu tannir ullatu?*
... a bathroom/fan/mosquito net   *...kuliyal arai / min viciri / kosu valai*

Is there a large room?   *edhaveda periya room eruka?*
Please clean it   *tayavu sethu sutham seiyavum*
Are there clean sheets/blanket?   *suttaman talkal / porvai ullana?*
Bill please   *bill tayavu sethu*

Travel
Where's the railway station?   *rail nilayam yengai?*
How much is the ticket to Madurai?   *Madurai ticket eva lavu?*
When does the Madurai bus leave?   *Madurai basu yeppo porappadom?*
How much?   *Evva lavu?*
Left/right   *itatu/valatu*
Go straight on   *nera ponga*
Nearby   *arukil*
Please wait here   *inge ye kattirungal*
Please come at 8   *ettu manikku varungal*
Quickly   *virai vaga*
Stop   *nirutta*

Time and days
right now   *ippo*
month   *maatham*
morning   *kaalai*
year   *aandu*
afternoon   *mathiyam*
evening   *sayan kalam*
night   *eravu*
today   *indru*
tomorrow/yesterday   *naalai/nettru*
day   *nal*
week   *vaarum*
Sunday   *Nayirru kilamai*
Monday   *Tingat kilamai*
Tuesday   *Sevvai*
Wednesday   *Bhudan*
Thursday   *Viyalak kilamai*
Friday   *Vellik kilamai*
Saturday   *Sani kilamai*

Numbers

1	*ondru*
2	*irandu*
3	*mundru*
4	*nanghu*
5	*aindhu*
6	*aaru*
7	*elu*
8	*ettu*
9	*onpathu*
10	*pattu*
11	*padhe nonnu*
12	*pani irandu*
13	*padhen moonu*
14	*padhe nallu*
15	*padhen aindhu*
16	*spadhen aaru*
17	*padhen elu*
18	*paden ettu*
19	*padhem bodhu*
20	*eruvadhu*
100/200	*nooru/yeran nooru*
1000/2000	*aayiram/irandu aayiram*
100,000	*latcham*

Basic vocabulary

Words such as airport, bank, bathroom, bus, doctor, embassy, ferry, hotel, hospital, juice, police, restaurant, station, stamp, taxi, ticket, train are used locally though often pronounced differently eg *daktar, aaspitiri*.

and *marrum*
big *perisa*
café/food stall *oonavu kadai*
chemist *marundhu kadai*
clean *suttamana*
closed *moodiya*
cold *kulirchi yana*
day *dinam*
dirty *asingam*
English *aankilam*
excellent *sirandha*
food/to eat *oonavu*
hot (spicy) *kaaram*
hot (temp) *soodu*
luggage *saaman kalai*
medicine *marundhu*
newspaper *seidhi thal*
of course, sure *uru tiyana*
open *thirakavum*
police station *kaaval nilayam*
road *salai*
room *arai*
shop *kadai*
sick (ill) *noyarra*
silk *pattu*
small *chinna*
that *adhu*
this *idhu*
town *nagaram*
water *thannir*
what *enna*
when *eppo*
where *engay*
which/who *edhu*
why *yain*
with *edhodu*

Eating out

Eating out is normally cheap and safe but menus can often be dauntingly long and full of unfamiliar names. Here are some Tamil words to help you.

Restaurants

Please show the menu *Tayavu ceytu menu katta*
No chillies please *kaaram poda vena*
…sugar/milk/ice …*sakarai/paal/panni katti*

A bottle of water please *ondru batal tannir kudanga*
sweet/savoury *innipu/uppataiya*
spoon, fork, knife *karandi, mulla, katti*

Tamil styles of cooking

Many items on restaurant menus are named according to methods of preparation, roughly equivalent to terms such as 'Provençal' or 'sauté'.

kozhambu curry or gravy based
kootu vegetables in coconut-based thick masalas
poriyal sauteed dry vegetarian dishes

Typical Tamil dishes

aatu kari kozhambu mutton curry
chettinadu milagu kozhi black pepper chicken curry
meen kozhambu fish curry usually with a tamarind and tomato base
sambaar spiced lentils curry eaten with dosas and idlies.
vartha kozhambu tamarind curry
poondu kozhambu garlic curry
thayir saadam tempered curd rice
rasam spiced watery soup (inspiration for the mulligatawny)

Meat and fish

chicken *kozhi*
fish *meen*
meat *kari*
prawns *yerra*

Vegetables (sabzi)

aubergine *kathrika*
cabbage *gose*
carrots *kerat*
cauliflower *poo gose*
mushroom *kaalan*
onion *vengayam*
okra, ladies' fingers *vendaka*
peas *pattani*
potato *uralai*
spinach *keerai*

Rice

saadam plain boiled rice
biriyani partially cooked rice layered over meat and baked with saffron
khichari rice and lentils cooked with turmeric and other spices
pulao/pilau fried rice cooked with spices (cloves, cardamom, cinnamon) with dried fruit, nuts or vegetables. Sometimes cooked with meat, like a biriyani

Roti – breads

chapati (roti) thin, plain, wholemeal unleavened bread cooked on a tawa (griddle), usually made from ata (wheat flour). Makkaikiroti is with maize flour.
nan oven baked (traditionally in a tandoor) white flour leavened bread often large and triangular; sometimes stuffed with almonds and dried fruit
parota fried bread layered with ghi (sometimes cooked with egg or with potatoes)
poori thin deep-fried, puffed rounds of flour

Sweets

These are often made with reduced/
thickened milk, drained curd cheese
or powdered lentils and nuts. They are
sometimes covered with a flimsy sheet of
decorative, edible silver leaf.

barfi fudge-like rectangles/diamonds
gulab jamun dark fried spongy balls,
soaked in syrup
halwa rich sweet made from cereal, fruit,
vegetable, nuts and sugar
khir, payasam, paesh thickened milk rice/
vermicelli pudding
kulfi cone-shaped Indian ice cream with
pistachios/almonds, uneven in texture
jalebi spirals of fried batter soaked in syrup
laddoo lentil based batter 'grains' shaped
into rounds
rasgulla (roshgulla) balls of curd in clear
syrup
sandesh dry sweet made of curd cheese

Snacks

bhaji, pakora vegetable fritters (onions,
potatoes, cauliflower, etc) deep-fried in
batter
chat sweet and sour fruit and vegetables
flavoured with tama rind paste and chillies

chana choor, chioora ('Bombay mix') lentil
and flattened rice snacks mixed with nuts
and dried fruit
dosai South Indian pancake made with rice
and lentil flour; served with a mild potato
and onion filling (masala dosai) or without
(ravai or plain dosai)
iddli steamed South Indian rice cakes, a
bland breakfast given flavour by spiced
accompaniments
kachori fried pastry rounds stuffed with
spiced lentil/peas/potato filling
samosa cooked vegetable or meat
wrapped in pastry triangles and deep fried
utthappam thick South Indian rice and
lentil flour pancake cooked with spices/
onions/tomatoes
vadai deep fried, small savoury lentil
'doughnut' rings. Dahi vada are similar
rounds in yoghurt
zamindar a landlord granted income under
the Mughals
zari silver and gold thread used in weaving
or embroidery
zarih cenotaph in a Muslim tomb
zenana segregated women's apartments
ziarat holy Muslim tomb
zilla (zillah) district

Index

Notes

Notes

Titles available in the Footprint *Focus* range

Latin America	UK RRP	US RRP
Bahia & Salvador	£7.99	$11.95
Brazilian Amazon	£7.99	$11.95
Brazilian Pantanal	£6.99	$9.95
Buenos Aires & Pampas	£7.99	$11.95
Cartagena & Caribbean Coast	£7.99	$11.95
Costa Rica	£8.99	$12.95
Cuzco, La Paz & Lake Titicaca	£8.99	$12.95
El Salvador	£5.99	$8.95
Guadalajara & Pacific Coast	£6.99	$9.95
Guatemala	£8.99	$12.95
Guyana, Guyane & Suriname	£5.99	$8.95
Havana	£6.99	$9.95
Honduras	£7.99	$11.95
Nicaragua	£7.99	$11.95
Northeast Argentina & Uruguay	£8.99	$12.95
Paraguay	£5.99	$8.95
Quito & Galápagos Islands	£7.99	$11.95
Recife & Northeast Brazil	£7.99	$11.95
Rio de Janeiro	£8.99	$12.95
São Paulo	£5.99	$8.95
Uruguay	£6.99	$9.95
Venezuela	£8.99	$12.95
Yucatán Peninsula	£6.99	$9.95

Asia	UK RRP	US RRP
Angkor Wat	£5.99	$8.95
Bali & Lombok	£8.99	$12.95
Chennai & Tamil Nadu	£8.99	$12.95
Chiang Mai & Northern Thailand	£7.99	$11.95
Goa	£6.99	$9.95
Gulf of Thailand	£8.99	$12.95
Hanoi & Northern Vietnam	£8.99	$12.95
Ho Chi Minh City & Mekong Delta	£7.99	$11.95
Java	£7.99	$11.95
Kerala	£7.99	$11.95
Kolkata & West Bengal	£5.99	$8.95
Mumbai & Gujarat	£8.99	$12.95

Africa & Middle East	UK RRP	US RRP
Beirut	£6.99	$9.95
Cairo & Nile Delta	£8.99	$12.95
Damascus	£5.99	$8.95
Durban & KwaZulu Natal	£8.99	$12.95
Fès & Northern Morocco	£8.99	$12.95
Jerusalem	£8.99	$12.95
Johannesburg & Kruger National Park	£7.99	$11.95
Kenya's Beaches	£8.99	$12.95
Kilimanjaro & Northern Tanzania	£8.99	$12.95
Luxor to Aswan	£8.99	$12.95
Nairobi & Rift Valley	£7.99	$11.95
Red Sea & Sinai	£7.99	$11.95
Zanzibar & Pemba	£7.99	$11.95

Europe	UK RRP	US RRP
Bilbao & Basque Region	£6.99	$9.95
Brittany West Coast	£7.99	$11.95
Cádiz & Costa de la Luz	£6.99	$9.95
Granada & Sierra Nevada	£6.99	$9.95
Languedoc: Carcassonne to Montpellier	£7.99	$11.95
Málaga	£5.99	$8.95
Marseille & Western Provence	£7.99	$11.95
Orkney & Shetland Islands	£5.99	$8.95
Santander & Picos de Europa	£7.99	$11.95
Sardinia: Alghero & the North	£7.99	$11.95
Sardinia: Cagliari & the South	£7.99	$11.95
Seville	£5.99	$8.95
Sicily: Palermo & the Northwest	£7.99	$11.95
Sicily: Catania & the Southeast	£7.99	$11.95
Siena & Southern Tuscany	£7.99	$11.95
Sorrento, Capri & Amalfi Coast	£6.99	$9.95
Skye & Outer Hebrides	£6.99	$9.95
Verona & Lake Garda	£7.99	$11.95

North America	UK RRP	US RRP
Vancouver & Rockies	£8.99	$12.95

Australasia	UK RRP	US RRP
Brisbane & Queensland	£8.99	$12.95
Perth	£7.99	$11.95

For the latest books, e-books and a wealth of travel information, visit us at:
www.footprinttravelguides.com.

 footprinttravelguides.com

Join us on facebook for the latest travel news, product releases, offers and amazing competitions:
www.facebook.com/footprintbooks.